What reviewers are saying about
In the Wake of the Storm

Ms. Severin has written one of the most informative and sensitive books on trauma and what is truly needed for people to transcend from the depths of despair to empowerment and personal growth. *In the Wake of the Storm* is a captivating story of family love, loss, and heart-rending renewal. Readers will experience a gamut of emotions ranging from sheer terror as Terri describes in vivid detail what it was like for the last twenty-seven seconds in the lives of the sixty-eight people on board who were to meet their final destiny, to outrage at the insensitivity of the airline industry and an outdated corporate system. Anyone who has ever experienced preflight jitters will be mesmerized and unable to put this book down. As a therapist for twenty years, I have witnessed great emotional pain in people's lives; now, having read *In the Wake of the Storm,* I have a greater understanding and appreciation of where our work must begin, as well as how we, as human beings, can better care for one another. A must read!

Marci Kagan
Master of Social Work (MSW)

This very insightful book gives a very different look at the extensively publicized crash of Flight 4184. As a fireman, I spent several days at the accident site doing what needed to be done at the time, never realizing what the families were going through. I had believed that, surely, the airline was doing everything it could to relieve pain and grief. This book will serve as an essential guide for airlines and any of those who respond to tragedies, forcefully arguing that true and timely help is much needed by families that remain "in the wake of the storm."

Glen "Butch" Cain
Fireman/First Responder for Lake Township Fire Department
Newton County Building Commissioner

As a former airline captain for a major carrier and now as an aviation disaster attorney, I recommend Terri's book for everyone who works in aviation, law, counseling, or in any profession working with people. Her generously shared insight offers priceless lessons and enlightenment.

Donald L. McCune
Former Captain, Northwest Airlines
Aviation Attorney, Motley Rice LLC

On October 31, 1994, we were watching the news while awaiting the night's first trick-or-treaters. When we heard about the crash of Flight 4184 in Roselawn, Indiana, my husband, Barry, immediately called the Red Cross, where he was chairman of logistics. We were informed that all personnel and equipment were to be prepared to assist with the operation the next morning.

An amazing amount of volunteers and staff showed up at the fire station to help, displaying a true outpouring of compassion for the victims' families. The National Guard, fire departments, the Red Cross, friends, neighbors, and too many others to mention put forth a truly heartfelt effort to support, feed, and comfort any and all that were in need. But the psychologists, therapists, EMTs, firefighters, paramedics, and others present could not have anticipated the magnitude of what they were about to undertake.

Being an EMT myself, I had seen many horrific tragedies. But nothing had prepared me for what I was about to see. I only went to the crash site once to help with the search: I could not bring myself to go back. To this day, that scene stays in my mind and in my heart.

As bad as the experience was for us as workers, we couldn't even imagine the despair and devastation endured by the families. Our hearts went out to all those who lost loved ones in the crash, and we kept them in our thoughts and prayers throughout the recovery process. We would like to thank Terri, not only for having the courage to document her traumatic ordeal in *In the Wake of the Storm*, but also for acknowledging the care and effort put forth by the various agencies working together at the crash site. Reading this account filled us with hope and promise, for Terri's honest and encompassing approach paid tribute to the work that we, along with countless other volunteers, do, and reminds us that there is purpose and meaning beyond every difficulty that we encounter.

Sandy Hostetler, EMT
Former Red Cross Volunteer

Barry Hostetler, EMT
Former Red Cross Chairman of Logistics

In the Wake *of the* Storm

LIVING BEYOND THE TRAGEDY
OF FLIGHT 4184

THERESA ANN SEVERIN

7/10

To Lisa —
With love and
magic on our healing
journey! I'm so glad we
were partners this weekend!
Love,
Terri Severin

NORTH
CROSS
PRESS

Arlington Heights, IL
northcrosspress.com

ISBN #: 978-0-9796062-0-5
Library of Congress Control Number: 2008925235

Printed and bound in the United States of America.
EB 1 2 3 4 5 6 7 8 9 10

To the loving memory
of my sister, Patty,
and her son, Patrick

Dedicated
to her surviving son,
Jonathon

Preface

When I first began documenting my experiences in the years following the crash of Flight 4184, I was intent on preserving the memory of my sister, Patty, so that she may always live on for her son, Jonathon. However, as I embarked upon this project, my purpose seemed to magnify in scope, and as often happens throughout the writing process, I found myself touching on many different issues that were illuminated in the aftermath of this tragedy. Initially, this expanded focus remained localized to the impact these occurrences had upon me and my family, but eventually I realized that our story was in many ways inextricably linked to those whose lives were also forever transformed by the events that took place on October 31, 1994.

This account examines my own journey down the road to recovery and the regaining of hope, as I chronicle my battle to overcome the shock and loss I suffered, not only from the immediate impact of my sister's and nephew's deaths, but also American Airlines' mishandling of the post-crash situation. While I direct a great deal of criticism at this corporation for the ongoing pain we were all forced to endure, such inconsistent and flawed approaches for dealing with the families of victims of air disasters were not isolated to American Airlines; rather, their lack of knowledge, sensitivity, and understanding on this issue was reflective of an industry-wide problem. I came to realize that the terrible management of the overall situation was not the product of individuals, or even of one specific company, but of a misdirected and outdated corporate system that allowed for the human cost in this tragedy to be overlooked.

Thus, my goals became directed toward exposing the flaws inherent in the corporate mentality, so that others never have to undergo the same perpetual trauma that all those associated with the crash of Flight 4184 have come to know. Because of the ongoing support, commitment, and consideration of government officials such as Jim Hall and Mary Schiavo, along with the dedication of the families, these aims were eventually realized with the passing of legislative reforms in the aviation industry.

Throughout my experience, I coped with the fluctuating emotions that result from any agonizing loss, and my narrative details the difficult process facing anybody trying to rebuild an identity after so many defining parts of life have been shattered. In the end, I set out to write a tribute not only to the love and life of my sister and nephew, but also to uncovering and remedying the injustices that plagued my struggle, so as to allow for the emergence of hope for a better tomorrow.

...So that we may never forget...

Foreword
by Jim Hall

From 1994 to 2001, I had the distinct honor of serving as Chairman of the National Transportation Safety Board (NTSB). The NTSB is an independent federal agency charged by Congress with investigating every civil aviation disaster in the United States, as well as significant accidents in the other modes of transportation—railroad, highway, marine, and pipeline. Since its inception in 1967, the NTSB has examined more than 124,000 aviation accidents and over 10,000 surface transportation accidents, and has also assisted many foreign governments with their own investigations. In its issuance of over 12,000 recommendations for all transportation modes, the Board has established a solid reputation for diligence and impartiality. For more than seven years, I headed this organization that serves as the "eyes and ears" of the American public for aviation and other transportation accident investigations across the country and around the world. Now, as a transportation safety and security consultant, I continue my commitment to promoting safety in our nation's transportation system.

When I announced my retirement from the Board, media and industry analysts speculated that perhaps one of my "most lasting legacies will be the change in how family members of victims of major transportation accidents are treated." While this is, and continues to be, a cause I champion, the overhaul of this system cannot be credited to me. Rather, the advancement of this goal and the significant legislative progress made during my tenure regarding the treatment of families in the aftermath of airline accidents is largely due to the relentless collective work of Terri Severin, other surviving family members, and organizations representing their interests, such as The National Air Disaster Alliance. Before October 1996, when Congress passed and President Clinton signed the Aviation Disaster Family Assistance Act of 1996, the Safety Board's primary mandate was to inspect transportation accidents. It was only through the work of these families that the Aviation Disaster Family Assistance Act of 1996 became a legislative priority, giving the Safety Board the additional responsibility of aiding the families of victims of commercial aircraft accidents occurring in U.S. territory. Terri's book does a wonderful job of describing the problems faced by families, providing both an intimate account and historical context.

The October 31, 1994 crash of an American Eagle ATR-72 in Roselawn, Indiana, which took the lives of all 68 persons aboard, was a great tragedy. It was a tragedy not only for the 68 victims, but, like all accidents of this kind, it was devastating for the hundreds of loved ones they left behind. My involvement with this disaster began just hours after it occurred, when I stood in the muddy soybean field in which flight 4184 had come to rest. Through the rain and mist that dark night, I was able to make out what appeared to be the tailcone of the fallen aircraft, not knowing at the time that in the morning light it would prove to be the only large piece of the plane remaining. Since then, I have had the opportunity to meet many of those who lost their loved ones, as the Board examined the crash, and updated individual family members on the status of our investigation. One of those individuals was Terri Severin. In the months following the catastrophe in Roselawn, Indiana, Terri became an impromptu spokesperson for the surviving family members, uncovering and exposing major failures by the airline in the handling of the victims' remains. It was through the work of Terri and other family members that the full scope of the Roselawn tragedy became clear. Compounding the devastation from the disaster was the airline's callous behavior.

Before October, 1996, in addition to Roselawn, I visited the scenes of three other major fatal airline crashes: USAir Flight 427, which killed 132 just outside of Pittsburgh, Pennsylvania on September 8, 1994; ValuJet Flight 592, which killed all 110 aboard in the Florida Everglades on May 11, 1996; and TWA Flight 800, which killed 230 off the coast of Long Island, New York, on July 17, 1996.

As beautifully articulated in, *In the Wake of the Storm,* the airline emergency response teams, in all four disasters, on occasion lacked organization, coordination, and perhaps even compassion. However, it was only through the strength and courage of these surviving family members working together, that we learned of the horror stories relating to their treatment—constant busy signals from the airline's 800 accident information number; misidentified remains; personal effects being mishandled; unidentified remains not treated with dignity, including the holding of mass burials without informing families; and using confidential information obtained during this grieving process in court against the families.

Internationally, family members of victims, including Terri, began to organize and demand more accountability in the aftermath of tragedies. They outlined five major concerns in the areas of initial notification of the accident, including the recovery and identification of victims, disposition of unidentifiable remains, returning of personal effects, and access to investigative information.

In response, the Board created the Office of Family Assistance to fill the void. It functions as a coordinator in the integration of the major resources of the federal government and other organizations, to support the efforts of the local and state government, and to assist the airline in meeting the needs of aviation disaster victims and their families. Family counseling, victim identification and forensic services, communicating with foreign governments, and translation services are just a few of the areas in which the federal government can help local authorities and the airlines deal more effectively with a major aviation disaster.

We designed our family affairs operation to harness the assets and abilities of the federal government and to work in cooperation with the local medical examiner or coroner, who has the responsibility of recovering and identifying victims. We focused on the recovery and identification of remains specifically because of the emphasis every family member placed on this—recognizing that in the immediate aftermath of a crash there is no greater interest for those who have lost a loved one. With all due respect to our investigators, for the victims' families the cause of the crash is a secondary issue. The NTSB fully recognized that the family affairs efforts must be focused on the quick and accurate identification of remains. Sadly, it took the passage of legislation at the behest of families, and the intervention of the NTSB, to appreciate the necessity and importance of this process. Nonetheless, these survivors and family members can take solace in knowing that their compounded grief, which moved them to action, has prevented similar future harms, not only in the United States but worldwide, as foreign governments around the world followed our lead and adopted legislation based upon the Aviation Disaster Family Assistance Act of 1996.

This story goes beyond Terri Severin's success in forever altering the airline industry's approach to families. It is an inspiring account that transcends grief, providing hope in the wake of tragedy and embracing life after experiencing a great loss. No one involved in these accident investigations can truly understand what families go through in the aftermath of a tragedy, nor do we presume that issuing a final report resolves their grief. However, our perspective is forever enlightened by the family members who bravely come forward and continue to share their stories with the public. As Thomas Jefferson, America's third president and one of its Founding Fathers, once said, "The care of human life and happiness is the first and only legitimate object of good government." I believe this phrase embodies the goals and mission of the NTSB's Office of Family Assistance.

Jim Hall
Former Chairman of the National Transportation Safety Board
Managing Partner of Hall & Associates LLC

Introduction

by Mary Schiavo

Accident – *n*. an undesirable or unfortunate happening that occurs unintentionally and usually results in harm, injury, damage, or loss; casualty; mishap. [1]

Several years ago I stopped calling aviation disasters "airplane accidents." There are airplane crashes, collisions, or disasters, but not accidents; nor are there incidents or mishaps. Accident implies there is no fault. Accident implies an unavoidable occurrence. Accident implies no one will be blamed or held accountable. Accident fails to describe the devastation to the lives not only of those killed or injured in the crash, but also the lives of their families.

A plane crash has an impact that extends beyond the families of those lost or injured. A horrific plane crash shakes our nation and the world. The government, politicians, law enforcement, safety groups, attorneys, the courts, big insurance companies, and of course the airlines, airports, and other aviation interests all have a stake in the outcome. Each interested party wants something different from the investigation, fact finding and fault finding, and each interested party has a different notion of what should be accomplished with the closure of the case.

I have had the occasion to work on aviation cases in many capacities. As the Inspector General of the U.S. Department of Transportation my goal was to identify systemic, nationwide, and overarching holes and loopholes in aviation safety and security. As a criminal investigator and prosecutor, working with my special agents and in conjunction with the Federal Bureau of Investigation, I investigated and prosecuted aviation crimes. As an Assistant U.S. Attorney I prosecuted those who refused to follow the laws of aviation. As an aviation writer and television aviation commentator, I often get the first calls after an aviation disaster and have to draw on experience and sketchy clues to shed light on what may have caused the crashes or collisions. And as an aviation disaster attorney, I sift through the evidence and make cases against those whose action caused or contributed to the air crash or collision and the horrific loss of life and injury, both to those on the plane, and to those on the ground.

I have noticed throughout my aviation work in various capacities that "closure" is a word often casually tossed about. Government officials use it when they want to quickly move on from the crash to whatever other news is on the front page. The courts and judges use the word "closure" to encourage families to settle so they can take another case off the docket. Most of all I hear attorneys for airlines speaking about "closure," usually to convince families to take a less than acceptable settlement they are offering but which always comes with a denial of responsibility, fault or guilt.

And so I have come to realize that, in the minds of many, "closure" equates with escaping responsibility, fault, blame, and accountability. The closure they seek is for their own benefit. They see it as a closing of a book, the ending of a case, wiping the slate clean, or turning the corner...for themselves.

But for families of plane crash victims, closure does not come so simply and painlessly, if at all. It cannot be bought with a no-fault check. It cannot be decreed by a court and the opinion of a judge. It neither starts nor ends at the times and stages as set forth in the psychologists' resource, *Diagnostic and Statistical Manual of Mental Disorders IV.* In fact, of the hundreds of families I have represented in airplane disaster cases, not one has ever reported obtaining "closure." What they have told me is that they learned to live with the new reality, a reality that their lives have been forever altered...against their choice, without their consent, and against their will. They learn to remember, so they will not be surprised when something personal triggers a flashback to a happier time, so they will not reach for the phone and start to dial only to remember their loved one died in a plane crash. They get used to their new life so they do not relive the pain each time they forget their old life is gone. They get used to their loss, but there is no closure. Closure is what others say or do so they don't have to think about it. Families think about it whether they want to or not. The plane crash is always there, and always will be. Families learn how to cope with it, but it takes a very long time.

In her book, *In the Wake of the Storm,* Terri Severin helps us begin to understand the devastation of aviation disasters, whether we are airline personnel, government regulators, accident investigators, courts and judges, attorneys, care givers, or kindly souls who just want to help. Her journey shows us what the reality is like for families forced to live and re-live an airplane disaster and how much time everything related to an airplane crash takes, be it the investigation, the fact findings and hearings, the litigation, and the getting through the anniversaries, birthdays, holidays, and countless little things everyday that remind us of the loved ones lost. I encourage you to go on this journey with her so you can understand, help, and maybe change the world in the process.

Mary Schiavo
Former U.S. Department of Transportation Inspector General
Aviation Television Commentator
Aviation Attorney, Motley Rice LLC

[1] *Dictionary.com Unabridged (v 1.1)*
Based on the Random House Unabridged Dictionary, © Random House, Inc. 2006.

1

I remember that even when I was growing up, I realized how lucky I was for all the things with which I was blessed in my life. I had two of the most wonderful parents a kid could ask for, and even though I only had one sibling, Patty, I knew that I couldn't find anybody in the entire world with a better sister. As we got older, Patty and I would often discuss the unusually close nature of our family, expressing gratitude for the love by which we were constantly surrounded. Regardless of life's ups and downs, I was kept grounded by the fact that I could always rely on the endless support and understanding of my sister. My conception of life for so long was inextricably linked to the wholeness of our family; eventually, Patty and I had children of our own, and we raised our two families as one loving unit, strengthened by the continued assistance and presence of our parents, who helped to instill in our children the traditions and teachings that had shaped the impressions that Patty and I held of the world. Life was beautiful, fair, joyous, and consistent with everything I had come to believe…the sky was a translucent shade of blue, and the rays of sunshine beaming down into my life were only occasionally and temporarily blocked by passing clouds…but unbeknownst to me, an ominous forecast was looming on the horizon. I can still recall that last moment of calm just before the storm…

It was Monday, October 31, 1994, and another Halloween was upon us. My house was filled with a building sense of anticipation, as my twelve-year-old son, Jimmy, and my nine-year-old son, Andy, excitedly transformed themselves into two daunting creatures, while my seven-year-old daughter, Nikki, refashioned herself into an angelic fairy princess. We were waiting for Patty and her two boys, seven-year-old Jonathon and four-year-old Patrick, who had all been in Indianapolis accompanying Patty on a business trip, and were scheduled to fly back to Chicago in just enough time to join us for trick-or-treating.

My children's energetic enthusiasm continued to mount as the moment they had looked forward to all year long approached. As I scurried around making last-minute costume adjustments I snapped several pictures of them bringing life to their characters, making sure to save several shots on the roll of film for the imminent arrival of Patty and her boys. These captured moments would be added to the many photo albums that already documented our lives.

On this day, the festive and cheerful atmosphere inside my house directly contrasted with the near-freezing temperatures, heavy winds, and driving horizontal rain outside, all of which created the harshest weather conditions of any Halloween I could remember. Nevertheless, it was still Halloween, and nothing could diminish the children's youthful exuberance, or the enjoyment Patty and I always felt from observing the passing of our beloved holiday tradition over to this new generation.

As I waited for everyone to arrive, I sat and watched my children experience the magic of Halloween and the uninhibited forces of imagination, reminiscing about growing up with Patty and the wonderful occasions we had shared together. Each year, Halloween had begun with numerous costume fittings, continuing until our mother's sewing and embroidering had been completed to perfection. We would start trick-or-treating early in the morning, pausing only for lunch or to make a quick stop home to replace an overflowing bag. For us, this holiday had extended well beyond October 31, as we would sit on the floor and trade goodies from our sugary stockpiles for weeks afterward.

Our Halloween rituals were indicative of the close bond between us that filtered into every aspect of our lives. Patty and I were known as "Irish Twins," meaning that we shared the same birthday, January 12, although Patty was born one year after me. Our unique connection had developed at an early age, partially arising out of our mischievous natures; we had always managed to find fun and excitement, while occasionally generating scenes of commotion.

Growing up, our family had attended church every Sunday morning; on one day in particular, just after arriving home, Patty pleaded with Mom to wear her new Sunday shoes and white socks to go out to play. Patty's angelic blue eyes and white-blonde hair endowed her with great powers of persuasion, causing Mom to eventually relent. I, on the other hand, had been content with wearing comfortable clothes along with my perfectly broken-in blue play shoes.

Within minutes, Patty and I had made our way to the top of a big dirt hill at the local park, where we always had fun playing with our friends. Upon arriving, one of our playmates had summoned Patty and dared her to run down the hill full speed and then out into the adjacent field. I watched as Patty started her decent, picking up momentum as she flew down the hill, but once she reached the bottom she had suddenly come to a screeching halt, appearing frozen in time as I watched her sink into wet, sloppy mud that slowly enveloped her new Sunday shoes, and then continued to swallow up her brand new white socks. She knew at that moment that she had made a huge mistake.

Without a second thought, my play shoes and I had started down the hill, following in Patty's footsteps. When I reached my sister, I took hold of her hand and pulled her free of the quicksand-like predicament, while simultaneously making sure to keep moving in order to avoid also getting stuck. I led her over to where our friends were huddled and told her to wait there. I then proceeded to run all the way home, where I snuck Patty's play shoes and another pair of socks out of the house, along with a paper bag for the freshly muddied Sunday shoes and socks, and hurried back to the park. Exhausted and out of breath, I handed Patty the dirt-free garments, satisfied with myself for having successfully prevented Mom from discovering the mishap, and relieved that I had been able to be there for my sister when she needed help. When Patty and I returned home, we cleaned the shoes, and to complete our foolproof plan, we threw the mud-stained socks into the bottom of the hamper, where they were sure to remain hidden. Of course, it wasn't until years later that we realized that the hamper was not responsible for magically replenishing our drawers with a stockpile of freshly washed clothing…for only our mother had such powers.

Our scheming plans usually wound up backfiring, but that certainly never stopped us from attempting to elude the watchful eyes of our parents. One year, Patty broke her arm from falling off the top of a swing set, and when it happened, I remember my horror at how distinctly her bone protruded from her wrist. Even though her injury significantly altered her daily routine, Patty had taken it all in stride, tailoring her activities to having the cast on her arm. Our upcoming combination ballet, tap, and acrobatic recital had been revised at the last minute, so as to accommodate Patty's new six-week restrictions. Swimming, on the other hand, had been banned altogether, as she was given strict orders not to get her cast wet. Of course, as far as we were concerned, going in the pool was prohibited only during the times Mom or Dad were looking out the window into the backyard, where we had a pool with water that came to a height just above our knees. Even though Patty couldn't swim in the pool with her cast on, she and I reasoned that it would still be okay to run across the yard, jump in the pool, run through the pool, and then jump out the other side. In typical childhood fashion, we figured that no harm could come from any such activity. At first, this swimming improvisation worked well, right up until the moment that Patty tripped jumping over the side of the pool. As she instinctively put her hands out in front of her to catch herself, she wound up firmly planting her hands at the bottom of the pool. We had suddenly realized why Patty was told to stay out of the water, for we both watched in amazement as this hard and seemingly indestructible cast instantly began to melt away.

Even after long days of play, there were times when Patty and I had still not been ready to say good night to each other. So, just before being tucked into bed, we would conspire to play a card game or two. To avoid suspicion, we would lie still for a couple of minutes after our mom had left before quietly getting up and pretending to use the bathroom. One time, I had been sitting on the toilet with my cards in hand, while Patty stood nearby with hers; in constructing this setup, we figured that

4

if Mom came upstairs, we would still be able to appear free of any wrongdoing. Sure enough, the game was going well when we heard Mom's footsteps climbing up the stairs. We remained unfazed, as we had so diligently laid out our great plan. Moments before Mom turned the corner into the bathroom, I slipped the cards onto my lap and concealed them with my pajama top, assuming that I would be safe as long as Mom didn't make me move. Meanwhile, Patty had quickly hidden her cards under the waistband of her pajamas, covering the bulge with her pajama top, and then we both looked at each other satisfied, believing we had inconspicuously hidden the evidence. As I was in the middle of innocently explaining to Mom that we had only gotten up to use the bathroom, Patty's cards had suddenly come loose from her waistband, flowing through the legs of her pajama bottoms and then piling onto the floor. I can still see Patty's startled expression as she stared at the two mounds of cards collecting at her feet. We couldn't even talk our way out of this predicament, as we had both been so stunned at our carefully devised plan having slipped right through the legs of Patty's pants!

As an adult, such memories of the youthful adventures that Patty and I had embarked upon would instantly bring a smile to my face and fill my heart with love for my sister. The closeness between us that had defined our early years transcended into adulthood, as Patty and I ran a business together, helped to raise one another's children, and lived only blocks apart. And as I stood watching my children zestfully prepare for trick-or-treating, I could only hope that some day they would be able to look back on these experiences with the same fondness that characterized my memories of Patty.

Around 3:45 p.m., a knock at my door jolted me back into the moment. Since Patty and her boys did not walk right in, I suspected the door must have been locked. I opened the door with a smile, ready to welcome them home and compliment them on their timely arrival. However, the eager smiling faces I saw were not those of Patty, Jonathon, and Patrick, but those of my children's friends, who anxiously bounded into the house to hurry my children along so they could all get started trick-or-treating.

Just minutes before 4:00 p.m., I snapped a couple more pictures of the motley crew in my kitchen before they all took off. Everything typical of our Halloween celebrations seemed to be in place—everything, that is, except for Jonathon and Patrick. Even though Patty and her boys had not yet returned home, as far as I was concerned they would just be getting a later start on the fun this year. I had no reason to believe otherwise, as Patty and I had trick-or-treated a lifetime of Halloweens together.

❧ ❧ ❧

While I was lightheartedly watching my children make their way out the door, over at my parents' house, my father was feeling restless. He had told Mom that he felt something was terribly wrong…something having to do with Patty.

Around the same time that Dad was relaying his sense of apprehension to Mom, down in Indianapolis, Patty was also experiencing feelings of uneasiness concerning her upcoming flight, arising from a disturbing discussion she'd had earlier that morning with her friend, Eric, who had accompanied her on the trip to Indianapolis.

The previous night, Eric had dreamt of an airplane crash, which he had shared with Patty upon waking; during the time before they left for the airport, Patty had expressed her anxiety over his unsettling premonition and spent the morning wondering whether or not to return on their scheduled flight. Despite her misgivings, Patty decided to proceed with her plans to fly home anyway, so as to ensure that she and the children would make it to my house in time for the highly anticipated Halloween festivities. Early in the afternoon, Patty, her two boys, and Eric headed for the airport. Upon arriving, they walked into what looked like a mob scene, with long lines everywhere. Patty and Eric decided to split up into two different lines, agreeing that whichever moved fastest would determine their mode of transportation home. Eric waited at the United Airlines ticket counter, while Patty stood in the line of a car rental agency. The United Airlines line won out.

At that point, Patty called Mom at the office to mention that her trip had not gone as expected, and that she had already stayed longer than she originally planned. Luckily, the standby tickets Patty had purchased gave her the flexibility to delay her flight home in order to do a little extra work on the assignment. Patty told Mom that she would be back in time for the boys to go trick-or-treating, and then inquired as to the weather conditions at home, most likely trying to gauge whether her boys' night would be affected by the storm. Mom had informed Patty of the torrential rains and sleet, insisting that since the weather was so bad she needn't hurry home.

Patty had acknowledged Mom's advice, but said she didn't want to disappoint her boys, especially since Patrick was already dressed in his Ninja Turtle costume, and ultimately decided to take the next available flight. She assured Mom that the details for their trip had all been arranged, and that although they held four United Airlines tickets, their intended flight only had two available seats, forcing a separation in the group; thus, she would be traveling with one of her boys, while Eric would fly home with the other. Because of the shortage of seating on their desired flight, American Eagle honored their other two tickets on a flight conveniently due to depart just fifteen minutes after the United flight. As it turned out, the American Eagle flight had also been full until a woman and her young son decided to drive a rental car back to Chicago instead of fly, thus opening up the two seats needed.

❦ ❦ ❦

After placing the phone call to Mom providing her with an update on their travel arrangements, Patty stood with Eric and her two boys in the Indianapolis airport, discussing who would take the earlier United Airlines flight, and who would shortly follow on American Eagle Flight 4184. They decided that Eric and Jonathon would take the first flight, and then they would all reunite when Patty and Patrick landed at O'Hare just fifteen minutes later.

Before they separated, another passenger assigned to the American Eagle flight overheard their flight accommodations and approached Patty to see if Jonathon would be interested in trading flights with him so Patty could travel with both of her boys. The passenger, Brad, wanted to take the United Airlines flight, because its earlier departure time would have helped him secure making his connection at O'Hare. However, Patty refused his request because she wanted Jonathon and Eric to stay together, and thus Brad took the American Eagle flight as scheduled.

At approximately 2:00 p.m. Chicago time, Patty and Patrick accompanied Jonathon and Eric to the United Airlines gate. Just before Jonathon boarded the plane, he extended his hand to Patrick for a "high-five" response. Having been cued to initiate their familiar ritual, Patrick slapped his brother's hand and giggled with delight as Jonathon immediately started shaking it, pretending that it stung from Patrick's strength. After the boys finished their customary farewell, Patty gave Jonathon her usual reassuring hug and kiss, whispering the words, "I love you," into his ear. Then her oldest son disappeared with Eric down the boarding ramp.

Patty and Patrick hurried over to the American Eagle gate, where she rushed up to the ticket counter and asked, "Is there still time?" Having received an affirmative answer, Patty scooped Patrick up in her arms and raced outside, carrying him across the tarmac to board the plane.

❧ 2 ❧

I spent the afternoon greeting the flow of trick-or-treaters arriving at my house; amid this activity, I heard my back door open several times, but instead of Patty, Patrick, and Jonathon walking into my house as I expected, my children appeared, seeking some temporary relief from the miserable weather conditions before again bounding back outside to resume their quest for treats. Jimmy, Andy, and Nikki's excitement, which had been building as they prepared for their Halloween adventures, was increasingly dampened while trick-or-treating, as they found themselves battling against the blowing winds and freezing temperatures of the rainstorm that chilled them to the bone. Eventually the weather won out, and everyone returned home by early evening, much sooner than was typical for this day.

At approximately 5:00 p.m., Dad came over, looking sick, with his face completely drained of color. This disturbing appearance contrasted sharply with Dad's usual strong and vibrant demeanor. He had served in World War II and been in law enforcement most of his life, but the balanced, calm manner that I was accustomed to seeing in him was suddenly absent. With a sense of urgency in his voice, he said there had been a plane crash coming from Indianapolis to Chicago, and wanted me to call the airport to see if Patty had been on that plane. Although startled by his uncharacteristic lack of composure, this information did not alarm me, since I knew something so terrible could never happen to our family.

Thus, surrounded by the flurry of children's footsteps and ringing doorbells, I found myself on the phone with the Indianapolis airport, trying to fulfill his request despite all the commotion that was surrounding me. Dad sat at my kitchen table with his head in his hands, completely distraught. At that moment, as much as Dad knew something had gone horribly wrong, I had remained entirely convinced that Patty was just fine, believing that my dad was somehow overreacting.

I remained calm and unconcerned as I was transferred from one representative to another, trying to track down Patty, which was quite a difficult task considering I did not know any of her flight information. Even though she had given Mom her travel plans earlier in the day, neither Dad nor I had been updated on these details, and anyways, Patty had not given Mom the flight number. In the absence of concrete particulars, I told the operator my sister's full name, Patricia Henry, and asked that she be paged in every possible area of the airport. There was never an answer. At one point an airline employee did say they had just heard of someone by the name of Pat Henry being addressed, but that direction eventually led to another dead end, as I learned that Pat Henry was the name of an airline spokesman working that night.

After spending some time on the phone with the airport, I realized that I was getting nowhere, and decided to hang up so that I could try to track down Patty at home. I called her number over and over again, but there was never an answer. I figured that she was surely in route to her house, as it was getting late, but my steadfast composure was slightly jarred by the panic-stricken look that remained on my dad's face. We decided to turn on the TV to see if we could find out any specifics about the plane crash, and quickly learned that the downed aircraft belonged to American Eagle. That was a relief, because I knew Patty held United Airline tickets. However, I still decided to call a phone number listed on the TV screen to get information about the crash. I dialed the number. Then the waiting began.

While I was on hold, my mind drifted back to five days earlier when the circumstances of this trip had arisen. On Wednesday, October 26, 1994, Patty had been at work in the office of our family's investigative agency. She had already spoken with many clients and was about to leave for the day when she received one last phone call from a frantic woman wanting some help regarding an upcoming divorce. Normally, we didn't accept this type of personal work; our clientele typically consisted of large corporations, insurance companies, and law firms. But in this instance, the desperation in the woman's voice had moved Patty to take the assignment. Moreover, while Patty's job did not typically involve traveling, she was so compelled by this woman that she decided to handle the case in person, arranging to fly down to Indianapolis with Jonathon, Patrick, and her friend Eric, who was to watch the boys while she worked.

Before completing her plans, Patty had come to me to explain why she was driven to take such an assignment. During the course of our discussion, she reminded me of the years she had spent debating as to whether or not to stay in her marriage. Her views on family, parenting, emotional support, and finances had differed greatly from those held by her husband, causing her to question the vows she had taken before God, and whether her loyalty to those vows should take precedence over her loyalty to herself. Our religious upbringing had weighed heavily on her, as we had been taught that we were to stay married until death do us part…but she had come to realize that would have meant being trapped in a life of unhappiness. It had been hard for her to believe that God would have deterred her from finding contentment, and she had wondered whether she would be forgiven for deciding to preserve her own well-being over her marital commitment.

Patty's marriage had eventually ended in divorce during the summer of 1994, just two months prior to her taking this assignment. Afterward, Patty had begun the long process of changing names and beneficiaries on legal documents. During one of our conversations during that time, we discussed the role each of us wanted the other to play in the event that one of us should die, covering issues concerning ownership of houses, cars, personal belongings, and our business; however, most of our focus was directed toward the future of our children. Patty had clearly stated to me that her ex-husband, Frank, had removed himself from the lives of their sons following the divorce, and thus, if she were to die before her children were grown up, she wanted me to take care of and raise them. I in turn had asked Patty to do the same for my children in the event my husband and I died while they were still young. We had both laughed thinking of how much additional work Patty would have gaining three more children than I would from acquiring only an extra two.

Therefore, during this conversation prior to finalizing her plans for Indianapolis, Patty admitted that the freshness of her own ordeal had ultimately sparked a heightened sense of compassion in her for the woman, as well as a desire to extend assistance that might ease some of her desperation.

The morning of Friday, October 28, a few hours before Patty and her boys needed to leave for the airport, she and Patrick had met me at work for a short time. While Patty had been on the phone confirming her tickets on United Airlines, Patrick and I played a little game. He would sneak up to my desk, and when he was sure I wasn't looking, he would snatch part of the snack I was eating before running back to his mother's side. I would then turn, notice some of my food was gone, and search for it all over my desk. Watching me, Patrick would grin from ear to ear and break into laughter. Finally, I would give up looking for my missing food and would continue with my work. When my back was turned, the same scenario would replay, occurring several more times until Patty had finished with her phone calls.

Sometime after 10:00 a.m., Patty, Patrick, and I had left the office for my house. About twenty minutes later, they headed home to pack for the early afternoon flight. It had taken Patty several minutes to convince Patrick that it was time to leave, assuring him that he could play with the Matchbox cars and parking garage the next time he came over, as these were some of his all-time favorite toys. After Patty and I said goodbye, I tightly wrapped my arms around little Patrick and gave him a kiss on the cheek, and in an instant they had been on their way.

During the time I was mentally traversing through all of these situational twists that had led Patty to Indianapolis, I almost forgot that I was still on hold until my dad suddenly burst out of his chair, unable to sit still any longer. Each minute I was on the phone had seemed like an eternity to him, and so he decided to go pick up Mom and then drive to O'Hare. When he finally left my house, my previously calm nerves had been rattled by his overwhelming sense that something had gone dreadfully awry with Patty.

An hour and a half after my dad left for O'Hare, it was close to 7:00 p.m., and there had still been no word from Patty; since she had said she would be back in time to start trick-or-treating, I was at this point somewhat alarmed by her continued absence. As I lingered on hold with the airline, I couldn't understand why they wouldn't just answer so that I could have the confirmation I needed in order to support my initial conviction that my sister had not taken that ill-fated flight. On our second phone line, I persisted in calling her house, but there was never an answer. As time went on, I began to feel more and more desperate for any response at all, either from the airline or Patty.

In order to remain composed, which was difficult considering that my patience was dwindling from the excessive amount of time I had been detained on the phone with the airline, I tried to concentrate on the fact that Patty held United Airlines' tickets. I even entertained the idea that maybe something more appealing than returning home had come up for her and the boys at the last minute, as it was certainly in Patty's nature to be spontaneous. But mostly, I held onto the thought that bad things like airplane crashes simply didn't happen to people in close, loving families like ours.

❧ ❧ ❧

Meanwhile, my parents had arrived at the airport and pulled up to the American Airlines terminal, where they brought their vehicle to an abrupt stop in the "no parking" zone, for at that moment, Dad's growing sense of desperation overrode the threat of being towed.

They dashed inside and approached the first American Airlines' ticket agent they saw, urgently asking if their daughter and grandson had been on that downed flight. Moments later, an airline representative arrived and escorted Mom and Dad to another area of the airport. On the way, Dad commented that it didn't look good, at which point Mom's earlier attitude of nonchalance gave way to sharing Dad's grave fears. Without offering Mom and Dad any information, or even the smallest suggestion of hope, the representative merely showed them into a room and requested they sit and wait.

❧ ❧ ❧

Back at home, I was still waiting as well, having been on hold close to three hours; finally, I heard a live voice on the other end of the phone. I let out a long sigh, hardly able to believe how relieved I felt at the prospect of at last getting some answers. All I wanted to hear were words substantiating my desperate hope that Patty was not on the downed flight, but was just in the midst of large delays because of the crash and bad weather. The operator began asking for the names, proper spellings, and my relationship to those I was concerned had been on the flight, as well as for my name and phone number. After I responded, the woman said she had no information for me, but would call me back as soon as anything was known. Then, as abruptly as the silence of being on hold had been broken, the line went silent.

I couldn't believe it…all that time waiting and yet still no answers. I didn't understand how the airline could put people through this type of torturous suspension. I called some close friends looking for comfort and reassurance—anything that would diminish the sense of panic I felt creeping up on me and trying to take over.

More and more time elapsed, still with no word from Patty. I raced to answer my phone every time it rang, longingly anticipating to hear Patty's voice on the other end. Each instance that I picked up the receiver only to hear a voice other than Patty's, the horrible, nauseous feeling inside me expanded.

Throughout the evening, while I was nearly glued to the phone in hopes of receiving that one message I so badly needed to hear, several calls came in that seemed to be out of the blue, from friends that I hadn't heard from in a while contacting me to see how I was doing. I shared my anxiety over the plane crash and not having heard from my sister, thinking it strange that these people seemed to know I could have used some kindhearted words of consolation at that moment. In the midst of these calls, my husband, Tom, had returned from work, staying home long enough only to pack his suitcase, as he was scheduled to drive out of town for a business trip.

At this point in the night, my children were gleefully sprawled out on the living room floor with their Halloween treats, just as Patty and I used to do when we were their age. But this year, it was as if I heard their laughter only from a distance, muffled by the anguish, fear, and helplessness with which I was confronted.

❧ ❧ ❧

Approximately four hours had passed since Mom and Dad's arrival at O'Hare. Their eternal wait had been broken only by the onslaught of American Airlines' representatives repeatedly bursting into the room to ask the same questions over and over. "What are the correct spellings of your daughter's and grandson's names? What do they look like? What were they wearing? What items did they have with them?" Each time that my parents tried to seek out additional information, the only communication that they received from the airline involved questions, questions, and more questions.

Periodically they glimpsed other families housed in separate rooms across and down the hall from theirs whose worries had also been continuously shelved by the airline, and whose faces reflected the same look of grave distress that my parents felt. A short time later, a chaplain entered their room to pray with my parents, as he was making his way from one family to the next, all sharing the same concern. The families prayed out loud. They prayed in silence. They prayed to be spared from the impending tragedy that loomed just around the corner.

Meanwhile, in another area of O'Hare, Eric and Jonathon had been stationed at the designated meeting place where they had agreed to rejoin Patty and Patrick, but what was to be just a fifteen-minute wait had turned into hours. They checked the screens to see if Patty's and Patrick's flight status was indicated as delayed, but all of the monitors had been blacked out. Not knowing why they hadn't arrived, and afraid to ask about the status of the flight because of his dream the night before, Eric and Jonathon had eventually just headed for home.

꽃 꽃 꽃

While my parents were fretfully praying with the chaplain at O'Hare, I had remained at my post by the phone, praying for it to ring. At last, a call came in, and as with each ring of the phone, my heart skipped a beat and my breathing stopped in anticipation of hearing Patty's voice. But instead I heard my mom, who was calling to tell me that she and Dad were still at the airport…still waiting. She said she would call back as soon as they knew anything.

Shortly thereafter, I heard the sound of my back door opening. The children were already asleep and my husband was out of town. Patty had finally come home. She had missed Halloween, but there would always be next year, and the important thing was that she had made it home safely. In my emotional frenzy, I rushed to greet her, but as I turned the corner I saw Tom, not Patty, standing before me. He had decided to stay home until the situation was resolved.

Late into the night, as I had still received no word from Patty, no additional calls from my parents, and no response from the airline, I found myself struggling to prevent my mind from taking off with the worst-case scenario. Again, I called on friends for consolation, but no words or actions could temper the feelings that were beginning to anchor in the pit of my stomach. I was overcome with waves of sickness that resembled what Dad must have felt when he had come to my house earlier in the day to tell me about a plane crash.

꽃 꽃 꽃

At O'Hare airport, approximately five hours after my parents had been escorted into a waiting room, they were met by one more airline representative, but this one was different than all the rest, for this one brought answers. Giving him their full attention, Mom and Dad listened acutely with every fiber of their beings as he said, "There has been a plane crash. It has been confirmed that Patricia Henry and Patrick Henry were on board the flight. There were no survivors."

Dad responded with, "Could you repeat that?"

૭ೇ ૭ೇ ૭ೇ

Minutes later my phone rang. It was Dad calling to tell me that he and Mom had just received verification that Patty and Patrick were on that downed flight. I don't remember any other words spoken. We hung up. I screamed.

ॐ 3 ॐ

I collapsed onto my bed, consumed in a fit of hysteria. I desperately tried to convince myself that this couldn't be real...it couldn't be happening. How could such a tragedy have befallen my sister, my nephew, my family, and me? How was I to go on without Patty? She was such a part of my world...such a part of me...imagining a life without her seemed inconceivable.

Earlier in the evening, the Monday-night football game on television had served as a background for the Halloween festivities. Each time I walked through the family room, I had glanced at the Chicago Bears playing the Green Bay Packers, and then at the special news coverage about an airline disaster. In that moment, I had thought only minimally about the crash, having been in the midst of celebrating Halloween with my children; the television broadcast had seemed completely removed from my life. Another news bulletin had indicated that due to the severe weather conditions, the recovery efforts had been suspended, and were not to resume again until daylight. I had not been able to figure out what difference it would make when the rescue attempts would recommence, for after all, the news report stated that there were no survivors.

However, hours after the initial broadcast, I found myself repeatedly replaying those short TV segments about the crash in my mind. In my state of raw grief, thoughts were jumping around in every direction, ranging from the devastating impact of the news to my desperate search for hope, any hope. I was consumed with frustration over not having taken more time to stop and listen to all of what had been relayed during the news bulletins, for then I would have had the information that I wanted…the information that I needed.

One of the details that I had retained from the earlier news broadcasts was that the search for survivors had been halted after authorities declared the crash fatal. At the time, I had not allowed myself to be impacted by what I heard, but upon receiving the devastating and shocking truth that Patty and Patrick had been on board that flight, this particular fact suddenly sent paralyzing waves of pain through my body. Even though everyone on board the plane was presumed dead, it seemed to me that nobody could really know for sure, seeing as how the recovery efforts had temporarily ceased; thus, I frantically began thinking of possible ways to get help for Patty and Patrick that night, not the next day—for while I could accept that this crash had been fatal to everyone else on board, I simply refused to believe that it had caused the deaths of my sister and nephew. Images repeatedly formed in my head of a site filled with horrific destruction so severe that, at a glance, or maybe even a closer look, not even the slightest sign of life was apparent. And yet somehow, I managed to grab and desperately cling to the thought that Patty and Patrick had survived. I pictured them injured, perhaps quite severely, but inexplicably still alive, helplessly lying in the dark marsh-like field, exposed to the bitter-cold rainstorm, and waiting for assistance. Waiting to be rescued. Waiting for nothing, as no help would arrive until the light of dawn. An onslaught of questions churned through my mind. Could they sustain life without medical treatment until morning? How could I get to them? How could I help? I wanted to go and find them…I wanted *anything* that would afford me some measure of control, but all I could do was remain stuck, feeling useless and powerless.

As I lay on my bed in this frenzied state, Tom walked out of the bathroom, flossing his teeth. Through uncontrollable sobs, I somehow relayed to him the information I had learned from my dad's phone call just minutes earlier. He paused only long enough to listen and then returned to his task. Startled by his indifference to what for me was Earth-shattering news, I was about to call someone who could offer me some support when my seven-year-old daughter, Nikki, walked into my bedroom yawning and rubbing her eyes. Earlier that evening, she and her two brothers had been tucked into bed knowing that Patty, Jonathon, and Patrick had not joined us for Halloween as planned. From the news broadcasts on TV they had also been aware of a plane crash, as well as the fact that I had been on the phone continuously trying to get information. Realizing that my children had yet to be told, I got up and approached Nikki as she entered my room.

"Was Aunt Patty in the plane crash, Mommy?"

"Yes," I answered, "She and Patrick were in the crash."

"Are they in the hospital?"

I couldn't help but think of what a typical question that was for a seven-year-old to ask, for to a child, isn't a doctor viewed as someone who can make everything better, almost as if he had the power of God? If mom couldn't fix something, it was taken to the higher power of a doctor, where all that was broken got mended. But in an instant, this innocent conception of magical cures and unfailing security was shattered for Nikki. Patty and Patrick were irrevocably thrust beyond the power of any mom's or doctor's healing remedies.

Struggling to speak, I responded with words that took all my strength to form and utter, "No, they are not in the hospital. Patty and Patrick are now up in Heaven with God."

Silently, Nikki turned away, and with her little head hanging down started back towards her room. I couldn't even go with her. I couldn't even comfort my own daughter. Instead, I asked my husband to go and be with her, and having finished flossing his teeth, he went.

As they were heading down the hall, my friend, Amy, called to see whether we had heard anything. Through my hysteria, I struggled to again utter those words that gave credence to Patty and Patrick being gone—not just on a trip, but forever. When we hung up, the calm demeanor that Amy had maintained while on the phone with me immediately gave way once she placed a phone call to my church. Thankfully, the patience and compassion extended by Sister Paul Anne eventually made it possible for her to relay the message about Patty.

A short while after receiving Amy's call, Mom and Dad came over directly from the airport. We met in the doorway of my bedroom, and they embraced me in the robotic fashion that had allowed them to drive away from the airport and reach my house. Tears fell. No words of solace were attempted, for what could have possibly been said? They stayed for only a few moments before heading to Patty's, where hours earlier Jonathon and Eric had arrived bewildered and nervous as to why Patty and Patrick had not shown up at their designated meeting place.

Upon returning home, Jonathon had expected at any moment to see Patrick bounding through the door with his usual smile, ready for an evening of marathon play, and as she had done thousands of times before, Patty would follow right behind to greet him with the warmth she constantly seemed to emanate, for Jonathon had no reason to believe that this night would be different than any other. Calm and a little tired from his travels, Jonathon had reached to turn on the TV, with no way of knowing that with the flip of a switch, his life would be turned completely upside down.

All at once he had been bombarded with a news broadcast that threw his life into a state of distortion more comparable to a nightmare than any reality he had ever known. For Eric and Jonathon, the information disclosed in the special report hit with a crushing force of unimaginable proportions, suddenly clarifying the horrifying truth as to why Patty and Patrick had never returned home. Immediately, Jonathon had realized he would never see his playful little brother or his beautiful, loving mother ever again. Even though he had been aware of the magnitude of the news, at that moment, he had not been able to comprehend the full impact of what he had just heard, and so all he could do was cry. He cried tears that in the past had helped soothe any of his scratches, bruises, or emotional pain by summoning his mom's comforting and perfect remedies. Whether it was with a band-aid, a hug, or a gentle kiss, Patty had always had whatever he needed. But that night, Jonathon's tears didn't bring his mother to him, and they never would again, regardless of how hard he sobbed. After what seemed like an eternity, Jonathon eventually gave way to exhaustion, which led to sleep.

When my parents entered Patty's house, they greeted Eric, and upon finding Jonathon asleep in his mother's bed, they decided to let him stay in his only possible place of temporary escape. They told Eric they would be back for Jonathon in the morning, and left.

As the night wore on, my earlier sense of desperation in needing to help Patty and Patrick, the only two possible survivors of the crash, began to fade, turning my feelings of helplessness into hopelessness as I gradually faced the cold, harsh truth of my sister and nephew being gone forever.

At some point, the priest called. I found myself providing information without feeling any effect from it whatsoever, as my emotions seemed like they had faded into nonexistence. I felt no comfort from the priest, but then again, I felt nothing at all.

Throughout the night, I both made and received several other phone calls. In the early morning hours, I finally drifted off to sleep, knowing that the person I had always understood myself to be would never again fully awaken, for part of me would forever lie with my sister, Patty, and my sweet nephew, Patrick.

4

My escape into sleep lasted for only an hour or two; immediately upon waking, I struggled to identify an ominous and unrecognizable sense that seemed to linger over me. I felt dissociated from my own reality, and completely disoriented as to what had actually occurred. Had I had a nightmare? What was this awful feeling that gripped me? Why did my face feel so swollen? Within moments, I realized that what had seemed like a nightmare was actually the truth of my newly altered existence.

I crawled out of bed with eyes so puffy they would barely open. As I walked into my living room, I was met with a new day that starkly contrasted with the driving winds and freezing rain that less than twenty-four hours earlier had swept across the Midwest. This new day brought a crystal clear sky and a sun that shone so bright I had to shield my eyes from it. The instant I saw this serene and picturesque setting, I lashed out at God, wondering how He could ever again let the sun shine…how dare He allow the deep blue sky to envelop us with its beauty? And if God truly was all-loving-and-powerful, then how could He take my sister and nephew…how could this have possibly been allowed to happen?

But as these thoughts entered my mind, I struggled to retract them, for even in the depths of my anguish, I knew that God had always been there for me in the past. I also wanted to believe that He would be there to help me through this incredibly tragic time.

I wandered through the house, purposeless and numb, wondering how I was ever going to again find meaning in my life. The first thing I forced myself to do was to break the devastating news to my boys, crumbling part of their loving, playful world. Then I was back on the phone. The words were all the same, and the feelings didn't change much either, as I was virtually numb. Between phone calls, an entourage of friends and acquaintances found their way to my door. At times, even large school buses were parked on my street, as some of the bus drivers Patty and I knew from school came by to pay their respects.

I found myself acutely observing how each person expressed their condolences, watching as they searched for language to convey their sorrow and deeply felt sympathies. I felt as though I was hearing them speak in slow motion, aware of the fact that each word had been purposely chosen to relay a specific message. While the words never touched me, never eased my pain, the gesture of showing up at my door, calling, and sending cards meant more to me than I was capable of communicating.

My friends also watched over me, questioning what I had to eat and drink. The answer was always the same—nothing. I had to be coaxed like a child by these caring friends, for even taking in the tiniest sip of water was difficult, as my body seemed to have shut down, leaving no room for anything.

While I accepted many condolences and spoke with concerned friends and acquaintances, I later came to realize that I had temporarily kept those closest to me at a distance, as their outpouring of love and tenderness was just too much for me to handle. I refused to allow myself moments of vulnerability that would open me up to my overwhelming heartache. I also knew I was not going to rely on my parents for support, for from the moment I received confirmation of Patty and Patrick being on the plane, I decided I wanted to be as strong as I could for them. I was aware that my feelings, however intense, could not begin to compare with how Mom and Dad felt in losing both their daughter and grandson...for in the circle of life, parents usually leave this earthly realm well before their children and certainly before any grandchildren, and this reversal of the expected natural cycles of life and death only emphasized the tragic nature of the situation in which we now found ourselves.

Early that morning, Mom and Dad called me upon returning to Patty's house to pick up Jonathon, who was still asleep in his mother's bed, not yet consciously alert to his waking nightmare. On the phone, they communicated their apprehension about removing him from his peaceful haven, and we expressed our wishes that we could somehow prevent him from facing all of this pain. Eventually, my parents gently woke him, struggling to be as soothing as possible when bringing the details of his new reality into focus. Mom told Jonathon that God had taken his mother and little brother to Heaven, and then held Jonathon while he cried.

Shortly thereafter, Mom and Dad led Jonathon out of Patty's house for the last time, while Eric stayed behind. Not only would Jonathon never again see the smiling faces of his mother and brother, but he would also never again be back in the comfort of the place he called home, where he had made so many memories. The living room's hardwood floor, upon which rested many green plants, had always given the room a warm and welcoming feel. The kitchen was typically filled with tasty snacks, drinks, and the aroma of Patty's delicious cooking. The bathroom conjured up images of the fun Jonathon and Patrick had had splashing in the bathtub. The two downstairs bedrooms had been filled with the many stuffed animals Jonathon and Patrick collected over the years, and Patty's upstairs bedroom held fond associations of playing on her waterbed, along with the security the boys felt when they fell asleep in this comforting place. Their big backyard contained an outside stove, where many fires had given Jonathon a sense of camping out in the woods, and this had also been where he and Patrick had played their favorite game of hide-n-seek, which always brought a smile to Jonathon's face.

But no more memories were to be made here, and no more laughter was to be heard. As he walked away on that bright November morning, Jonathon could only embrace these recollections of the life he had shared with his mother and brother as his most precious belongings, and then his home as he once knew it was instantly transformed into yet another memory.

Jonathon's residence from then on would be my house. It was a place with which he was very familiar, and one that offered a variety of playmates and lots of toys, pets, and love. It was also the place where, just months earlier, Patty had said she wanted Jonathon and Patrick to stay in the event anything was to happen to her.

Upon arriving at my house, Mom and Dad led Jonathon inside. I met him with a huge hug, and in spite of the devastating loss that Jimmy, Andy, and Nikki were enduring, they also gathered around their cousin. They must have instinctively understood that while they felt an enormous amount of pain, the effect that this disaster had upon Jonathon was far greater than anything they could imagine. They showed Jonathon love and concern so genuine that it could have only come from children.

The next thing I knew, the four of them ran outside through the back gate and into the park, as if it were just any other day. There they were, watched over by the warmth of the brilliant sun, perfectly blending into the exquisite tranquility permeating all of nature. Jonathon and his cousins played for hours, running, laughing, and carrying on. I realized that even in the midst of indescribable grief, the beauty in such a scene, like the beauty in all of God's creation, was still temporarily able to resonate inside of me.

Unfortunately, the majority of the day stood in complete opposition to that serene picture, as my house was filled with the continual sounds of the ringing phone and chiming doorbell. I felt as if I was trapped in a powerful and swiftly moving current that had instantly rerouted the direction of my life, and it was all I could do to try and keep my head above water.

In the midst of what seemed to be a pounding torrent of chaotic activity, both the local schools and the police department called to say that the media was trying to reach me to get my story, but I was set against giving any form of public address. In my opinion, there was no way to express the lifetime of love and sisterhood that Patty and I had shared, or to try and put words to the feelings of a seven-year-old who was suddenly without his only brother and his mother. I concluded that all the broadcasters wanted was a display of uninhibited emotions, which I was not willing to give. The schools and the police assured us that they respected the privacy we were seeking, and would try to protect us from the media onslaught.

Sometime mid-afternoon, we received several phone calls from an airline representative informing us that American would be holding a memorial service for the crash victims at a local church the following day, and would be providing a limousine for our transportation. Also, two women from the airline's Care Team, a specialized group of personnel who were available to assist families in the aftermath of a tragedy, were to come to my house and collect information to aid them in the identification process.

Toward the end of this steady stream of phone calls and visitors, Jonathon's father, Frank, arrived at my house. While seeing him jolted my thoughts of the difficulties between him and Patty following their divorce, I nonetheless wanted to be respectful of Jonathon's only surviving parent. However, I knew that my ultimate responsibility lay in acting in Jonathon's best interest, which included fulfilling Patty's wishes that he live with me, at least until a final determination was made by the court.

After I spent hours aimlessly drifting through surges of commotion, the skies finally darkened, and we regained some solitude from the silence of the night. The doorbell eventually stopped chiming, the phone stopped ringing, and everyone returned home. Somehow, I had made it through the first full day of my new life, having found some form of protection in the numbing sensations ensuing from my shock. I tucked all four children into bed, as they too were exhausted from a day that seemed too unbelievable to comprehend.

At about 11:30 p.m., I was startled by yet another chime of the doorbell. When I opened the door, I came face to face with a retired coworker and good friend of my father. "I'm sorry to bother you at this late hour," he said, "but my wife and I have just heard some disturbing news, and we just had to come over to hear you confirm that it isn't true."

As his wife sat in the front seat of their car in her bathrobe, he looked at me, studying my face for the slightest change in expression as he uttered the words, "Is it true that Patty..." but before he could even finish the question, I answered with, "Yes, it's true."

His face turned ashen as his gaze fell from me to the ground. His words, "I'm so sorry," were barely audible as he turned with a lowered head and made his way back to his car.

⚜ 5 ⚜

The following morning, Mom and Dad attended the service held by American Airlines, along with the other families and many airline employees. I did not attend. I would not attend. As far as I was concerned, their memorial could not change the grim outcome of the crash, for which, in my grief-stricken state, I held this company responsible. Afterwards, Mom and Dad told me that the ceremony had felt superficial, for almost as many media personnel were present as those paying their condolences, and it took away from the authenticity of the event.

The day after the service, the American Airlines' Care Team representatives were scheduled to come to my house. On the phone, they had offered to retrieve Patty's car from the airport parking lot. In what seemed to be no time at all, the representatives were able not only to obtain keys for Patty's car, but also to locate it amongst the thousands of other parked vehicles at O'Hare before driving it to my house. I thought it almost miraculous that they had accomplished this task in what appeared to be an effortless manner, and I simply couldn't understand why American Airlines seemed to be saving miracles for returning cars instead of returning passengers to their families.

The two women from the Care Team were very respectful and pleasant. They said they were there to "help us in any way they could," as well as to collect information for the identification process. Mom, Dad, Tom, and I sat with the Care Team representatives at my dining-room table. The women began by telling us that they only had a limited amount of information about the "accident" at that point, but promised that they would keep us apprised of any new developments. When they

29

described this disastrous and devastating crash as an "accident," I felt a surge of anger run through me, because in my mind, the word accident denoted a minor mishap, or a fixable mistake, but certainly not a fatal tragedy. However, the fact that these women were stumbling to find the right words in order to best communicate with us somewhat helped to assuage my frustration, because it was evident that they were struggling with this situation as well. While there were few details to be had, they were able to inform us that the crash had been so catastrophic that nearly everything was destroyed; therefore, the identification process could take several weeks, and it would most likely be impossible to identify everyone from the plane.

It was hard to take in their words. I couldn't fathom how the plane crash could have been so destructive that almost no recognizable remains existed. My common sense had told me that things don't simply disappear, and so I sat there wondering where everything and everyone had gone. I heard the words, but just could not connect them with Patty and Patrick.

In spite of the emotional upheaval generated by these details, I had to put these confusing thoughts on hold, since the airline representatives said that they needed to collect some personal information. I was asked to explain the purpose of Patty's and Patrick's trip to Indianapolis. They also wanted to know what Patty and Patrick were wearing at the time of the crash, the jewelry they had with them, the types of clothing they had packed, and whether they had anything of value with them, including cash. The women requested a description of their luggage, or any other carry-on items they may have brought. I was to supply them with doctor's names, dental and birth records, an overview of all health problems and surgeries, as well as the location and causes of any scars. They inquired about the causes of deaths for our deceased relatives, and read through a long list of illnesses and addictions, asking if they existed in our family.

While I was eager to assist with the identification process in any possible way, I could not help feeling confused by this line of questioning. Many of these inquiries seemed contradictory to what we had been told just moments before, for if everything had been destroyed, then why did the airline representatives need to know what luggage Patty and Patrick may have carried or what they were wearing? Why did they need to know the purpose of their trip to Indianapolis? Why were they asking about Patty's and Patrick's overall physical well-being, and what did the health of my relatives have to do with my sister and nephew? If Patty and Patrick had been killed on the street by a truck, the truck driver's employer would most likely not have asked me for such information. I could not fathom why these representatives were sitting in my home and prying into my family's personal information, and all the while representing the corporation that in my mind was liable for the deaths of my sister and nephew. But even though this series of questions did not sit right with me, these two women appeared genuinely concerned for our family, and thus I somehow managed to convince myself that the airline would do the "right" thing and act in our best interest.

The Care Team women concluded their visit by inquiring as to whether we had any questions; I looked over at my parents blankly, for in this overwhelmed and distraught state, I had absolutely no ability to even process the information I was given, let alone formulate responses or questions. Before leaving, the two airline representatives gave us several phone and pager numbers and told us that we could contact them day or night. They reiterated that they were there to assist us through this extremely trying time.

❧ ❧ ❧

Amidst trying to handle all of the upheaval arising from the tragedy, I needed to start planning a service to be held at our church. It would be called a "memorial" instead of a "funeral" service, as there would be no caskets. My parents had left the arrangements up to me, as they did not have the strength to focus on details surrounding the preparations. My friend Barb supported me each step of the way, helping me to select pictures of Patty and Patrick that clearly reflected the love and joy that defined their lives, and together we created two large collages to display in church.

Such preparatory obligations got me through yet another day of my new life. Although I managed to efficiently take care of business, I intermittently experienced jolts of pain so intense it almost felt as though I couldn't breathe. By the time night fell, it seemed as if I had spent the entire day in some sort of trance, as I simply felt stunned at having survived another twenty-four hours without my sister.

❦ ❦ ❦

Even though it felt like our lives had effectively ended, we had to find a way to keep on living. In those first days following the tragedy, Mom, Dad, and I began assuming diverse roles that formed a pattern, creating an illusion of some semblance of control and normalcy in our lives. Mom divided her time between work, assisting me in handling circumstances concerning Patty and Patrick, and helping to care for the children. We openly talked about matters at hand; we never discussed our emotions. Dad kept to himself, although whenever we needed his guidance or support in any way, he was there without question. Tom went to work each day while I looked after the children, who were staying home from school. Mom continued to bring the kids to piano lessons so that they too could maintain some façade of their usual routines.

This incredibly busy daytime schedule allowed me to stay as far away from my feelings as possible. However, at night, in the silent darkness, when everyone was sound asleep, my tormenting sense of loss would creep up on me like a dark plague, piercing me in a way that would leave me feeling totally incapacitated, as the intense and inescapable agony paralyzed every fiber within me. Each night I spent hours on the phone with friends questioning whether I could find my way back from a place so dark and so low. Sleep only came to me after having drained myself of all emotion, but even then it would only last for a few hours. Somehow, by early morning, my strength would reform, and once again I would be there for Jonathon, my children, and my parents.

❧ ❧ ❧

Somewhere in the midst of time blurring past, the final day of planning for the memorial service at our own church had approached. While working on the finishing touches for the ceremony, I met with the priest to cover some specifics about the mass. I needed to let him know of the closeness between Patty and me, and of the strong bond that had defined the relationship between her and her boys. But most importantly, I wanted to emphasize the unique bond within our family, and the love and respect Patty and I had always held for our parents, urgently explaining how important it was to include this information during the mass. He said he understood. I thanked him and we parted company.

When I got home, I called him to say I didn't think I had relayed how significant it was that he integrate into the service the fact that Patty and I used to often talk about having the best parents in the world. He thanked me for calling back, and again assured me that he would fulfill my request. I thanked him a second time and hung up.

A short while later, I found myself back on the phone, speaking with the priest for a third time. I reiterated that I knew we had already talked about this, but it was just too important for me to leave any room for miscommunication. Again, I told him how much our parents had meant to Patty and me throughout our lives, and expressed my wish that this be explicitly stated during the mass. Patiently, the priest once again acknowledged my concerns. As I hung up, I couldn't help but smile at the redundancy with which I insisted upon including this detail. Even though I was aware that I sounded slightly ridiculous, I felt that it was important to honor the love and happiness that would forever characterize our family.

I allowed my thoughts to drift back to our home growing up, which I had always associated with feelings of warmth, joy, and security. Our house was constantly filled with the aroma of Mom's cooking—she had amazing culinary skills, which we had all enjoyed thoroughly, whether in the form of dinner, fresh pastries, or desserts. Sewing had also been a gift of Mom's, and thus when Patty and I were young, she had made most of our clothes. She usually fashioned the same style of clothes for both of us to wear, but my outfits were usually pink, while Patty's were made out of blue fabric, probably to match her blue eyes.

Each day, as the echo of Mom's words, "Daddy's home," rang through the house, Patty and I would drop whatever we had been doing and run full speed to greet him as he returned from work. Our dad had always been fit and strong, and during one of the games we played, Patty and I would jump up and down on his stomach at the same time, as we had loved to frequently test out the strength of Dad's muscles.

The closeness Patty and I had shared with our parents as children transcended into adulthood. A typical day involved Mom and Dad stopping by my house on the way to the office, as they worked part time at the family business my husband and I owned. Mom usually brought something with her, whether it was household necessities or something for the children, while Dad ordinarily just came to socialize. It was also common for Dad to take Jimmy, my oldest son, out to breakfast before driving him to school each morning.

Since Jonathon and my daughter, Nikki, were only six months apart in age, the two of them had been in the same pre-school class, where Dad had volunteered; taking turns, the students, several at a time, would sit on Dad's lap or lean up next to him, and attentively listen to him tell stories like the ones I remembered listening to as he tucked Patty and me into bed at night when we were young. Dad used his tales as a subtle way of teaching important lessons or sharing valuable information. Dad also performed his magic tricks for Jonathon's and Nikki's class, making balls disappear, discovering lost pennies behind students' ears, and having a guillotine crash down on his finger without any injury. The students loved having Dad in class as much as he loved being there.

...Sometime during my re-living of these happy memories, I drifted off to sleep...

❦ ❦ ❦

I awoke early the next morning, and mechanically proceeded to get myself and the children ready for the day's events. An outsider looking in would have thought this morning was just the beginning of another typical day; the kitchen rumbled with the usual sounds of spoons clanging against colorful ceramic bowls, juice being poured into the children's favorite glasses, the avalanche of different cereals filling the bowls, and small talk from sleepy children still trying to wake up. It almost seemed like they were heading off for another day of school, while I prepared to head to the office.

Except that this day was to be nothing like our usual routine. A short drive would not deliver us to a school or an office, but to our church, a place I associated with many fond memories, as Patty and I had grown up only two doors away. The attached complex was where we had attended grammar school, as well as swam competitively. It was where I was married, where my children were baptized and confirmed, and where up until the previous Thursday night, Patty had taught swimming lessons. On this day, however, we weren't arriving for a celebration or a swim, but rather to recognize and honor the beautiful lives of my sister and nephew.

Upon entering the church, I was met by Sister Paul Anne, who knew our family well from the many school visits Mom had been requested to make due to Patty's sometimes overly zealous behavior as a child. Sister Paul Anne had also been present at the various celebratory functions during our adult years; in contrast, at that moment she stood before me not to rejoice in life's blessings, but to mourn an indescribable loss. After offering her genuine condolences, she informed me that there were flowers in the church from American Airlines, for whatever reason understanding this would be important for me to know. Immediately, I felt as though the corporation had imposed upon my family's privacy; after some consideration, I decided that the flowers could stay, but that the card would need to be removed, as I wanted no reference made to the airline that I saw as having caused the need for this service.

Turning around, I noticed the two women from the airline's Care Team, whose presence I saw as another intrusion. I vehemently felt that they should have asked ahead of time if they were welcome to attend, but I chose to let it go.

The church was filled to capacity, as for a holiday mass. Friends, relatives, coworkers, Patty's swimming students, and classmates from as far back as grammar school were among those present, many of whom had traveled from out of state to offer their condolences.

Funeral services were not foreign to me; in the past several years, I had attended them for my grandmothers, grandfather, aunts, and uncles—but this service differed considerably from the others. Previously, we had been able to somewhat mentally prepare for and accept a death that was due to old age or ill health, and had always been left with a sense of closure after having celebrated and paid homage to a long, full life. Additionally, this service remained separate from those that had come before, in that Patty and Patrick did not lie peacefully in a casket, stripping us of the chance to be in their presence one last time. Upon walking away from this service, I would still be stuck wondering where they were, wondering how nothing could be left of their physical bodies that once contained so much life. But the most significant discrepancy between this service and all the others was that this one was for my beloved sister, Patty, and her son, Patrick. In the throes of my grief, I found it very difficult, if not impossible, to understand their deaths as existing within the natural progression of life.

However, my inability to accept what had transpired was not going to prevent the service from taking place, nor would it change the facts of my new reality. Thus, I took a deep breath and slowly let it out, then took my seat just as the mass began.

I made sure I heard the words the priest spoke, but did not allow them to penetrate me, as I feared that once my grief was exposed, I would not be able to keep it contained. The priest read three letters written by friends, each one sharing the beauty that so naturally emanated from Patty and young Patrick:

There was a serene calmness about Patty that made her so easy to love. She had a gentle smile and nature. Her casual way of dressing somehow added to her great beauty.

She was a loving daughter. I often sat with Patty and her sister, Terri, and I listened to them tell one story after another about their family. It was obvious from my first visit with Patty that she had the most wonderful parents a child could have. It is of no wonder that parenting her own children came so easily to her.

I frequently saw Patty around town with Jonathon and Patrick. She was always smiling when she was with them, seeming calm with her children and sure of herself as a mother. When her children were young, I remember their faces constantly snuggled up against hers, and their fingers holding on to her blonde hair.

One could not help but feel almost privileged to be with Terri and Patty when they were together. It was hard to know where one started and the other left off. The two of them functioned like one unit.

Patty glowed with a beauty that came from inside as well as outside. Her precious smile and gentle nature will live on in the hearts of those who knew and loved her.

The shock of the death of Patty and her son Patrick has numbed me and my wife, leaving a sense of emptiness and pathos we will never overcome. We are grieving for all of Patty's and Patrick's family. Two wonderful people have been senselessly taken away from us.

"Go-for-it" Patty and I taught swimming together at the church for about three years each Thursday evening. She was my mentor and will remain so.

Patty absolutely pushed the children with her famous "peel offs," a system of racing used to strengthen endurance, improve strokes, and increase self-esteem. Her swimmers made the pool look like a hurricane had hit as they swam back and forth, while Patty stood guard, carefully watching. Patty loved it, and so did the children!

When I filled in for Patty while she was having her second baby, Patrick, her students always wanted her back as a teacher. To my surprise, they even demanded those most difficult "peel-offs."

Patty had one special child she taught. Suffering from pervasive developmental disorder—an especially difficult behavioral disability—this boy was a good swimmer but a most challenging student. At first Patty believed him to be just another troublemaker. He spent more time crying and kicked out of class than in class.

The boy's father had tried to avoid the embarrassment of once again having to tell his story. But it was unavoidable. Patty, after hearing the truth about the boy, became aggravated, wanting to know how she was expected to teach him without knowing his problems. She was correct, of course.

From that night on, she took control of the young swimmer, guiding him each lesson, inspiring him each lap, pushing him each stroke. As a result, he later became a three-time gold medal winner in the Special Olympics. Patty had a unique gift for drawing the best out of each of her students, especially those with special needs.

I saw Patty for the final time three weeks ago at a soccer game. Giving her a kiss on the cheek and a big hug, I remember thinking how much fun she was, how much her "go-for-it attitude" meant to all those around her, and what joy she emanated. I only wish I could see her one more time in the pool with the children she so dearly loved. I just wish I could see her with her sons, Patrick and Jonathon. I just wish I could see her one more time.

Patty's most outstanding feature would have to be her enormous, generous smile. Always readily available, it attracted you to her at once and surrounded you with a sense of warmth, trust, and well-being. It was a manifestation of her highly adventurous nature, her strong gusto for life, and her abounding love for her children and family.

No two sisters could have meant more to each other than Patty and Terri. They were obviously raised with a tremendous respect for family and drew upon the strength of their relationship throughout their lives, touching many with the love and devotion they expressed for each other. When one was down the other was always close at hand to help lead the way back up.

They worked together, raised their families together, and shared all of life's ups and downs. They understood and lived the meaning of the words love, sharing, giving, and caring. The values instilled in them by their loving parents held them in good stead as they raised their own families and contributed to the betterment of our schools and community.

Patty's smile, her gusto for life, her strength of character, her love and devotion for her family, and her drive to experience, do well, and enjoy—these are the treasures of life that she lived and the memories of her that God has blessed us with.

When the priest finished reading the letters, he began to describe the special connection Patty and I shared with our parents. Even I smiled when I heard him say that if he didn't get this right, not only would I be after him, but Patty as well.

After the priest had finished speaking, Jimmy, who had volunteered to read a passage and play the piano, spoke beautifully and performed angelically.

After the mass, many friends and relatives commented on the beauty of the service; I was told that it inspired people to write letters to loved ones expressing their feelings. The reception afterward gave us the opportunity to reunite with everyone present and share many happy memories.

In spite of the day's events having gone as well as could be expected, I lacked the sense of closure I typically felt after a funeral service, for I knew that Patty and Patrick had not been laid to rest. I had not been able to see them and pay my respects, leaving me with no way to say goodbye. In actuality, this service had functioned mostly as a formality.

From that moment on, I began to question my conception of the word closure as signifying completeness. Instead, I was embarking upon the slow process of learning to understand it as an arbitrary idea, with a meaning that seemed impossible to realize, as I could not imagine myself closing the door on the life that I had shared with Patty.

❧ 6 ❧

Two days after the memorial service, I awoke aware that this morning marked the end of my first whole week without my sister; somehow, another Monday had arrived, and the sun had continued to rise and set exactly seven more times since the crash. I was increasingly astonished by the extent to which my life had been radically transformed. It seemed as though I had encountered a massive paradigm shift, forever altering my family and heart, and yet the world at large seemed to be unaffected by this shift, as peace, love, and beauty continued to exist for others, while I was paradoxically trapped in what felt like a bleak, hopeless, and unchangeable new reality.

Even though I was reluctant to acknowledge the permanence of my situation, I realized that many tasks needed attention. I decided that I would begin by clearing out Patty's house. As Mom and I gathered their belongings, Patrick's toys and stuffed animals seemed to be every-where—little figurines remained ready to be brought to life, train sets lay dormant in their boxes, waiting for the next time they could spur the creativity and imagination of a four-year-old. By the day's end, only a few items remained; one, a clay wolf, stood out from all the rest. Patty knew that I loved wolves, and earlier in the year had bought a clay wolf that stood about three feet high, positioned with its head tilted back as if howling. She had asked my friend Amy to paint it, after which she had planned to give it to me as a surprise. I deliberately chose to leave the sculpture behind, so that special care could be taken in moving it to my house.

After leaving Patty's, Mom and I slowly began sorting through the belongings that we had gathered. As I sat surrounded by the memorabilia of my sister's life, I was suddenly overwhelmed by the idea that these cherished objects would forever after serve only to remind me that Patty would live on solely in my memory. Suddenly, I became overwhelmed by a world of recollections, as each item I looked at and touched held associations of the bond that Patty and I shared.

Her pewter dishes were just like the ones stacked on my kitchen shelves, and looking at them generated thoughts of the Thanksgiving dinners that Patty had made, which were thoroughly enjoyed by everyone. Whether it was a large dinner or a pancake brunch, Patty seemed to have the magic touch when it came to cooking—a touch that Dad would point out to me from time to time, suggesting I take notes. But I never did; I figured there was no point, since Patty was always around.

As Mom and I attempted to straighten Patty's clothes strewn here and there about my house, images of my sister dressed in various outfits popped into my head, and I smiled at how she had always appeared so comfortable, so approachable to others. Looking through her wardrobe, I decided that I wanted to wear something of Patty's every day in hopes of continuing to feel connected to her, as well as finding some sense of comfort and relief. One of her blue shirts reminded me of Mom's method of differentiating our socks and other garments when we were young. Always in the same, inconspicuous place, Mom would sew a few stitches, using blue on Patty's clothes and pink on mine, to distinguish each item.

As we got older, Patty and I would frequently exchange clothes, rummaging through one another's closets until we found an item to borrow. It was fun feeling as if we had a new wardrobe without ever having to go shopping. This process of swapping clothing reached its pinnacle when we were in our early twenties, when, after Dad's retirement, he and Mom moved out of state, giving Patty and me an opportunity to share an apartment together, where it seemed that we had a limitless array of ensembles at our immediate disposal. We discovered that this was only one of the many perks of living on our own, and those years proved to be both amusing and educational. For instance, we figured out that a garbage disposal was for the disposal of food only, and certainly not for a bouquet of flowers from Patty's boyfriend that had long since withered and died. We learned that leftovers pushed to the back of the refrigerator would eventually develop a life of their own, which is where those surgical gloves that Patty brought home from the pharmaceutical company she worked for came in handy. Not only did our refrigerator seem to be alive and growing, but we had also been per- plexed as to why our freezer space was mysteriously diminishing until one day we realized it was forming ice that we needed to remove. Easy enough—Patty and I took a hammer and chisel and banged away until we got most of the ice removed, but unfortunately, we had also banged away large pieces of the freezer's interior; we were later informed of an- other, much more gentle method called "defrosting." We found out that Comet scratched and took all the shine out of the sink and bathtub sur- face, but by the time we eventually heard of a product called Soft Scrub it was too late. We discovered that pizza was not only a great dinner, but an easy breakfast as well. I realized that the oven was not the best place to hide dirty dishes when unexpected guests came over, for when Patty came home and preheated it for her evening meal, the dishes became much harder to clean with chunks of old food baked onto them. Patty recognized that I would stop washing her dirty dishes, and when she came home to what appeared to be a clean apartment with an empty, shining sink, she no longer had to wonder where the heaping pile had gone, for it was right there in the oven! We learned how much fun par- ties were at our apartment, how nice the police could be, and how toler- ant most of the neighbors were who lived below us. We more than thrived; our landlord barely survived.

The box containing Patty's assorted penguin collection brought back recollections of all the years we spent in the water. "The Penguins" was the name of the swim team that Patty and I belonged to from child- hood into our teen years, during which time we would compete wearing black swimsuits with a white panel on either side in the front. Dad spent all of his available time at our aquatic workouts, and he used to joke that he had a hard time distinguishing who was who in the pool, since we all looked like penguins.

I thought back to when Patty and I taught Dad to swim after he came to us in the pool one night for some pointers as to how he could best stay in shape. Observing his stroke so we would know where to begin, Patty and I had begun laughing uncontrollably, for in Dad's attempt to swim forward, he inexplicably wound up propelling himself backward. Patty and I had never seen anything like it. Once we composed ourselves, we began instructing him, and before long he was able to swim laps, soon covering the distance of a full mile, a routine which he maintained five days a week for years. He loved it, and we had thoroughly enjoyed seeing his accomplishment.

I continued getting lost in different memories, generally pleasant ones that testified to our adventures and our love. But mostly, I reflected upon Patty's naturally sensitive and generous spirit, which guided her through motherhood, as well as defined her endless capacity to reach out to others. Her universal kindness came into play while Patty was driving with Jonathon and Patrick one day about a block from her house, and passed a woman walking down the street who was elderly, frail, and appeared to be confused. Patty stopped to ask if she could be of assistance, and when the woman explained that her house was in the area but she couldn't find it, Patty helped her into the car. As they drove up and down the block looking for her house, the woman, Martha, told Patty that her family had put her in a nursing home, making it clear that it was against her will to go there, and that she was homesick. Martha went on to vocalize that it had taken her almost a year of saving small change to collect enough money for a one-way cab fare from the nursing home to her house, and began to longingly describe the special memorabilia she had sitting on her fireplace mantle.

As Martha relayed her story, Patty pulled up to a house with overgrown grass, weeds, and a row of untrimmed bushes lining the driveway. The place looked very unkempt—in fact, it looked about a year's worth of being unkempt, and it was Martha's. Patty accompanied her to the door and watched as she unlocked it with the single key she carried, and together they entered. Martha immediately made her way to her fireplace, where Patty watched her pick up and hold those mementos she so dearly cherished.

Shortly afterward, Martha was settled back into her home, where Patty kept her well stocked with groceries, and would often prepare her food. Patty also hired a weekly lawn service to care for the premises. Since they only lived a block from each other, it wasn't an uncommon sight to see Martha come walking through the backyard shrubs into Patty's yard just to say hello. Through Patty, I came to know the peace Martha enjoyed by being back in her own home.

During the process of sorting through Patty's things, a prescription bottle tossed in a drawer filled with miscellaneous items caught my attention, since it was uncommon for Patty to take so much as an aspirin. As I looked closer, I noticed it was a medication to help her sleep, and it was from the time when she and I had been at odds with each other. Instantly, my thoughts traveled back to that tumultuous time, not long after Patty's divorce during the summer of 1994. She had begun to take more and more time off from work, but since she was president of the nationwide investigative agency that Tom and I owned, and an integral part of the operation, her absence had a definite impact on the running of the business. She had also begun dating Eric, who was jealous of the relationship I had with Patty. Before we realized what was going on, friction had developed between us.

I was angry over what had seemed to be her taking excessive amounts of time off of work, but what I hadn't understood at the time was that she had probably needed a break from her hectic schedule and the pressures ensuing from her divorce. Patty had always been very committed to whatever it was that she chose to do, consistently putting 100% effort into her work, and when she got home she put that same level of dedication into her boys. The fact that Patty and I had not discussed her needs led me to misconstrue her reduced hours as just wanting to be with Eric, when in reality, she probably used the time off to recover from the emotional upheaval of her divorce.

Months went by that were totally unlike our lives to date. I had never imagined such a rift emerging between us, but it seemed that there was never a good time for us to talk. One afternoon, early in October, I received a call from her saying she wanted to meet. Although I missed having the special connection with my sister, I was still upset with her. I called Dad for advice, and he simply said, "If you don't meet with her, you may regret it for the rest of your life." I called Patty back.

The next day we met at the park behind my house. From across the field I saw her pulling up in her car, and I began to walk toward her. Somehow, even from this distance I could feel all the walls she had put up over the past couple months disappearing, causing mine to instantly vanish. Without hesitation we embraced, and in that moment I felt whole again. How good it felt to have the riches returned to my life…not those of a nice house or successful business, but the riches of my family…the riches of my sister.

These reflections forced me to consider how I could have been so upset and stubborn with someone I loved so much. At that time, I had chosen to fill the canvas of my life with anger and hard feelings toward my sister, tainting the strokes I had used to paint those moments. Sitting amid the tokens of her memories, I felt as if I had thrown away the gift of many precious days and weeks without my sister, and there was nothing I could do to have that time back.

Mom and I spent hours sifting through Patty's belongings that day, and would dedicate even more time over the coming days and weeks, as this process could not be rushed. By honoring Patty's and Patrick's belongings, we also paid tribute to their lives.

Another week managed to slip by as we continued sorting through Patty's and Patrick's things, receiving condolences, grieving, and waiting—waiting for whatever information the airline had to offer.

7

When the American Airlines' Care Team representatives had come to my house, they told us that we had to wait another week or two for "final confirmation" that Patty and Patrick had actually been on the flight, which seemed odd, for we were already told that the passenger list showed they had boarded the plane. Moreover, Jonathon and Eric knew the flight they were taking. But the biggest indicator that they had been on that plane was the fact that they never returned home—so how much more proof could we have possibly needed?

Exactly two weeks after the crash, we received a phone call, not from our assigned Care Team women, but from someone else at American Airlines, who informed us that everyone on American Eagle Flight 4184 had been identified. Hearing those words brought that inconceivable Halloween night of fourteen days ago back into focus…scary attire, doorbells ringing, and tasty treats had instantly been overshadowed by questions, anxiety, fear, and hysteria….all of which was resurrected upon receiving word of this final confirmation.

This new airline representative also asked where he should have the two caskets sent. His words hit me like a jab to the stomach, and I felt like I was gasping for air; temporarily stunned into silence, I sat there frozen as his words, "the caskets," resounded through my mind. We had previously been told that the crash resulted in the near total destruction of everything and everyone on the plane, so his mention of caskets left me completely and utterly baffled. Still too unraveled to speak, I handed the phone to Mom, who in her bewildered state gave him the name of our church. Afterward, she tried phoning the Care

Team women several times, in order to determine why someone else from the airline had called, and why he was having caskets shipped to us. But the phone and pager numbers the women had given us had either been disconnected or were not being answered. At that point, we became even more confused as to why we couldn't reach the two representatives who had sat in my house and told us that they would be our lifeline during these trying times. Their promises to offer us support, provide us with updated information, and help us in any way they could had come to an abrupt end, leaving us with no clue as to why.

We had not discussed any burial arrangements, given that we had previously been told that the crash resulted in near total destruction, and that very few, if any, remains were going to be identified; however, upon receiving this last call, the horrific nature of the crash led Mom to adamantly decide she wanted their remains cremated, as we did not have their bodies to lay to rest. Mom called the representative back to express our wishes, but he responded that if we desired a cremation, there would be an additional two-week delay due to the paperwork involved. I was both irritated and confused as to why they hadn't discussed these options with us earlier so that their paperwork could have been completed in a timely fashion, and instead had taken it upon themselves to make such an important and deeply personal decision for us in assuming that we wanted caskets.

The thought of having to wait again was just too much to bear, for only fourteen days earlier I had been anxiously suspended for hours on the phone with the airlines, Mom and Dad had endured unbearably long hours at the airport, and we had waited for the final confirmation that Patty and Patrick were actually on board that flight. And then, after having obtained this affirmation, we were asked to put ourselves on hold for an additional two weeks if Patty's and Patrick's remains were to be handled in the way we felt was most respectful. But we simply refused to again shelve our own needs and prolong the rituals that would help us to move forward. Mom called the new airline representative back to say that we would forego the cremation, not because we wanted to, but because we needed to, as waiting another fourteen days seemed impossible.

A short while later, the priest called to say that the church could not accept the caskets. At his suggestion, Mom, still in her confused state, called a local funeral home to arrange having the caskets delivered. We then began making preparations for the second service, which was to be held privately on the following day. Not even Jonathon or my children knew it would be taking place, for as far as we were concerned, they needed to grasp onto the loving and peaceful sentiments that characterized the previous memorial.

During the early morning hours preceding the service, I should have been in bed sleeping, but instead, I was sitting on my bathroom floor, leveled by emotions so dark and severe that they surpassed the worst physical pain I had ever experienced. My anguish was partly caused from speculating as to what my parents must have been experiencing, and it intensified with the knowledge that in just a short time we would be at yet another service, again revering the lives of Patty and Patrick, and again saying good-bye.

My agony over the effect that these circumstances were most likely having on my parents prompted me to compose a letter to them in an attempt to ease their pain. While writing, I thought only of their well-being, and tried to appeal to what I thought they would understand and what might assist them with their grieving process. The tone and language of the letter was meant to encourage them to lean on their faith as a means of helping them heal. Just before they arrived at my house that morning, I finished rewriting the letter, as I had stained the initial copy with my tears.

The ceremony at the cemetery was to be much different than the memorial service. We would no longer have the distractions of playing hostess, keeping the media at bay, overseeing certain aspects of the service, and being watchful of the children—in short, we would be stripped of all interruptions that had allowed us to make it through the first service with as much grace as possible.

On our way to the chapel, I found myself plagued by disturbing questions as to what was in Patty's and Patrick's caskets. I urgently tried to dismiss such thoughts, for I just could not allow myself to come to terms with the gruesome implications. I instead decided to hold onto the image of my sister with her long, flowing blonde hair lying serenely inside the casket, right next to the smaller one that housed her son, whom I also pictured at peace.

As we gathered before the caskets, I remembered being with Patty just hours after she had given birth to Patrick. Despite being exhausted, she was feeling euphoric and blessed by the infant she held in her arms. Jonathon, too, was feeling proud of his first-time status of being a big brother. As I recalled the sense of oneness and closeness generated by the celebration of a new life coming into the world, I became fixated on the vastly contrasting senses of coldness and separateness symbolized by the two steel caskets that stood in commemoration of two incomprehensible deaths.

Along with my parents and I, only Patty's ex-in-laws, Tom, and a friend of mine from work, John, were present at the service. The year before, John had been diagnosed with terminal cancer. Patty had told me that when he died, she wanted to attend his funeral service with me, so that she could be at my side for support. Ironically, my friend ended up standing at my side during my sister's service.

The collages of Patty and Patrick we had put together for the other memorial were much easier to look at than the harshness represented by the caskets, for the pictures had celebrated life, whereas the coffins served only as a reminder of death and loss. Thus far, the priest's words seemed to have been fading in and out as they competed with my memories and feelings. But as I focused on what he was saying, I realized I was hearing familiar words; in fact, they were the very ones I had written just a short while ago to my parents:

Dear Mom and Dad,

   I used to think the words of a priest at a funeral service were, as we say, just words. As time has passed, though, I have learned that the priest offers words of truth.

   At first, having loved ones called away to be with God seems like such a tremendous loss to those who are left behind. But by truly having faith in God, we can know that Patty and Patrick are now completely at peace and a part of His pure love. They are in a perfect place that only God could provide. We also must remember that He knows what is best, even though at this moment we may not quite understand.

By this event, Patty and Patrick may have been spared from something on Earth of which we cannot have any knowledge. And God, blessing us as He has by giving us each other, has probably helped all of us, especially Patty and Patrick, by this occurrence.

I have met a lot of people in my life, and without a doubt I can say that our family has truly been fortunate. Patty and I often talked about the complete and unconditional love you hold for us in your hearts, and about feeling the same way about you. We knew that we each had the very best parents and the very best sister ever, and were very proud of our family.

In my mind, the priest's most important teaching is to hold onto the idea that Patty and Patrick are still alive, but have just moved to a new house, a house of the greatest honor. One day each one of us will be welcomed into it, but for now God has decided that our job, our purpose, remains here on Earth. And just as a child must learn to accept his parents' decision as to what is best for him, we must do our best to fully accept the decisions God has made for Patty, Patrick, and us.

I know none of us would want Patty and Patrick to still be here if that wasn't what was best for them. It hurts us terribly, but it might have hurt them more by staying, and we love them both too much to be selfish.

With God's guidance and love, along with the ongoing support we have for one another, we will get through this loss, living on with the memories of Patty and Patrick forever in our hearts.

Love, Theresa

With my letter having been read, the ceremony was complete. Afterwards, I went to Patty's house to retrieve the few items I had left behind. Mainly, I wanted the wolf, so that I could hold and cherish this object that was an expression of Patty's love for me.

I hadn't known about the wolf until after the crash, when Amy told me that Patty had bought it especially for me, in order to convey how lucky she felt to have me as a sister, as well as to gratefully acknowledge the stability and harmony that I had helped her find in her life. Patty had also said she hoped I knew how much she loved me, and that she wished this gift of the wolf would help me to understand all that was in her heart.

As soon as I opened the door to Patty's house, I noticed that someone else had been there. Not only had the few remaining items been moved, but there was also no sign of the wolf. In a complete frenzy, I began searching each room of the house. I finished hunting downstairs and then raced up to Patty's bedroom, leaping over several steps at a time, peeking into each nook and cranny of the second floor. I returned to the living room, standing in the middle of the empty space with my mind racing, wondering who had been in the house, and why they would have taken my wolf. At that moment I noticed a brown paper bag leaning against one of the living-room walls; glimpsing inside, I found hundreds, maybe thousands, of shattered pieces of the wolf I had come to take home with me. I just stared at them in disbelief…for how could this have happened? I had never seen a wolf like that before, nor would a replacement ever suffice. Somehow, I had to come to terms with the fact that, just as my sister was gone, so too was this very precious token of her love.

❦ 8 ❧

Having attended two services without coming any closer to that elusive and seemingly unattainable idea of closure, I found myself struggling to recover meaning in my daily existence. The purposelessness that I saw as characterizing my new reality eventually attained a significance that I began to realize had been there all along, but that I hadn't been able to see through my swollen eyes and despairing shock. I became cognizant of the fact that the mere presence of the children was motivating me, as early each morning I found the strength to respond to their calls. It was my love for them that released me from the depths of my despondent state, and I devoted myself to my job of guiding and supporting Jonathon and my three children. Along with managing everyday trials and tribulations, they were faced with new lessons to learn that were not intellectual, but emotional. As I helped the children grapple with concepts of loss, grieving, and coping, I was hoping they might come to understand change as the only constant in life, with some transformations being larger than others. I tried to assist them in realizing that it was our job to go on living in spite of the fluctuations around us, and that mastering the art of flexibility and acceptance of change would allow them to move through life with more confidence and greater ease. These new lessons were not easy ones; in fact, they were the most difficult ones our family had ever been forced to undertake. However, I maintained that we would all get through this difficult situation, because we had one another's support and love, along with our faith.

In spite of the horrific tragedy that had occurred, I needed to help Jonathon and my children perceive death as a natural part of life—a transformation that allows the soul to move into a different reality with which we are less familiar. I explained that our physical bodies house our souls during the time that we live here on Earth. When we die, our bodies, the vehicles of transport, are left behind as our souls move on to their new lives. We talked about our belief that Patty and Patrick were still alive, but had just traveled to some other place. They remained a part of our lives, but in a way with which we were less accustomed.

Although we often spoke about the incredible impact of our loss, I thought it was also necessary to celebrate the time we had been privileged to share with Patty and Patrick, as opposed to dwelling on what we would never again have. I felt it was very important to keep them in the forefront of our minds, and so even if we were just in the car driving somewhere, I would ask the children what they guessed Patrick might have been doing at that time. Their responses were always positive and always on a grand scale. Patrick, from everyone's point of view, always had endless toys to play with, and boundless adventures ahead of him.

Preparing for dinner, I frequently asked the children what they thought Patty and Patrick were dining on that night. Again, the responses were overwhelmingly better than anything we could have possibly had to eat. One evening, Andy launched into Patrick's magnificent dinner menu, exclaiming, "Patrick is starting his meal with the chunkiest peanut butter and the sweetest tasting grape jelly sandwich ever made." Jimmy then chimed in, "And after he eats as little or as much of the sandwich as he wants, Patrick then has the juiciest char-grilled steak and the biggest lobster waiting for him to devour." Nikki eagerly added, "Instead of having to eat green vegetables, Patrick has great big, salty fries piled high on his plate." Barely able to wait for Nikki to finish, Jonathon jumped in, "Patrick is also drinking his favorite cherry Kool-Aid, with ice cubes in the shape of different animals floating around in his drink. And when he is finished he has the biggest and reddest Kool-Aid mustache that he is allowed to wear as long as he likes." As the children's enthusiasm grew, Jonathon raced on to the details of the delectable dessert that accompanied this grand meal, "Patrick is going to have five large scoops of his favorite chocolate ice cream." Nikki then blurted out, "And piled on top is lots of chocolate syrup under tons of whip cream." Bubbling over with excitement, Andy exclaimed, "There are so many juicy cherries that they are spilling over the sides of the bowl." Just when I thought they had finished with this lavish creation, Jonathon assuredly declared, "And he won't even get a tummy ache!"

On most days, the children somehow continued on with their lives in an amazing fashion, protected by their own internal defense mechanisms and cushioned with lots of love. They were all so courageous—especially Jonathon.

As he stepped into his new life, he also needed to rebuild his identity, for until recently he had held the status of being the son of his vivacious, beautiful mother, and had wonderfully maintained the role of being a big brother to Patrick, accepting the responsibilities that it had entailed. But Jonathon was presented with the task of having to entirely reform his identity under traumatic and vastly altered circumstances.

I was acutely aware of the ways that both adults and children spoke to Jonathon during this critical time, knowing that the wrong words could negatively impact his recovery and well-being.

In spite of how well the children fared during the daytime, nighttime always seemed more difficult, for distractions during the day helped create a barrier, protecting everyone from their deepest emotions, but at bedtime tears were shed and feelings discussed. These were the times when we sought comfort from God, trying to find reasons for our unexplainable new reality.

The day before Jonathon was scheduled to return to school, I paid a visit to his class. I did so because I wanted to let his teacher know that Jonathon was living with me, and that either my parents or I would be transporting him to and from school each day; also, I felt it was important for Jonathon's classmates to fully understand what had happened in his life. I wanted him to be able to go back to school without his friends bombarding him with questions, as well as to help his classmates avoid feeling awkward about approaching him.

Thus, I faced the hardest thing I had to do since the death of my sister and nephew as I stood before his class of wide-eyed second-graders, who seemed to be taking in every movement I made. On this day, however, the heightened levels of alertness required of a second-grade teacher proved to be unnecessary, as the class sat in quiet anticipation, anxiously awaiting the update on their classmate and friend.

As I began to speak, I provided only the facts without any emotion, attempting to prevent my unbearable grief from taking over. I talked about to the airplane crash on Halloween, and explained that Jonathon's mother and only brother had died in it. I told Jonathon's classmates that he had a new place to live, with me, my husband, and our three children. As the students listened, their serious expressions barely seemed age-appropriate, and their quiet attentiveness was clearly in opposition to the typical energy of a second-grade class.

As I stood before the innocent children, I'm sure I appeared collected and calm as I delivered my message, but inside, I was struggling not to display my overwhelming sorrow. What I wanted to do was scream out that I shouldn't even be speaking those words, as each one seemed to give more validity to the unbearable and unbelievable. I wanted to yell that it was MY sister and best friend of thirty-seven years, along with MY nephew, who had died on that flight. I wanted to shout out that it felt like not only had Patty's and Patrick's lives been taken from me, but that my own life had been taken from me as well, and it was only my body that had been left behind.

Hearing myself announce their deaths was so painful that I wanted to turn and run out of the room to escape the reality of what I was saying. The words dead and died sounded so horrifyingly final, without any hope of an afterlife. For some reason, these were the words I used when speaking to the class, although I could not manage to use them when speaking with Jonathon or my children.

Feeling as though I could hardly endure another moment standing before the class, I opened up the floor for questions. The silence was instantaneously broken as several hands shot into the air. "How old are your children?" asked a small-framed, dark-haired boy. Then another boy piped in, "Where do you live?" Next, a short, blonde-haired girl wearing a pink oversized sweater shyly raised her hand and inquired,

"How is Jonathon feeling?"

As torturous as this process was, I took my time answering each child as directly and thoroughly as possible, continuing to fight back my emotions, for this talk needed to be all about Jonathon—his life, his loss, and how he was affected. His classmates did not need to know how I had been impacted by the tragedy.

The questions continued to come at a steady and rapid pace: "What kind of pets will Jonathon have?" "How big are the dogs?" "Where will Jonathon sleep?" "Does he like his cousins?" In the same matter-of-fact manner that the children asked the questions, they also accepted my answers.

When I had finally responded to what I thought were all the children's questions, and was prepared to make a speedy exit before my despair erupted, one last hand was meekly raised by a cute, freckle-faced, fair-skinned girl who sat directly in front of me, as she shyly asked, "Will you be Jonathon's new mom?"

Mustering the composure to reply took more courage and strength than I thought I would be able to summon. After a long pause, fighting back my tears, I explained, "I could never replace Jonathon's mother. She loved and raised him as no one else could, but I will do my very best to be there for Jonathon and provide for him in every way possible."

After my response, I left as soon as I could. The moment I stepped outside the front door of the school, I nearly collapsed from the tremors of pain that had been relentlessly jarring my body while I spoke. I couldn't let go of that last question, and I was floored by the levels of implications that it contained. "Will you be Jonathon's new mom"...I knew that there was no good answer to that. On the one hand, I was honored to think that Jonathon might look to me as he had to Patty for the love, guidance, and support that only a mother could offer; on the other hand, I had no intention or desire to ever pretend that I could replace Patty as Jonathon's mother, and I was devastated by the fact that she wouldn't be able to raise her son and watch him grow into the person she had hoped for him to be.

❧ 9 ❧

As a consequence of my own pervasive sense of loneliness and profound melancholy, I became increasingly attuned to the importance of remaining aware of the various mechanisms we all employed in order to cope with our new circumstances, so that we could retain our capacity to empathize with one another's positions. I naturally maintained the bond that I had always shared with my parents, despite our different ways of expressing and managing our grief, as they were integral and indispensable to my conception of family.

While my parents adopted a more silent approach in their struggle to deal with the newfound conditions of their lives, the persisting angst they endured emerged in other forms. One day, during a conversation with Mom, I asked if she had any knowledge regarding the fate of the clay wolf. As it turned out, Mom and Dad had previously been at Patty's the day I had gone to retrieve the sculpture. Spotting the wolf and not recognizing it as either Patty's or Patrick's, Mom assumed that it must have been Eric's. Having no way of knowing that it was a gift of love from one of her daughters to the other, while in the grips of her vexation and despair, Mom opened the front door to Patty's house, picked up the wolf, and heaved it onto the steps below with all the force she could muster.

Hearing this story, I became infuriated, for Patty's gift had not even been broken accidentally. However, even in my heightened state of anger, I knew that her attempt to release her pent-up feelings was in no way directed at me, and so I stopped myself from allowing my frustration to explode. It would have been senseless to take my aggravation out on Mom, who had always supported me in such a sensitive and loving way, and who inspired me to incorporate these qualities in relating to Jonathon and my children.

Thus, I continued to retain my compassion for the position my parents were in, even though I did not always understand the ways they chose to manage their overwhelming sorrow. We continued to talk over the business at hand, but our feelings remained a topic we never discussed, which deviated significantly from my own coping strategies, as it was important for me not to only talk over the issues, but to express my feelings about them as well. It was not unusual for me to call my friend Amy and mimic a TV commercial by saying, "It's a Calgon night; come and take me away," which was our playful way of asking if the other was available for a walk that night. Either alone or with our kids and dogs in tow, we would venture out in all types of weather, commonly covering the entire spectrum of our emotions throughout the duration of our walks.

During one such nightly excursion, Amy asked me why I was not upset that Mom and Dad were not more open with me in communicating their sorrow, as she didn't understand how I could accept and forgive this lack of emotional connection. I quickly and yet definitively responded that my love for them allowed me to accept and respect whatever route their grieving process needed to take, as I knew that I could do nothing but love them unconditionally, the way they had always loved me.

Years later, Mom told me that the reason she hadn't talked about her feelings at the time was that everything had just seemed too unbelievable to be real; in her mind, if she didn't talk about Patty and Patrick being gone, then it couldn't have possibly been true, leaving open the prospect of having her loving family intact again, as it had been for thirty-seven years. The reasons for Dad's silence had less to do with denial, and were more a product of his absolute trust in the teachings of his faith, as he firmly held that Patty's and Patrick's lives continued on somewhere other than here on Earth. His unwavering belief in God, which for him justified the unknown, unexplainable, and unproven phenom-

ena in life, was put before him in the biggest test of faith he had ever encountered. Regardless of the differences between the ways my parents
and I grieved, the love that had always characterized our relationship
never faded, and I learned to incorporate all of our various healing
methods into guiding the children through this exceedingly trying time.

I began engaging Jimmy, Andy, Nikki, and Jonathon in a version
of a Native American tradition in order to help them realize and express
their feelings, which required a special object called a "talking stick" that
Jimmy had carved and varnished especially for this purpose. Sitting at
the dinner table, we would take turns passing the talking stick from one
person to the next, and whoever held the stick was the only person entitled to speak, while the rest of us were to listen without commentary.
Each child was encouraged not only to discuss any events of interest to
them, but more importantly, to express their feelings.

Initially, Jonathon was pretty quiet when we passed the stick, and
was quick to hand it off to someone else, which would inevitably result
in me passing it right back to him, as I refused to let him off the hook.
Before long, Jonathon sat at the table, eagerly awaiting the talking stick
to make its way into his hands. Eventually, everyone came to enjoy this
tradition so thoroughly that I had to establish a time limit for speaking.

I was able to devote so much time to the children as a result of the
thoughtful actions of close friends, who along with casual acquaintances
and even those we had never met who wanted to help in some way,
gathered together to eliminate some of my usual obligations. Each night
an entire meal was provided for us; we had everything from delicious
homemade stews, chicken and vegetable platters, and Chinese food
brought to our house. This unexpected assistance was especially appreciated during these difficult weeks.

Most of the dinners we received were without a dessert, a detail to
which I never gave a second thought. In fact, as far as I was concerned it
was better that way, since the children had various food allergies and I
was trying to keep sweets to a minimum. Each evening when the doorbell rang, Jimmy would promptly drop whatever it was he was doing
and run to the door to receive the meals. Years later, the reason for his ea-

gerness manifested. As it turned out, every meal that arrived at our house had included a lavish dessert, but feeling somewhat deprived of sweets, Jimmy had realized he was in the midst of a windfall of goodies, whether it was homemade chocolate brownies, carrot cake with ice cream, or chocolate chip cookies fresh from the oven. Of course, these desserts never made it into the kitchen, and instead ended up either stashed away in a drawer or hidden in the spare refrigerator downstairs. As he gobbled up all the treats, Jimmy was able to compensate for the fact that I kept their intake of sweets to a minimum. In this way, he was an enthusiastic participant in another lasting family tradition, for he naturally seemed to find his way into the practice of mischief that Patty and I had so freely engaged in as children.

✣ 10 ✣

The passage of time did not ease the turmoil that had anchored itself within me. I had always taken it for granted that my sister and I would attend our children's graduations and weddings together, and that we would grow old together, continuing to share in all of life's ups and downs. I struggled to find answers...I struggled to find tranquility. In my letter to Mom and Dad for the last memorial service, I had said that "Patty and Patrick are now completely at peace and a part of God's pure love. They are in a perfect place that only God himself could provide." But that letter was meant to comfort my parents, not me. Instead, it spoke to my inner conflict, because as far as I was concerned, the idea of Patty and Patrick being up in Heaven with God would have been just fine if it hadn't meant that I was left behind, forced to live on without them. Part of my search for understanding involved inundating myself with questions as to whether or not I could have done anything to prevent their deaths, and even though I knew I could never find such an answer, it was a thought that unavoidably arose out of the pain of my unfathomable loss. I needed Patty here with me, and no matter how hard I tried, I just could not accept a life without my sister.

Amid all the chaos generated by the many responsibilities that my new life entailed, my husband began putting pressure on me as to when I would have the garage and basement cleared of Patty's belongings, when I would stop accepting meals from neighbors and friends, and when our lives would return to normal. His questions served as a reminder of the coolness that existed in our marriage, and naturally illuminated his inability to offer me support. In my mind, his unanswerable inquiries only spawned more questions…for what was normal? And besides, how could my life possibly ever revert back to what it had been before being forced to undergo this unwanted metamorphosis? I didn't know what there was left to return to, as my world had been turned upside down and inside out, and I had no idea how I was ever to make the journey back to where I had been before the crash.

According to *Funk and Wagnall's Dictionary*, "normal" is an adjective meaning "conforming to or consisting of a pattern, process, or standard regarded as usual or typical; natural." Those days I found very little in my life that consisted of a pattern regarded as "usual" and "typical," and there was nothing "natural" about the present circumstances in my life, or the way they made me feel.

Before the crash, my time had been filled with photography and videotaping, which I loved, as well as journaling each of my children's lives through pictures, videos, and writing. Before the crash, I had been committed to taking my children to piano lessons each week, and practicing with them every day. Each morning I had gone to the office once the kids went off to school, and my afternoons had consisted of driving them to an array of athletic activities, including basketball, soccer, swimming, Tae Kwon Do, and Judo. I was also Room Mom, and volunteered for other school activities. My life had been filled with lightheartedness, work, and play, and above all I had been part of a close family that was characterized by deep love.

After the crash, I felt as if my world had come to a screeching halt, not unlike the instantaneous stop that the ground had provided for Flight 4184 just weeks earlier. I no longer had the desire to be creative through pictures, videos, and writing. Practicing the piano with the children had become difficult, to say the least, and I suddenly lacked the energy to involve myself with school activities. My daily trips to the office had abruptly stopped.

After the crash, I no longer found comfort in my home, which had been turned into a mini-construction site while my friend Sandy, who was a handyman, was converting our dining room into Jimmy's new bedroom, since Jonathon would now be sharing the bedroom with

Andy. And following a full day's work at my house, I somehow had to muster up the energy to head over to Patty's with Sandy, where he was helping me prepare her house and car to be sold.

When I was in public, I remember thinking how perfectly ordinary I must have appeared to everyone, for there were no obvious outward bruises or scars to be seen. On the inside, though, I felt nothing like what my physical appearance indicated. There was such upheaval in my life, and I carried such enormous emotional weight that it seemed ironic that people could still perceive me as "normal."

In spite of our world having been turned completely upside down, Mom and I continued to strive for something resembling what we conceived the idea of normalcy to mean. However, these endeavors were both mentally and physically exhausting, and ultimately proved to be futile, for we eventually learned that regardless of our persistent efforts, nothing could ever bring our lives back to what they had been before that fateful Halloween night. Although we grasped this truth intellectually, it took time for it to settle in emotionally, bit by bit, with every hour of each passing day.

What it came down to was that "normal" was a word that could no longer describe our lives. No attempts to carry on with life as usual could ever conceal these changes, or the ensuing pain that lingered inside of us. The extent of the upheaval could be measured by the very shift in the way we benchmarked time…for everything in our lives was forever after demarcated by the distinctions of "before the crash" or "after the crash."

❧ 11 ❧

With approximately four weeks having elapsed since the tragedy, we became increasingly concerned as to the whereabouts of the personal effects that Patty and Patrick had taken on board. In spite of the fact that much of the plane and its contents had been obliterated upon impact, we had been previously notified that there were items that had been deemed recoverable. Thus far, the airline had responded to my family's letters and telephone calls with reassurances that the process was underway, and that we would soon be receiving all retrieved belongings.

For me, these personal items carried tremendous importance, although I had no ability to formulate a concrete explanation as to why I so desperately desired to have these possessions. Maybe it was because they had been with Patty and Patrick at the time of their deaths, and so in some way helped me maintain a link to them, or maybe it was just because these objects belonged to my sister and nephew, and therefore held a sentimental value. Whatever our individual reasons, we all waited for the time we could hold their belongings and be comforted by the portraits of our past that they evoked.

However, this waiting was not without trepidation, as I was somewhat unnerved by the thought of what condition the items might be in, and what my reaction would be in seeing firsthand evidence of the horrific destruction. But regardless of my fears about how difficult this might be, nothing diminished the eagerness with which I awaited the return of their belongings.

Even though I wondered whether I was being too forward or impatient with the airline regarding this matter, I was concerned by their failure to deliver these items in the time frame they had indicated. However, their continued assurances eased my reservations, at least for the time being, as I assumed that the airline would do right by us, especially considering the circumstances. But then again, the fact that our Care Team representatives had suddenly disappeared and become unreachable added to the resonating doubts in my mind regarding the integrity of the airline's promises, given that those two women had committed themselves to be there for us in every possible way. The airline's sincerity seemed too good to be true, and, as we were about to discover . . . it was.

❧ ❧ ❧

During this time, I was also busy handling the many legal matters pertaining to Jonathon. As executor of my sister's will, I was responsible for handling Jonathon's suit against the airline; initially, I had signed up for representation with a small law firm, which had quickly directed me to a larger, more established firm that specialized in airline disasters. Mom and I attended the first meeting together, listening to how this firm would handle the process of litigation, and we also answered the attorney's questions that were part of a screening process to determine if he would accept our case. I dedicated most of my energy to keeping my emotions in check, but Mom wasn't quite as successful; she got up and walked out of the office shortly after we arrived. In completing the interview, I began what would come to be an all-encompassing journey through the legal system.

Concerns were also raised regarding Jonathon's future. Months earlier, Patty had decided that in the event anything were to happen to her, she wished for me to raise her boys, and had been in the process of changing her will at the time of her death due to her ongoing sense of uneasiness about the lack of involvement Jonathon's and Patrick's father, Frank, had in their lives. I was determined to adhere to Patty's wishes concerning Jonathon, and I understood what had to be done. It seemed natural for Jonathon to reside at my house, since he had always spent time with my children and me on a daily basis. Jonathon expressed how comfortable this situation was for him when he stated to teachers and friends that he had two moms, one having died in a plane crash. Thus, I found myself embarking upon another legal process as I filed for custody.

In preparation for the custody proceedings, many teachers, friends, and neighbors came forward with offers to write letters and testify on Jonathon's behalf. They all knew how devoted Patty and I had been to one another, and how close Jonathon was with his cousins; therefore, they expressed without hesitation that living with my family would be best for him. Many people commented to me that they were surprised and impressed at how easily Jonathon seemed to adjust to his new environment, as well as the degree to which he appeared to be coming to terms with his loss.

While this was mostly true of Jonathon's state during the daytime, at night he was overcome by enveloping melancholy; to help subside his pain, I initiated a bedtime ritual of recounting stories about Patty, offering a means by which I was able to at least partially compensate for the fact that she was no longer there to tuck him into bed. I began to share more and more memories with him about his mother and brother that testified to many years of mischievous fun.

One of Jonathon's favorite topics of discussion concerned the amusement he used to get out of engaging in games with Patrick when they were very young. While they were both typically very reserved in public, when they played together at home they allowed their extremely free-spirited natures to emerge. One of their favorite games was hide-n-seek, which had frequently taken place in their big backyard. First Jonathon would hide, and when Patrick found him it would then be Patrick's turn to hide, but Jonathon quickly discovered that locating Patrick didn't take much effort, as he always hid in the same place he had just found his big brother! Jonathon would grin reminiscing about all the fun he used to have serving as a role model to innocent and gullible little Patrick.

The telling of another favorite bedtime story would usually make me laugh to the point of tears. When Patty and I were in our early teen years, several of our friends owned horses, which they would occasionally ride in our large backyard when they came over. One time, Patty mounted one of the horses, but before she could command and direct it into our backyard, the horse took off. As she was unable to gain control over it, the horse proceeded to run down the block, which wouldn't have been so bad if the horse was on the street, but instead it raced through our neighbor's lawns, leaving crushed flowers, flattened and broken bushes, and small trees in its wake. All the while, Patty was desperately clinging to the saddle with a wide-eyed expression of shock on her face, powerless to stop the horse from continuing on its path of destruction.

During these adventuresome accounts, Jonathon would sit and listen intently to even the smallest of details, as if he were savoring every word. After I finished describing a tale, it was common for Jonathon to look up at me and say, "Tell me that again," which I would proceed to do with the same zestful elaboration.

Jonathon and I also enjoyed looking through my many photo albums, which always provided us with an wide array of topics for discussion. His stillness during my storytelling was replaced with the fervor with which he perused the pictures. Then, with an abundance of enthusiasm, he would share the stories of his family that the images evoked. These albums were a journal of our lives, and revealed the devoted nature of our family. While I had a readily-available storehouse of memories contained in the hundreds of hours of videos I had shot over the years, the thought of seeing these animated captions of my sister smiling and laughing was just too much to bear at that time, and so the videos remained stashed away.

Jonathon discovered that many others were also eager to commemorate the lives of his mother and brother, for in the months following the tragedy there had been an enormous communal outreach for our family, as all who had known Patty and Patrick sought to honor their lives in whatever way possible. I received notice that Jonathon's school had a tree planted as a tribute to Patty and Patrick, and during the dedication ceremony they also revealed a plaque inscribed with the names of my sister and nephew. The swim instructors and students Patty once taught also presented an inscribed plaque with a swimmer on it in her memory. It recognized Patty's loyalty and commitment to using her natural swimming talents in a way that helped to bring out the best in each of her students.

At this time, everyone who knew Jonathon was very protective of him, and I was especially adamant about avoiding his exposure to a frenzy of media attention. However, even though the police and the schools did what they could to respect our privacy, occasionally reporters slipped through the barriers. In one instance, several weeks after the crash, I had gone to Patty's house to meet one of her friends. Moments after our arrival, we were approached by a reporter who, after briefly apologizing for the tragedy, casually proceeded to ask questions. I insisted that I didn't know what he was talking about and that he must have had the wrong address. He was dumbfounded, but I stuck to my statement, and eventually he left.

❧ ❧ ❧

Before we knew it, the Christmas season was rapidly approaching, and we found ourselves again striving to simulate "normalcy" in our lives, which we pursued with infinite determination. Family activities had always been a grand occurrence; past seasons of love, laughter, joy, and togetherness were the barometer for measuring our success of recreating them.

Most years, Christmas had been held at my house, where we had plenty of room to accommodate family and friends. It also became a tradition that each year someone dressed as Santa would come to the house. "Santa" was an acquaintance of mine whom the children would not recognize, and who owned his own costume that fit perfectly, as if it had been tailored just for him. Annually, he made the rounds to a number of homes in the area, and always arrived at the front door with a sackful of gifts that had secretly been stashed for him in the yard.

Santa had always made his visits on Christmas Eve, just prior to the onset of his busy night. Upon his entrance, Jimmy, Andy, and Nikki played Christmas carols on the piano that they had been rehearsing for weeks, as the rest of us sang along. Typically, my children and I would perform duets together, and once in a while Santa and I would sit down and play together as well.

The celebration with Santa ended each year with everyone joining in on the Happy Birthday song, for as Jonathon's birthday fell just two days after Christmas, this was one way we had of keeping his own special day from being overshadowed by the holiday festivities. After Santa's departure, we would have a quick meal, after which Mom would begin passing out the gifts piled high under the tree. At a glance it was hard to tell who was having more fun—the little kids or the big kids!

During this first Christmas season without Patty and Patrick, we strove to rekindle the merriment of previous years, but the goal was immensely difficult. We went through all the motions of Christmases past, but they remained only motions, as a dull, lifeless aura prevailed throughout the day, leaving us with the harsh reality of another futile attempt to recreate the good cheer and celebratory happiness that in the past had come all too naturally. The old adage about hard work paying off could not have been further from the truth, for no matter how hard we tried, the jovial Christmas spirit seemed unable to infuse our despairing hearts.

The sting of our new reality just could not be eased. Our division of time continued to be described by those two simple words, before and after.

✣ 12 ✣

Two days after Christmas, Jonathon turned eight years old. We held his party at an arcade, which had all sorts of games for him and his friends to play. Again, we all went through the motions of a birthday celebration, but amidst the chaos of a typical party for an eight-year-old, a sullenness permeated the air; it arose from the absence of the one person who knew and loved Jonathon most in the world. From greeting the guests to thanking them for coming, we were keenly aware that Patty wasn't there to direct the party and dote on her son. The attempted festivities also intensified our grief over the absence of Jonathon's little brother, as no one could ever look up to and cherish Jonathon the way Patrick had. We included all the essential ingredients for a birthday party—family, friends, presents, games, and cake—but there seemed to be nothing celebratory about the occasion.

With Thanksgiving, Christmas, Jonathon's birthday, and New Year's behind us, I hoped to feel a sense of relief over having made it through these monumental occasions, but instead, a new tension began building within me that increased with each passing day. Exactly twelve days after the New Year began, this anxiety came to a crescendo.

January 12 was Patty's and my shared birthday, when we acknowledged our title of Irish Twins, of which we had always been quite proud. It was a day so special to us that we had looked forward to it even more than Christmas, as it was the occasion for celebrating the uniqueness of our sisterhood.

This year, the arrival of January 12 brought not festivities and excitement, but rather a pervasive sense of loss and loneliness ensuing from the realization that I would spend the rest of my life observing our birthday without my sister. Regardless of who attended the birthday party, my depression from this solitude couldn't be eliminated, because the one person I wanted there was Patty. My parents also struggled through this attempted celebration as they had through the others this holiday season, trying to make it as wonderful as possible for at least one of their daughters, impossible as they knew this would be to achieve.

During the weeks following my birthday, my friends slowly began to return to their own lives and families. To some extent they had put their usual routines on hold to be by my side and offer their support. I felt extremely fortunate to have such an array of good friends upon whom I could call at any time, and each had made substantial contributions in helping me through the most difficult months I had ever known. I accepted that they needed to get back to their lives, but at times that thought magnified my awareness of the fact that I would never again return to the life I had always thought of as familiar. This contrast only heightened my confusion about the direction in which I should proceed, and what I was supposed to do.

The only way I knew to move forward was with one small step at a time. Small repairs and minor adjustments to Patty's car and house made for an effortless sale to a woman whom I felt good about living there. Occasionally, I would stop by for a visit, and during one of these times she thanked me again for offering her the house, as she had recently become engaged to a man who lived just down the street, whom she otherwise never would have met. It felt good that life and joy continued to exist in the place that Patty once called home.

Even though I was able to manage the more concrete tasks set out before me, I still found myself no closer to re-forming my identity, or to figuring out a way to come to terms with my loss. There were times when I felt terrified that I did not have the endurance required to overcome all the adversity that had been thrown my way. But I came to realize that since the crash, I had been continually summoning more strength than I had ever known, allowing me to put my own feelings aside while attending to other matters, especially Jonathon and my children. This instinctive resilience also prevented me from collapsing at my parents' feet due to my incredible pain, knowing that I could not begin to imagine the anguish of losing a child. It allowed me to get through my nightly conversations with the children, and to stand in front of Jonathon's classmates. I simply did what I felt needed to be done.

Each day, the distraction of these obligations continued to act like a natural anesthetic, but at night this numbness would wear off and my strength would diminish, leaving me immersed in the agony of having lost my sister.

Then, one night, I had a very small, remote, and yet familiar feeling come over me, and I suddenly realized that all I needed to do was reach out to a single individual—the only person in my life that I knew could pull me out of this darkness that was so cold, scary, and lonely. Dragging myself off the floor, I crawled to the phone, knowing it didn't matter that it was the middle of the night, or that she would be sound asleep. At that moment I needed her. She was someone I could go to for anything, someone I could be myself with at all times, for she had the ability not only to listen to me, but to truly empathize with my feelings as well.

Feeling relieved and grateful that I had remembered to call this person with whom I shared such a unique bond, I picked up the phone and began dialing those all-too familiar numbers, knowing that in just moments her understanding and guidance would help me to feel better.

I dialed the first, second, and third numbers, just as I had thousands of times before. Then as I reached to dial the fourth number, I froze. In that instant, I suddenly realized that the help I was so desperately seeking was no longer available. My sister, my best friend, was gone forever.

ᘒᕽ 13 ᕽᘒ

Before I knew it, close to three months had gone by since the crash, and it occurred to me that it had also been approximately six weeks since the airline officials assured us that we would soon be receiving Patty's and Patrick's personal effects; at this point, I had become frustrated by what I perceived to be the lack of authenticity and truthfulness in the words of the airline. Initially, we had naively trusted that they intended to take the right course of action, but our innocent faith had faded, as we just didn't understand why the airline was not following through on their promises. I began to feel as though we were being strung along on a road to nowhere.

We finally made another inquiry, but this time, instead of telling us that Patty's and Patrick's belongings would be arriving shortly, the airline requested not only that we detail every personal item they had on board with them, but also that we supply the sales receipts to show proof of purchase. In addition, the airline wanted pictures of Patty and Patrick that showed them with these possessions.

I hung up the phone, floored by what I had just heard, and sat there trying to process the ridiculous nature of their request. Was this some kind of joke? I couldn't possibly be certain of what Patty and Patrick had with them, seeing as how I hadn't packed their bags. It suddenly seemed as though the airline's reassurances over the past couple of months had all served as delay tactics, but I could not begin to fathom why they would want to prevent us from obtaining these sentimentally valuable objects. The most gnawing question in my mind focused on why the two Care Team women, who had sat at my dining room table so earnestly promising their assistance, had not informed us that personal effects would not be returned without proof of purchase and a detailed list of everything Patty had carried onto the plane.

Not long after receiving that frustrating update, a letter from American, dated January 27, was sent to us that seemed to make time come to a screeching halt. All I saw were words swimming around on the page, informing us of a burial that had taken place months earlier for all the victims of the crash…a burial of which we had received no notification until this correspondence. The airline went on to say that a team of nationally acknowledged forensic specialists had been able to positively identify all of those on board, even though they had not identified all the individual remains. Further, they explained that the treatment of the remains was the responsibility of the Newton County Coroner (which was the county in Indiana where the crash had occurred), who had decided that an interment was "the fitting and proper resolution." On November 15 and 16, just two weeks after the crash, a nondenominational burial service for the unidentified remains had been performed by the Indiana Funeral Directors Association with the cemetery staff in attendance; the airline was not invited to participate. At this point, I struggled to follow the cohesive structure of the words, for the message seemed incomprehensible. The final blow came with the remark that the airline officials had decided not to advise families of this burial because they thought we had attended an adequate number of memorial services, and they wanted to spare us "additional pain."

As I lifted my eyes, I struggled to regain my capacity for comprehension. "Additional pain?" If the airline's intent had truly been to prevent us from enduring "additional pain," then throughout these past few months, their actions would have upheld their words; however, all the promises that they made to us thus far had been empty. We were never returned any recovered personal effects, the Care Team women had not been available to "assist us through this trying time," and they had not kept us updated on all new developments. Therefore, it was nearly impossible for me to regard the purpose behind the airline's silence about this mass burial as a genuine attempt to act in the best interest of the families. This lack of disclosure, compounded by their failure to consult us before presuming to determine the number of services that we would need or want to attend, vanquished any trust we might have had in this company's reliability. With this information, the number of victims of the crash seemed to multiply tremendously. Patty and Patrick were victims by consequence of having been on the plane, but we had become victims, too—victims of the indifference of a large and powerful corporation.

When I was finally able to resume reading the letter, I found out that the airline was arranging for a memorial stone to be placed at the burial site, and its unveiling was to be accompanied by a multidenominational service. They concluded with the assurance that they would provide us with ample notice regarding the date and time of the ceremony.

As far as I was concerned, all this translated into more waiting with no end in sight.

꧁ 14 ꧂

The airline's baffling disclosure of the mass burial was soon followed by the public hearing of the National Transportation Safety Board (NTSB) in Indianapolis. This hearing, scheduled to begin on February 27, 1995 was a fact-finding inquiry to assist the NTSB in collecting information to help determine the probable cause of the crash.

Tom planned on taking off work to attend the hearing. He seemed compelled by his curiosity regarding the details of the crash, which was consistent with his investigative nature. I had no initial intention of going, since I felt it was more important to be with the children. But, going about my business several days before Tom was due to leave, I began to notice something peculiar. Throughout the day I had the distinctly physical sensation that someone was following me around and tugging on my sleeve, as if one of my children were at my side trying to get my attention.

My attempts to ignore this impression worked only temporarily; the feeling would occasionally subside, only to occur again. After a few days, I noticed that this phantom-like calling seemed to be sending me a message, and inexplicably, I knew that it was a sign urging me to go to the conference. As crazy as the idea seemed, I could not ignore the sensation, and so I arranged for my parents to stay with the children, and the next day Tom and I were on our way to Indianapolis.

The hearing was held at a convention center at one of the hotels in Indianapolis. When Tom and I met the attorney representing Jonathon's airline case in the lobby outside the convention hall, it was already buzzing with people. He introduced us to the many reporters from newspapers, radio, and TV stations that were present. We learned that most of the other people congregating inside the lobby were also family members of crash victims. I met person after person whose eyes seemed to reflect the same deep despair and sense of bereavement that I carried, and was surprised by the instant bond I formed with many of these individuals.

After introductions, which included naming the family members we had lost in the crash, our discussions quickly turned to the issues we had encountered with the airline thus far. Almost everyone I spoke with was indignant about not having been notified of the mass burial until well after it had taken place, although we did make the shocking discovery that a few families had actually learned of its occurrence back in November. When these select individuals had first inquired about the details, the airline denied having any knowledge of such an affair, and only when these families persisted did the airline finally admit that a mass burial had been conducted. Although this confirmation had taken place only weeks after the burial, it was not until late January that the airline had finally decided to notify the remainder of the families.

We were also all infuriated by the airline's ongoing failure to fulfill their promise to return the personal belongings. Everyone, including myself, expressed a longing to get back those possessions, regardless of their physical condition. This certainly was not the first plane crash in history; however, the airline's seemingly flippant attitude regarding the personal effects suggested that the company was not prioritizing the families' concerns, but rather seemed focused on getting this inconvenience taken care of as quickly and efficiently as possible.

Additionally, through these discussions with other family members, Tom and I ascertained that in spite of the Care Team having told us to stay away from the crash site, several families had been brought to the field by the airline in order to perform religious ceremonies. It seemed unfair that those who had come forth more assertively were afforded what appeared to be preferential treatment, while we adhered to the company's request not to interfere with the clean-up and investigative efforts, and then had wound up feeling utterly dismissed. How could the airline personnel have been so inconsistent in dealing with the families? Why couldn't they have clearly laid out the facts, along with the options available to us?

As the conversations continued, I learned that many families desired the airline to purchase the farmland where the crash had occurred, as they considered it hallowed ground and were disturbed by the thought of it being cultivated; additionally, they requested a monument to be placed at the site to commemorate the tragedy. In spite of the fact that some of the families had secured a promise from the airline that this land would be purchased, we received word that the field had been cleared and released back to the farmer a couple months prior. Contrary to the airline's assurances, the tenant farmer who worked the field steadfastly maintained that he would be planting his crop again come spring.

Inching my way through the lobby, I was beginning to feel dazed from trying to keep everyone's name, relations, and story straight when a woman approached me, and upon introducing myself she immediately exclaimed, "You're the one!" I quickly discovered that I was talking to Jenny, the sister of Brad, the passenger that had approached Patty wanting to trade his American Eagle ticket for one of the United Airline tickets that Jonathon and Eric held, so as to assure making his connection at O'Hare.

Jenny explained that her dad had been seated in the waiting area that fateful day. As he waited to say goodbye to his son, he watched the array of busy travelers, including a tall blonde woman accompanied by a man and her two young boys. During his observations, he witnessed the loving relationship between this mother and her children. He had learned that her oldest child would be flying home on a United flight, the one his son had attempted to take, and he had also known that this woman and her youngest son would be boarding the same American Eagle plane as Brad.

Sometime after the crash, Brad's father focused on these once inconsequential details, recalling the tall blonde woman and her youngest son boarding the same plane as Brad, and he remembered her oldest son, who turned out to be Jonathon. In his mind, the significance of that scene became concentrated on the fact that the woman's oldest son, who boarded the United Airline flight, had in one terrible instant been stripped of his mother and brother. Jenny went on to explain that for the past several months, Jonathon's fate had been the talk of the small town in Indiana where Brad's family lived.

Amongst the many people present at the hearing, the copilot's parents were also in attendance. They were the only family members I was apprehensive about meeting, because I wasn't sure how to feel about knowing that their son had held the controls of the plane in his hands. The type of aircraft operated on Flight 4184 was made by the French manufacturer Avions de Transport Regional (ATR), and was referred to as an ATR 72; this plane was a turboprop, which means that it was powered by propellers instead of jet engines. I knew that this type of aircraft had previously encountered icing problems, and that in December, just weeks after the crash, the Federal Aviation Administration (FAA) had ordered the grounding of all ATRs flying in areas forecasted to have icing conditions, which effectively applied to the entire American Eagle fleet operating in the Midwest and northern parts of the country. Regardless, since the investigative efforts to date had not revealed who or what had caused the crash, I still felt uneasy about meeting the copilot's family, especially when thinking about whether or not the pilots had assumed any kind of responsibility in the tragedy.

Despite my reservations, I found myself standing face to face with the parents of the copilot who had played some role, however minor it may have been, in carrying out the destiny of my life and family. My initial impression was that of a clean-cut, middle-aged couple who seemed as hesitant to meet me as I was to meet them. As we began speaking, the immense pain they carried was immediately evident, and they extended condolences that were unquestionably sincere. During our conversation, they confirmed that they were in fact apprehensive about meeting the other families, as they feared their son being blamed for the crash. My initial misgivings soon dissipated, for I quickly came to realize that the pilots and their families were also victims in this tragedy, and I was able to see the kindhearted nature of this couple.

After a morning of shared stories and inquiries amongst the families, we moved into the main conference room where the hearing was to convene. Its purpose was to assist the NTSB's process of figuring out the probable cause of the crash by supplementing the facts, conditions, and circumstances discovered during the on-scene investigation, in order to help the agency make recommendations to prevent similar tragedies. While the hearing was not to be used as a determination of liability, various parties could be ruled out as causal factors of the crash during the investigative proceedings.

Included among the parties participating in the NTSB's analysis were the FAA; the aircraft manufacturer ATR; the Air Line Pilot Association (ALPA); the National Air Traffic Controllers Association; the National Weather Service; and Simmons Airlines, Inc. (which does business under the title of American Eagle, and these two companies had jointly operated the plane used on Flight 4184). The AMR Corporation is the parent company of American Airlines, which in turn is the parent company of American Eagle. Simmons is one of four air carriers owned by AMR that flies under the American Eagle name, but it was American Airlines that had contact with us beginning the night of the crash, that had sent their Care Team members into our homes, and that had been directly involved with us in the aftermath. Additionally, Patty's ticket had been honored by American Eagle, and she had boarded an American Eagle flight. It wasn't until some of the legal matters arose that the name Simmons was first introduced to us, and even then it was vastly unclear what role, if any, they played in this whole situation. We never saw the Simmons name on a plane, and the correspondence we received was on AMR, American Airlines, or American Eagle letterhead. Therefore, this account generally refers to American Airlines instead of the specific other carriers.

The conference room was divided into several areas. There was a section of reserved seating for the more than thirty families in attendance, and a separate area for the general public. Positioned in the front of the conference room were tables where the aforementioned parties were seated. There were also several raised platforms, which housed the

Board of Inquiry (consisting of four senior NTSB officials), the Safety Board Technical Panel (which was comprised of fifteen people and led by the NTSB's chief investigator of the crash), the witness stand, and the news media. The witnesses were experts in fields pertaining to specific elements suspected to have played a part in the crash, and were selected to testify based on their abilities to offer the best available information on aviation safety. They were to first be questioned by the Technical Panel, then by the designated spokesperson for each party represented at the hearing, and finally by the Board of Inquiry. At least fifty reporters, along with approximately twenty-five television cameras, were grouped together at the media platform to cover the duration of the hearing.

Tom and I found a seat near the front among many of the families we had just met. We wanted to be able to hear and see everything.

When the hearing commenced, the NTSB's chief investigator of the crash, Gregory Feith, was called as the first witness. Part of his testimony consisted of a graphic video presentation recreating the aircraft gyrations from several different perspectives. We were informed that before the start of the crash sequence, when the flight was considered controlled, the cockpit voice recorder had documented a single chime alert, which was thought to indicate that the aircraft was accumulating ice. The pilots had responded by activating the equipment installed for de-icing, called airframe boots. The video used flight instruments to provide a demo of what the pilots would have seen during the different rotations of the aircraft. During this presentation, we heard a version of the actual cockpit voice recorder transcript, with conversation considered non-pertinent edited out.

The re-enactment began with approximately one minute of the controlled flight prior to the first roll, when the plane had been in a holding pattern at 10,000 feet, with the flaps at 15 degrees to reduce turbulence; at 3:56:27 p.m., the pilots had received clearance from the air traffic controllers to descend to 8,000 feet. As the plane descended, the speed exceeded the maximum operating speed for having the flaps at 15 degrees, and a warning sounded. The pilot's training had stipulated that they could have either decreased their speed or retracted the flaps, and because of their expectation of impending release from the hold, the pilots chose to retract the flaps. The retraction of the flaps disturbed the airflow over the wings, creating a massive change in air pressure; this retraction also affected the aileron, which is the control service located near the tip of the wings that is used to keep the plane level and to help steer the aircraft.

Compounding the disruption of airflow triggered by the retraction of the flaps was a ridge of ice buildup that accumulated too far back on the wing for the de-icing equipment to reach. The design of the wing and the inadequate design of the de-icing boots (which allowed the ridge of ice to build) caused the airflow to separate from the wing, impairing the aileron's ability to properly function. Along with contributing to the lack of critical lift needed to keep the plane flying properly, this ice ridge deflected the airflow over the wing and away from the aileron itself in such a way that the aileron was rendered ineffective in its role of stabilizing the airplane. The aileron's reaction was a sudden and violent movement for which the autopilot could not compensate.

When the aerodynamic forces became too great, the autopilot detected that it could no longer maintain the preset parameters, and so the autopilot disengaged. The autopilot had masked the aerodynamic forces created by the retraction of the flaps and the ridge of ice buildup, leaving the pilots unaware of these forces, and so upon the autopilot disconnect, at 3:57:29 p.m. the aircraft simultaneously rolled violently 77 degrees "pitched right-wing and nose-down." The flight crew managed to regain control for only two or three seconds before the aircraft then experienced a second unrecoverable full roll "right-wing-down," and from there began spiraling Earthward. The pilots' dialogue was broken up by "intermittent heavy irregular breathing," which was accompanied by repeated thuds, beeping, and wailing sounds. As the plane spiraled downward in a "nose-low pitch," thumping sounds followed by rattling could also be heard. With the continued rapid increase of air speed during its plummet to Earth, the plane exceeded its maximum operating speed. The ground proximity warning system sounded as the plane froze on the video projection screen. The outer ten feet of both wings and the horizontal tail separated from the plane moments before it struck the ground in its "steep nose-down, nearly inverted attitude" (the picture of the plane in relation to the Earth) at approximately 425 mph. From the onset of the first roll, the events that transpired had been nearly instantaneous, for the crash was documented as having occurred at 3:57:56 p.m. The video ended with a loud, crunching sound.

By the time the video was over, tears were flowing down my face. I had just witnessed exactly what my sister and nephew had gone through in the last moments of their lives. They had experienced not just some turbulence, but an actual violent rolling of the plane on two separate occasions, and then a screaming dive down to the Earth. Many of the family members, myself included, were frustrated by the extremely technical description of the flight sequence, which added to our already bewildered states arising from the emotionally draining subject matter of the hearing, as well as the overwhelming volume of information with which we were being presented. While I was extremely confused by the language supplementing the visual demonstration, I came to learn that all this basically meant that a variety of factors had worked in conjunction with one another to disrupt the smooth flow of air over the wings, which eventually resulted in an unrecoverable roll.

I watched the video from the perspective of a mother trying to do anything possible to protect her child. I grew sick imagining my sister's initial panic at the aircraft's first violent roll, and the overwhelming fear that must have engulfed her at the onset of the second roll. Surely her thoughts had gone instantly to Patrick, for isn't it typical for a parent to want to console their child? And yet what tools had been available for Patty to protect her youngest son at that point? I also pictured the overhead bins popping open as the second roll took place, and everyone's baggage and personal items flying about the cabin, along with people yelling, screaming, and possibly praying out loud. And in my mind I saw my sister sitting in the plane, clutching Patrick as she looked out the window, watching in horror as she and her son plummeted faster than the speed of the falling raindrops.

Envisioning the terror that Patty must have sustained triggered my thoughts back to earlier that year, when I had been driving down a busy road, and came to a stop, waiting to turn left. When I had initially come to a halt, there was no one behind me, only oncoming traffic. After waiting about a minute, I happened to glance into my rearview mirror and saw a car driving up quite fast from behind. Within a matter of just two to three seconds, my mind had assessed the entire situation. Not only was this evaluation detailed, but it also seemed as if it had been in ultra-slow motion. I had first decided that the driver did not appear that he was going to stop, or that he had even begun to slow down. I figured he was going thirty-five to forty miles an hour. I hadn't been able to fathom how he didn't see me, but all that mattered was concentrating on the best course of action. I focused on my own vehicle, and had mentally gone through some safety checks: were my wheels facing forward, so that if I got hit I would not be pushed into oncoming traffic? Was my seat belt on and was it snug? Were both my hands on the steering wheel to assist in holding myself in place? I then punched the accelerator, glancing in my rearview mirror just as the car ran right into me.

With the video of the crash still replaying in my mind, I tried to translate my sense of heightened awareness that day to what my sister must have experienced just prior to impact. What sort of time distortion had she felt? If my entire assessment of the impending car accident had taken place in just two to three seconds, I couldn't begin to comprehend what Patty must have endured during the twenty-seven seconds from the first roll of the plane until impact. I wondered what thoughts, memories, impressions, and details had stood out for Patty during those twenty-seven seconds that must have seemed like a lifetime. Had she only been able to think about the imminent crash, or did her family and friends enter her thoughts? Was her mind filled with regrets, or had she been able to feel happy and satisfied with her life? Had she realized that she was going to die? In the car accident, I had some control over the sequence of events, in that I had been able to lessen the impact by my ability to react quickly. My sister, on the other hand, had absolutely no power to influence the outcome of the situation. I couldn't even imagine the helplessness and hysteria she must have felt, especially as a mother with the innate instinct to keep her child out of harm's way.

By the end of this first day of testimony, I felt like sprinting away from the convention room, feeling more rushed than I had ever been to leave anywhere before in my entire life. I could not wait to crawl into bed and fall asleep, so that I would no longer have to watch the video incessantly replaying in my mind.

ৡৢ ৡৢ ৡৢ

Tuesday morning, the second day of the hearing, Tom and I took our seats once again to listen to testimony. We had decided to stay only briefly so that we would have time to drive out to the crash site, as this was my first opportunity to pay my respects to my sister and nephew at the place where their lives had ended. We mentioned our trip to other family members, but they all chose to stay and observe the proceedings.

At the beginning of the hearing, a spokesman said he had a special announcement to make, and everyone in the audience immediately gave him their undivided attention. He then proceeded to wish one of the investigators a happy birthday. As he spoke, I was overcome by a rush of agitation and sadness. How could anything celebratory be a part of this hearing? I wanted to stand up and say that only one month prior I had struggled through my first birthday without my sister, but I knew my distraught feelings would override my ability to relay my thoughts clearly, so I just sat there in silence.

A short while later, my husband and I left the hearing for the crash site, located some 120 miles northwest of Indianapolis. The field in which the tragedy had occurred is situated in an unincorporated area just outside the small rural town of Roselawn, but for all intensive purposes is simply referred to as having taken place in Roselawn. Our route took us through what seemed like endless stretches of farmland. Coming to a stop on the road that bordered the eastern edge of the crash site, I noticed a small grouping of flowers and several crosses against a barbed-wire fence. Seeing this informal memorial triggered a stabbing pain that arose from my inexplicable loss. The exact location of impact was approximately one-third of a mile west of the main road, from which a gravel road extended out into the field, having been laid for the sole purpose of providing investigators access to the site.

Since Tom had already visited the site, he was aware that new dirt had been brought in to fill the craters created by the impact of the crash, for due to the fact that the field had been declared a biohazard, the old dirt had to be taken away and disposed of at a biohazard dumpsite. There was one large crater, and a smaller one close by. Some areas of the field were fairly firm, while others were soft and slimy. Tom had suggested that we purchase knee-high rubber boots, because even though it was the end of February and very cold, the field was still quite muddy.

I had felt ambivalent about attending the public hearing in the first place, and I found myself feeling extremely apprehensive as we began the long walk down the gravel road. The end of it led directly into the open field where my sister's and nephew's life had come to an abrupt end just four months earlier. The previous day, I had watched a video re-enactment of the chain of events that had brought Patty and Patrick to their deaths in this exact place, and now I felt as though I was picking up where the video had left off.

As we trudged through the once-mature soybean field, I felt thankful that we had brought boots, for the mud in several areas of the field was so thick that it seemed more like quicksand. Attending to each step deliberately so as not to get stuck, I headed toward the larger crater, which was the point of impact. At a glance, the field blended into the miles of other farmland that extended in every direction; only under close examination were the details of the recent past revealed. During my trek through the field, I discovered many scattered pieces of the plane and some personal belongings; among the objects I picked up were frayed wires, switches, wire bundles, mangled pieces of the interior and exterior of the aircraft, and an armrest from one of the seats. Included amongst the personal items we found was a luggage tag, a torn coat sleeve, a watchband, a metal pocketknife, and a pearl. There was so much that I couldn't carry it all, and eventually, we had to go back to the car and retrieve some bags. Signs of the crash were still readily apparent, even after all the time that had passed, and even after the field had been cleaned up. I had not expected to see so much evidence of the tragedy, and I was most definitely not prepared to handle such a destructive scene.

Before long, I had made my way across the field, while my husband was quite a distance away. Standing in the mud and pools of water, I was once again aware of the tugging-like feeling I had experienced prior to the trip, and I couldn't help but wonder what purpose I was supposed to fulfill in coming here. About a minute later from across the field, Tom yelled, "You're not going to believe what I found."

I rushed over to where Tom was standing, and I could hardly believe my eyes...for body parts were still strewn about the freshly laid soil. In spite of how disturbing a sight it was to behold, I persisted in gathering the remains as reverently as possible, for in my mind, I couldn't help wondering if I was collecting the remnants of my sister and nephew. By the time we left, we had bags full of human remains, plane wreckage, and personal effects. I found it disconcerting that we had effortlessly retrieved so much in such a short time, as it unleashed the possibility that more might be uncovered if the area was thoroughly scoured, which contradicted the airline's earlier assertions that the field had been fully cleaned. While I was aware that the magnitude of the disaster caused the process of clearing the site to be enormous, the fact that debris was still so visible, as well as the fact that the farmer had negated the airline's promise to declare the site as hallowed ground, led us to again feel deceived and disregarded by this large corporation.

Shortly after leaving the site, we stopped at a small convenience store, and I waited in the car while my husband went inside. He soon returned carrying a bag of ice, some drinks, and a small cooler. He opened the bag of ice and dumped it into the cooler. What I expected to see next were the newly purchased soft drinks secured inside; but, to my surprise, Tom reached for the fragments of human remains we had collected and proceeded to bury them deep within the cooler. Since the remains had been frozen out in the field, he thought it best that they continued to be so.

Once back at the hotel, we called the coroner, arranging to turn over the body parts the next morning. We also contacted Stephen Fredrick, a former American Eagle pilot we had met the previous day who used to fly the same type of aircraft used on Flight 4184. He was interested in the day's events, and suggested that if we talked to the media it might strengthen our argument for setting the land aside as a memorial. Although I had wanted to avoid speaking with the press, my desire to expose the airline's lack of respect, not only for all of those who had been aboard the plane by preventing their remains from being honored, but also for their families, outweighed my reluctance to publicly reveal my emotions.

I began to recall my conversations with the other family members just the day before. Some of the people I had met were outspoken about the airline's injustices, while some had kept their feelings of frustration more to themselves. So many people were hurt by this situation that I could no longer sit back passively and wait for the airline to do the "right" thing. Tom and I agreed to do an interview in the former pilot's hotel room, as CNN was interested in the exclusive.

Even though the day had been exceptionally trying, before retiring we felt compelled to do whatever we could for those who had once been mothers, fathers, sisters, brothers, sons, and daughters that were now sharing our hotel room. As respectfully as possible, Tom and I gently rinsed the mud from each body part, and washed the personal effects we had collected.

As we settled in for the night, we began to notice an unrecognizable scent inexplicably starting to permeate our hotel room. We initially assumed the smell was that of jet fuel, or of something else that may have doused the personal effects. Eventually, we realized that this unfamiliar odor was the stench of decomposing body parts, for when we had rinsed off the caked-on soil, the remains had begun to thaw.

I stayed awake for some time, replaying the events of the day as I waited for sleep to take hold. Between the fresh images of the crash site and the odor that saturated the room, I felt as if I was lying amongst those who had perished out in the field. Our senses had been peaked throughout this unique and surreal day, from what we had seen and touched in the field, to the unusual odor in our hotel room. Shortly before the onset of sleep, one more sense would be activated, the one commonly referred to as the sixth sense.

❧ ❧ ❧

Upon rising the next morning, Tom revealed a peculiar perception he had the previous night as he laid awake with the blankets pulled up and the lights still on. "I saw what appeared to be a hand impression pressed into the blankets," he said, "and at the same time I felt pressure across my chest." He went on to explain, "I wasn't afraid, but I just knew it was someone from the plane." As for me, that night I dreamt that several passengers from the plane had come into our room. Their presence in my dream had filled me with comfort, and reinforced my will to ensure that they be properly buried.

While Tom and I were slightly perplexed by these strange encounters, we had to put these thoughts aside in order to prepare for our press interview. We arrived in the pilot's room at 6:30 a.m., and as we awaited the reporters for CNN, we gingerly displayed each and every item we had brought back from the crash site, including the several pieces of human remains. I had been feeling uncomfortable about the entire interview process, but once the cameraman and reporter appeared looking somewhat disheveled and still with wet hair, I breathed a sigh of relief. Their professional yet casual demeanors eased the stress of the interview process, and I eventually allowed myself to relax. The news report focused on our recovery of the personal possessions and body parts; we were factual about our findings, and expressed concern about the implications of what we had seen.

After the interview, we paid a quick yet very important visit to the copilot's family. Our purpose was to return one of the personal effects we had found at the crash site to its rightful owner, having washed and cleaned this item to the best of our ability. Standing face-to-face with the copilot's father and stepmother, we turned over the luggage tag bearing their son's name in as gracious and compassionate a manner as possible.

Their tears were accompanied by expressions of heartfelt appreciation.

Following this emotional exchange, Tom and I made our way to a secured area of the hotel where representatives from the airlines and ALPA (the pilot's union) were staying, in order to get to our scheduled meeting with the coroner. We had to obtain clearance from an armed guard to pass into the protected area; these extreme security measures took my husband and me by surprise, as there were no high-profile political figures present.

Upon entering the coroner's room, we were met by an unassuming, soft-spoken individual. We handed him the remains, and discussed our findings from the previous day. He identified that one of the pieces was part of the bone from a femur, the large thighbone. There was also a muscle and nerve bundle from the lower lumbar area, along with what appeared to be a heel bone. The coroner admitted he was not surprised that these emerged, for when something is driven into the ground with such force, the freezing and thawing of winter can cause items to be pushed back up to the surface over time. While this knowledge would seem to exonerate some of the airline's negligence, the sheer volume of debris Tom and I found, along with the fact that the nature of the aviation industry would make any airline inevitably aware of factors affecting crash sites, prevented us from taking a lenient view of their actions. The coroner assured us that the remains we had gathered would be properly entombed at the cemetery in the mass burial plot.

After making some inquiries, we discovered that he had been elected to the post of the Office of the Coroner, and acted under the direction of the state of Indiana. He was also the person who, several weeks ago in a letter, American Airlines had stated was responsible for the undisclosed burial of nineteen caskets of unidentified remains. The coroner talked about the daunting task of distinguishing each individual aboard the plane, explaining that he was able to identify all the individuals, but could not differentiate all of the two thousand body parts remaining from the sixty-eight people aboard the plane.

The coroner then handed us a sheet of paper. As I looked at it, my initial impression was akin to looking upward into a sea of tranquility, or into the vastness of a late-night sky containing thousands of stars and planets that all appeared as tiny specks, some clustered together and others standing alone. But after this first glance, the picture that came into focus instantly contradicted these grandiose images of a twinkling sky. He informed us that each numbered speck on the page corresponded to a numbered stake that designated the location of a piece, a fragment of an individual once on board the airplane. As I looked more closely, I saw Patty's name written by several of the specks. My eyes were then drawn to the right, where Patrick's name was written next to one of the specks. Immediately, I jumped off the chair and raced to the bathroom, where I was overcome by rhythmic waves of nausea.

When I returned, the coroner continued on to calmly explain that the concentration of stakes in the field had become so great that a decision had eventually been made to mark areas where groups of body parts were found, instead of designating the location of each individual fragment. The sixty-eight people on board the plane had been scattered over an area of approximately ten acres, and therefore to identify each particular remain was a task of nearly impossible scope and magnitude. He also said that the site had been declared a biohazard due to the large amounts of biological and other possibly hazardous materials that had been exposed following the crash. According to the coroner, it was only the second time in U.S. aviation history that an airline accident had been classified as a biohazard, and thus far, this crash had been the most destructive ever witnessed by the NTSB team. Unfortunately, I was beginning to get a clearer picture as to the extent of the devastation.

Tom and I then raised the subject of the undisclosed burial. The coroner matter-of-factly elucidated that he had been the person responsible for the proper disposal of unidentified remains, as well as for the identification process. However, it was American Airlines that had purchased the mass burial plots, and they were also in charge of informing the families of the funerary proceedings. He said he was surprised when he found out that the families had not been notified of the burial, as he and his team had worked very hard to respectfully prepare the remains for entombment.

When we questioned him about the personal effects, the coroner responded that actually quite a few possessions had survived the crash and been recovered, although they were not under his jurisdiction. After the personal items had been removed from the site and cleaned, they were inventoried and stored in boxes in a tractor-trailer. The coroner further revealed that upon completion of the body identification process, the airline officials went through all the items recovered and chose one or two per passenger that *they* considered valuable. Most belongings they decided to return were easy to identify because they bore a name, such as a credit card or driver's license. The company the airline had hired to remove fuel and plane wreckage from the crash site had then been instructed to destroy the remaining personal effects—those that the airline had deemed unimportant. The coroner disclosed that he had received a phone call from the president of this company, who was so uncomfortable with this directive to demolish items he was sure the victims' families would want returned that he had felt compelled to express his objections before carrying out the order. The coroner in turn contacted the airline to discuss the issue. The airline agreed to hire the company to go through the personal effects one more time, and supplied the company's president with a list of items that some of the families had requested including a saxophone and a wedding dress. The president then proceeded to sift through the objects, setting aside five document-sized boxes of belongings, some of which the families had requested, and others that he himself determined families would find to be of some value. Among those he saved were photographs, rolls of film that he had developed, credit cards, business papers, money, and a university band uniform with medals attached. The leftover items were subsequently incinerated, and the boxes of preserved personal effects were shipped via Federal Express to American Airlines corporate headquarters in Fort Worth, Texas.

When the coroner finished talking, I was dazed by what I had just heard. Since I hadn't packed Patty's and Patrick's bags, and therefore could not supply a list of belongings, did that mean I wouldn't get their possessions back? I knew that if I saw the items or even pictures of them, in an instant I could pick out which ones had belonged to my sister and nephew. The airline had failed to mention the fact that if I didn't supply this list, then all but one or two of their recoverable belongings would be destroyed.

I couldn't believe how presumptuous it was of the airline to make such suppositions. Who were they to infer what objects we would cherish, and how could they be so audacious as to assume the right to destroy our family's personal property? The items didn't belong to them. They were ours. Somehow, the airline seemed to have gained absolute control over decisions regarding the crash site and the families' possessions, and by ignoring our input they left us virtually powerless and voiceless.

The coroner said he was free to share information with us, and that our questions would continue to set the parameters for what he discussed. During the course of our conversation, I noticed a large notebook sitting on the table; upon inquiring about its contents, I learned that it contained pictures of the identifying indicator for each person on board the plane. The coroner informed us that Patty had been identified using fingerprints and a single tooth.

I sat for a long time debating whether to ask to see the pictures. On one hand, a part of me wanted as much information as I could get; I felt that if I didn't ask then I would miss out on this opportunity to know the facts. On the other hand, another part of me warned that once I learned something and established a picture of it in my head, I would forever carry that image and that knowledge. I desperately tried to protect myself from being exposed to any representations of my sister that were anything other than whole and beautiful, as she existed in my mind as nothing less, and I was terrified that viewing the photos would transform my mental portrait of her.

When the coroner said that one of Patty's identifiers had been a tooth, I immediately thought of the very small ridges that Patty and I both had on the bottom of our front teeth. We had joked about our ridges over the years, and in some strange way we grew to like them. Maybe because it afforded us one more way to feel connected. Then, several years before the crash, I had some dental work done and the ridges were removed. It didn't take long for Patty to notice the difference. She wasn't happy about it, and repeatedly asked how I could let this dentist file "our" ridges away.

As I sat before this notebook, I just had to know if Patty's identifier had been one of her front teeth with "our" ridges. I asked to see that picture. Scared to death, I slowly reached out for the open notebook and commanded my eyes to look at the picture. I stared at it for some time, feeling as though I had found my way into a parallel universe where everything outside of this single tooth had vanished. Finally, I returned from this distorted consciousness with the answer I wanted; the tooth with "our" ridges had not been the one used to identify my sister.

While I had forced myself to view one picture, I would not turn the page to see what was photographed as the identifying feature used to obtain her fingerprint, nor could I flip the page to see how Patrick was identified. I simply could not allow myself to be haunted by these images.

I knew that some families had the wherewithal to seek out every possible detail regarding the identification process in order to gain as much information as possible about their loved one. Through speaking with the coroner and seeing pictures of what the caskets contained, they had discovered that unidentified remains were put into caskets along with the piece identifying a particular victim, and together these remains were shipped to the families for burial. In fact, it was ascertained that some had received only unidentified remains, without any part of their family member in the coffin. One family discovered that female remains had been buried as their son; the casket was eventually exhumed and the family returned the remains to be placed in the mass grave. Through DNA testing, another family learned that their casket contained the parts of three different individuals, while another family received the ashes of the wrong person after cremation. And, contrary to what we were initially told, not all victims of the crash had even been positively identified.

Immediately I questioned what all this meant regarding the final resting place of my sister and nephew. Were they even in the two caskets that we had cried over at our own funeral service? Or were they mostly in the mass grave? Had they been hauled away to the biohazard dumpsite among all the truckloads of dirt, or did they lay scattered about the field, hidden under the new soil covering the crash site? Alternatively, perhaps they had been shipped to another family's hometown in England, Scotland, Germany, Sweden, Canada, Colombia, Mexico, South Korea, India, or somewhere else within the United States. How could I know for sure without exposing myself to details I wasn't sure I had the capacity to accept?

My thoughts then drifted to the two cemetery plots Mom and Dad had purchased for themselves that were situated right next to where their daughter and grandson were presumably buried. The location of those plots would be meaningless if that was not actually where Patty and Patrick had been laid to rest. By withholding information about the mass burial, and by deceiving the families regarding the reality of the identification process and the returning of remains, the airline officials had stripped Mom and Dad of one of their most important sources of comfort in trying to deal with this tragedy. I was nauseated by the airline's demonstration of insensitivity and their flagrant disregard for the fragile emotional state of our family.

Having seen and heard enough for the time being, Tom and I thanked the coroner for his straightforwardness in answering our questions. He assured us that he would be available if we had any further inquiries.

When we left the meeting, I felt angry, sickened, and deceived, all at the same time, and I found it difficult to sort through all this new-found information.

Meanwhile, the hearing was already underway. Although Tom was physically by my side as we walked down the hall toward the convention center, I was again aware of his detachment from any of my emotional needs. Even when I had left the table upset upon seeing Patrick's name on the paper, he had showed no support or signs of concern. He seemed alarmingly engrossed by the suspense-filled drama into which he had been thrust, as the circumstances surrounding Patty's and Patrick's deaths readily illuminated his true passion for investigation.

As we turned the corner into the hallway leading to the convention center, we heard someone yell, "There they are." Within seconds reporters, microphones, news cameras, and lights surrounded us. Some cameramen walked right beside us, while others squatted on the floor to get shots at certain angles as we walked by. There were reporters clutching notepads, and others holding microphones up to us. Behind the reporters were the families. Somehow, Tom and I had landed at the core of a media frenzy. Apparently, word had spread about the findings at the crash site the previous day, and everyone wanted our story. Most, if not all, of the reporters and families who just moments earlier had been at the hearing were now gathered in the hall. The flashing lights and clicking cameras seemed appropriate for some Hollywood production or celebrity's special appearance, but my wrenching emotions instantly reminded me of the tragedy that brought everyone here, neutralizing any apparent sense of glamour, and my sense of loss was compounded with each retelling of our story.

When it came time to break for lunch, we barely had time to eat, as we were scheduled to meet with a new group of reporters afterward. We had done so many interviews all morning long that it was hard to believe there was anyone that had not yet heard our account.

Jenny, Brad's sister, accompanied us to the room used for the interviews, and upon entering, she lunged forward in disbelief when she saw the display of the personal effects we had collected at the crash site. She started to cry as she picked up the watchband, exclaiming that it was her brother's. Jenny then held up a framed picture of Brad that she had been carrying all week and directed everyone's eyes to his wrist. On it was the same watchband that less than twenty-four hours earlier my husband and I had retrieved from the muddy field.

Following this last interview session, I was ready for a quiet afternoon of listening to testimony at the hearing. Unfortunately, once again I realized that I could not control my own agenda, as we were met with family members who were interested in hearing our story first-hand and seeing what we had found at the site. For the second time, we laid out everything we had brought back. People hovered over the table, eager to get a look, while Jenny shared her experience being reunited with her brother's watchband.

On the first day of the hearing, I had met a man whose elderly mother was on the plane. With a soft-spoken demeanor and pain-ridden eyes, he had shared some of his loving memories of her. He then mentioned the expensive, fine jewelry that she took with her on her trips— one of the items being a set of pearls she had inherited from her own mother. He told me about the black-velvet pouch she carried her jewelry in, and about how important it was for him to receive these valuables.

As this man, along with the other family members, gathered around for the display of personal effects, I saw his eyes fixate on the pearl we had placed on the table. Slowly he reached out and picked it up. Concentrating his full attention on this lone pearl, he turned it over several times, giving it a thorough examination. With tears in his eyes, he turned to me and said, "There is no way I can prove that this one, single pearl belonged to my mother, but I would like to believe it did. I would like to claim it as hers."

He walked away holding that one pearl as if it were the most priceless commodity he had ever come across. And it most likely was, for it had been his mother's. At that moment, the pearl temporarily filled his entire emotional bank that had been empty since the tragedy, just as the watchband had for Jenny. Each item was small, but represented something enormous, in that it provided a means by which they could feel connected to their lost loved ones, which had been difficult without having bodies to bury and honor.

Before we had finished our meeting with family members, another media commotion had begun in the lobby. I found out that a spokesman from American Airlines was issuing a news release in response to our findings at the crash site. The spokesman claimed that the airline was as outraged and shocked as everyone else that not all the remains had been cleared away, as they had hired a private biohazard firm, PWI Environmental, to do the clean-up, which had billed the airline several hundred thousand dollars for the job. Basically, I stood and watched as this spokesman passed the blame off the airline and onto PWI and the coroner by maintaining that the site was not under the jurisdiction of the airline, and that the airline had gone to great lengths and expense to return the property to its original state. His comments seemed to dance around the issues raised, failing to substantially address our complaints about the personal effects or the exposed remains.

Shortly thereafter, the president of PWI made his own statement to the media, arguing that his firm was responsible only for the removal of plane parts and the clean-up of the soil contaminated by hydraulic oil and jet fuel; they had not been hired to remove the human remains or the personal effects from the field, but only to clean the hazardous materials off of the belongings. Thus, he strongly objected to the airline's inaccurate statements regarding the role of his company. According to him, the biohazard firm had followed the airline's instructions stipulating that only certain personal effects were to be saved, and that everything else was to be destroyed.

In another press announcement, PWI's attorney said that he found the airline's account perplexing, because at the end of the clean-up efforts, representatives from the airline, the biohazard firm, and the Indiana Department of Environmental Management had walked the field and determined the work to be satisfactory. He concluded by saying that, in spite of the job having been completed in early January, the airline was still withholding full payment of their contract, and the biohazard firm was consequently suing the airline in an Indiana State Court. After I heard PWI's assertions, the airline's statements appeared rampant with inconsistencies, further detracting from their already severely compromised credibility.

Hard as it was to imagine, my husband and I found ourselves giving more interviews following the press releases made by the two companies. We continued to address the issues of personal effects, finding human remains at the site, and the undisclosed burial that had taken place just a couple weeks after the crash. We also discussed the wishes of many family members to see the field declared as hallowed ground and set aside as a memorial. We spoke about the airline's disrespectful treatment of the families, which seemed to be worsening with each passing day.

By late afternoon, the media had made their way to the crash site. Throughout the day, not only were special reports broadcasted about our findings, but reporters also described their own sightings. They described the smell of jet fuel when the wind blew in a specific direction, as well as having detected additional plane wreckage and personal effects.

...The dominoes just kept on falling...

In response to the discoveries at the site, the governor's office ordered the State Board of Health to re-examine the field. Also, the State Emergency Management Agency coordinated an immediate re-inspection and investigation of the site, during which state officials were to retest soil samples to determine if the field was a health or environmental hazard.

By nightfall, the initial whirlwind surrounding our visit to the crash site the previous day seemed to have progressed into a full-blown tornado. The first interview we had given at 6:30 that morning had created a chain reaction so large that by day's end we were awed by it all. I found myself being swept along in a swiftly moving current not unlike the one I had found myself in four months earlier. However, I was no longer struggling to survive each day of my changed life, but instead was engaged in a fight to get the small voices of the families heard by a multibillion-dollar corporation.

❧ ❧ ❧

The next morning, Tom decided to leave the hotel room before me. We were to meet up for breakfast before heading into the hearing. As I walked through the lobby on my way to breakfast, I couldn't help but notice that almost everyone I passed turned and looked in my direction. I heard whispering, which led to more head-turning. Initially, I figured it was my imagination. My next thought was that I must have looked pretty good in what I was wearing that particular morning. As the stares continued, I began to feel a bit self-conscious, checking to see if maybe I was wearing part of my breakfast, until I remembered I hadn't even eaten yet that morning. I then spotted my husband waving me over to him. On my way to the table, I felt escorted by almost every set of eyes in the restaurant. Once I was seated, Tom, speaking in a quiet voice, said he had something to show me. The next thing I knew, I was looking at the front page of a newspaper displaying a huge picture of Tom and me, featuring the story we had spent the previous day telling. Somehow, I had managed to give all those interviews without fully comprehending the fact that I was going to have to endure a bit of publicity, and I almost laughed at myself for not realizing why strangers had been eyeing me on my walk to breakfast.

We soon saw that every paper from the *Indianapolis Star* to the *Wall Street Journal* contained an article about our findings at the site, although many adopted different perspectives on the issues. A few accounts described the focal point of the hearing as having shifted to the crash site, some forty miles southeast of Chicago, as a result of our publicized visit. Others focused on the fact that our uncovering of additional human remains had occurred not long after the families were notified of the mass burial that was not disclosed until well after it had taken place. Some papers highlighted the circles of blame that ensued from our discovery; others reported that the presence of the victims' families was injecting a shattering human element into the otherwise highly technical NTSB testimony dominating the proceedings.

Due to information he learned the previous day, my attorney filed an emergency motion on my behalf in Federal Court for a protective order to preserve all remaining aircraft wreckage, personal effects, and records. He was concerned that the wreckage being incinerated could be critical evidence should a lawsuit be filed against the airline. The order pointed out that the airline had already destroyed plane parts after the NTSB no longer needed them, and that the airline could not provide an inventory of what had been demolished. The order also mentioned that personal items might have been destroyed along with those plane parts, and therefore mandated that the remainder of the belongings be preserved. I did not see how the airline had not originally been legally bound to preserve the evidence until a thorough assessment of the crash had been made, as I would have thought it to be a matter of course in our legal system. I couldn't believe that such an order was even necessary. However, upon further investigation, former American Eagle pilot, Stephen A. Fredrick, elucidated:

> *The airline used its clout with government authorities, who had in turn ordered PWI to release the aircraft wreckage back to AMR. American had begun destroying the wreckage, which was possible evidence if the case ever went to trial, and was denying experts a chance to view and investigate the remains of the ATR-72. Fortunately... because AMR had also not paid the disposal company for its work, the company had stopped the destruction.*

In response to a news release from my attorney about the order, an airline representative again came forward, stating that the only parts of the plane wreckage the airline had ordered to be destroyed were those not considered crucial to the NTSB investigation. He also declared that the only personal items discarded were those that were badly stained or appeared to be beyond repair, adding that they would not dispose of any more items from the crash. The spokesman concluded with the promise that many of the personal effects were being returned to families that very week, a statement that at this point I knew better than to rely on.

Back at the hearing, attendance remained high even as the week progressed. Tom and I had already exceeded our expected two-to-three-day stay when we took our seats for this fourth day of testimony. Engineering and test pilot experts were among those called to the witness stand. At midmorning, a break gave everyone an opportunity to get a breath of fresh air.

On my way out of the room, a young woman stopped me, explaining she was employed by one of the agencies working the crash site in the immediate aftermath of the tragedy. She was so soft-spoken that I had to lean in closer to hear her over all the noise created by people leaving the room. She sadly divulged that she had cried when she learned from our interviews the previous day that we had not received any personal effects, as she and the other workers had taken painstaking care with each item uncovered, so that they all could be returned to their rightful owners. Instinctively, they had all understood the significance these belongings would have for the families, regardless of their condition. The young woman repeatedly stated that there had been an abundance of personal effects—in fact, the field was full of them. With tears glistening in her eyes and her voice beginning to quiver, she whispered that she and the others working for the agency had been told not to talk about any of the activities that went on at the site. Although she risked getting into trouble by sharing these details with me, she just could not bear the pressure of keeping it all to herself any longer.

The young woman then described the on-site system regarding personal effects. As each one was found, it was logged in and washed to the best of the crew's ability. The items were then turned over to the biohazard company for a more thorough cleaning. With deep melancholy, she said she didn't understand why the airline had not returned these belongings to the families. It was easy to see the pain this woman felt over so much of her effort having been for nothing. We exchanged phone numbers, and I promised to keep her name quiet, as she feared work-related consequences.

As the hearing reconvened, my mind raced with the contradictions illuminated by the information disclosed during our conversation. This woman, with genuine emotion, had spoken of the great number of personal effects she and others had found, and of their handwritten logs listing all that was recovered. I couldn't see anything she would gain by telling me a story that wasn't true, and yet for four months, the airline had continued to claim that very few items had been retrieved. If that were the case, then where had the many belongings described by this woman gone? How would the airline benefit by not returning the personal effects? Was it too costly or time consuming to determine ownership of the items, or did they just not care? Each piece of new information I acquired seemed to deteriorate more and more of the airline's integrity.

During the hearing, we learned that part of the clean-up effort had entailed the removal of 65 truckloads of soil, which had been replaced with 120 truckloads of fresh soil. One family member had been at the site at the time, and clearly understanding the implications as each truckload of dirt was hauled away, she had cried out, "My son! Where are you taking my son?"

Listening to this story recalled a set of circumstances that had played out months earlier. Shortly after the tragedy, my husband had repeatedly asked the Care Team women about visiting the crash site. They had made it crystal clear that we should stay away, as our presence would only hamper recovery and investigative efforts. But at the end of December, on his way home from a work assignment, Tom had stopped by the crash site anyway. Even back then, there had been many bouquets, wreaths, crosses, and hand-lettered signs by the entrance to the makeshift gravel road that led out to the field, which was available to use, as the investigative efforts at the scene had been completed. No one had been present as my husband began driving down the road, but two vehicles were parked near a barbed-wire fence on the east end of the field, one being a flatbed truck, and the other an idling bulldozer. No signs indicated "Keep Out" or "No Trespassing." Tom passed the two vehicles and came to a stop not far from the point of impact. When he began walking through the field, he saw hundreds of metal pieces of the plane, some as large as twelve-by-twelve inches. The main impact crater had been partially filled with new dirt, but still contained quite a bit of water.

Since Tom had taken his camera with him, he started snapping pictures. Once back at his vehicle, a man who had arrived at the site just moments earlier approached him and identified himself as an employee of PWI Environmental. He told my husband there were no photographs permitted, and threatened to call the police if he did not turn over the film.

Tom had called me at home to ask for my advice, which I easily formulated. The film did not belong to this employee, nor did the land or the wreckage he was bulldozing. Tom had ceased taking pictures upon his request and was willing to leave, but the film was his and he should not give it up.

But when my husband had refused, the man fulfilled his threat to call the police, and then blockaded the only road out of the field with the bulldozer. An hour later, a state trooper had arrived, informing Tom that if he did not surrender the film, he would be arrested for trespassing. Thus, Tom turned it over and was given a receipt. The state trooper had promptly handed the roll of film over to the environmental company employee, who promised Tom that he would be contacted by the airline or biohazard firm regarding its return, and then permitted him to leave.

However, almost two and a half months later, there had been no update from either the airline or the biohazard firm about the film. My husband's letter of inquiry went unanswered.

I was confused as to why the site could not be photographed, and felt a growing suspicion that there was something to hide, which was reinforced by the fact that the state trooper had given the roll of film to the employee of the private firm. I was bewildered and disturbed by Tom's description of the circumstances at the site; most notably, the dumping of the dirt left me with many questions and a gnawing sense of uneasiness. There was no way to determine whether the earth had been sifted through for our family's belongings, or if any uncovered human remains were set aside for a proper burial. While I was aware that the soil needed to be removed, as it contained contaminated materials that were hazardous to leave exposed in the field, I was distraught by the idea of the dumpsite becoming yet another location for the disposition of our loved ones. I would have felt somewhat assuaged if the dirt had at least been respectfully buried, which would have afforded the victims a resting place where they could be commemorated.

I was so engrossed in these thoughts that I nearly forgot to pay attention to the ongoing testimony. When the hearing broke for lunch, on my way out of the room I was stopped by a gentleman who had just made his way out of the area reserved for the hearing's participants, who said he knew my story from the interviews I had given the day before. He extended his condolences, and informed me that although his purpose for being at the hearing was technical in nature, he had also worked at the site immediately following the crash. He explained that the destruction had been overwhelming, and at times difficult even to comprehend. Working in the midst of this great devastation, it was common for him to forget the element of human tragedy in the wreckage strewn throughout the field, for an inner defense mechanism seemed to kick in to prevent him from becoming overwhelmed by sentiment.

But this protection was not fully comprehensive. Even as we conversed, I observed some emotion beginning to stir in him as he detailed something he had seen each time he circled around the tail section of the plane. Lying among the wreckage, human remains, and harvested soy beans were two items that had instantly penetrated his self-protective barrier—little Patrick's Ninja Turtle gym shoes and one of his Ninja Turtle workbooks. It was certain that these had belonged to Patrick, as he had been the only child on board the flight. The man told me that he had young children of his own, and that each time he had seen Patrick's things, he was inescapably struck by the human toll in this tragedy, which emphasized the fragility of human life.

During the lunch break, media reports began coming in from the re-inspection of the crash site the governor's office had ordered the previous day. The State Health Commissioner said that eight pieces of additional bone fragments had turned up while he was walking the field. He also reported the presence of substantial amounts of aircraft debris, including wiring, electronic parts, and pieces of aluminum. Parts of a suitcase and clothing still littered the ground. The report concluded by quoting his remark, "You name it, it's up there." However, he still maintained that no evidence had indicated that the field posed a health risk, and thus the farmer could retain control of the property. At the commissioner's direction, the airline contracted with a different state-approved biohazard firm to clean up the debris at the crash site to the satisfaction of government authorities. We also discovered that the airline required this new biohazard firm to sign a confidentiality agreement. In short, they wanted to make sure that no employees would be allowed to talk to family members or give out any information.

When the fourth day of testimony resumed, we obtained further explanation regarding the icing problems on the wings, which flight tests conducted in December demonstrated could have caused an unexpected roll like the one incurred by Flight 4184. As previously mentioned, ATRs were equipped with rubber de-icing boots on the wings, which theoretically served to remove ice formations so that air could pass smoothly over the wings, thus ensuring that pressure remained stable over the ailerons; however, since frozen droplets were able to bypass the boots, the consensus amongst the NTSB investigators was that aviation authorities needed to set stricter standards for certifying planes to operate in icing conditions.

We listened as the aircraft manufacturer defended the quality of the aircraft, while simultaneously stating that new de-icing equipment would be installed by summer to make the fleet safer.

However, testimony also revealed that ice alone did not cause the crash. Investigators questioned whether the pilots had violated the sterile cockpit rule, which bans extraneous activity in the cockpit during critical phases of flight, as the cockpit voice recorder captured bantering among the pilots and flight attendants during the thirty-three minute holding pattern preceding the crash. For a variety of reasons, it was eventually affirmed that the plane's crew was not at fault, and it was decided that this issue did not require further investigation. The pilots' reputations were upheld as professional and capable.

After these extensive presentations from experts and investigators, testimony concluded for the day. When the hearing reconvened in the morning, the last remaining issues on the NTSB's agenda were to be addressed.

෨෴ ෨෴ ෨෴

The next day, which was the final day of testimony, my husband and I found our seats once again among the other families, the general public, and news media. Even though I tried to listen to the proceedings, my mind could only concentrate on what seemed to be the mountains of new information that we had encountered throughout the week of the hearing.

We had discovered that airline personnel had initially gone through the personal effects, removing only the items that they considered to be of value to the families. Through the efforts of the coroner and the president of the biohazard firm, PWI, five additional document-size boxes of belongings doomed for destruction were cleaned, labeled, and returned to the airline's headquarters in Texas, although the airline denied ever receiving these boxes. One of the families held a copy of the receipt verifying this information.

Each family member with whom we had spoken shared our concern over not having obtained any belongings. Despite all the airline's reassurances that we would be receiving these items, it wasn't until the discoveries my husband and I made at the site that the first personal effects were delivered, and by the last day of the hearing, the airline still had yet to return any of Patty's and Patrick's possessions. And when the news media began to research the matter, no one from the airline could be reached for comment.

By the time our lawyer entered the protective order to preserve the personal effects, four months had passed since the crash. The families questioned why attorneys would even have to intercede, and we were perplexed over why the airline thought the families would not want anything back in less-than-perfect condition. If perfection was what we sought, then purchasing brand-new items from the store would have sufficed.

After speaking with different family members and the coroner during the week, along with our trip to the crash site, the whole and beautiful images of my sister and nephew onto which I had so tightly clung vaporized into thin air. The knowledge I had gained during the week of the hearing, in conjunction with our findings out in the field, left no room for denial.

In November we had been informed that cremation of the bodies would take an additional two weeks, and we had decided against it because we were not prepared to wait that long to put our family to rest. However, we learned that any lingering remains out in the field were to be cremated from that point on which was inconsistent with and contradictory to the airline's earlier statements. Throughout the week of the hearing, continued revelations of the airline's excessively disturbing actions further denied us the usual benefits that time would typically provide during a healing process. It was difficult to comprehend how the airline's treatment of the families could have been so callous.

A short time into this final day of testimony, I realized that I could not take one more day of turmoil. I could not receive one more detail that would initiate an onslaught of more pain, nor could I listen to one more cold, mechanical discussion about this horrific, heart-wrenching tragedy. Because the investigators had already disclosed that they expected it to be months before a consensus was reached as to the probable cause of the crash, which wasn't to be revealed until another public hearing well into the future, I had no qualms about my decision to leave before the end of the day. With eyes full of tears, I got up and walked out of the hearing one last time. Then Tom and I quickly packed our bags and headed for home.

❧ 15 ❧

Once back at home, I welcomed the familiarity of being surrounded by family, and devoted myself to domestic concerns in my attempt to disengage my thoughts from what I had learned at the hearing. With the intent of fulfilling Patty's wishes, I set about preparing for a court date to obtain custody of Jonathon. Interrogatories and depositions had already been completed for the legal process, including the statements submitted by friends, neighbors, and teachers testifying as to where they thought Jonathon would grow and flourish most; they expressed enormous support for Jonathon to stay in a familiar family situation, in a place where, according to Jonathon, his "other" mom lived. To be able to remain with his cousins and be near his Grandma and Grandpa all seemed vitally important.

Jonathon's and Nikki's kindergarten teacher sent a letter stating that the two of them had replicated the behavior of a set of twins she had in one of her classes, constantly displaying care, love, responsiveness, and exceptional loyalty toward one another. She detailed the closeness between Patty and me, explaining that each of us had been a complete extension of the other, and that I, in so many ways, had been a mom to Jonathon for his entire life. Under the circumstances, she felt it would be in Jonathon's best interest to stay with me, where he felt most comfortable. Furthermore, she revealed that she had never once met Jonathon's father, Frank, throughout the entire year Jonathon had been her student.

Jonathon's current second-grade teacher told me he had asked Jonathon whether he should refer to me as his aunt, by my first name, or more formally by my last name. Jonathon instantly replied, "Call her

Mom."

I compiled many stories, letters, and notes in preparation for the hearing. I also came across a Valentine's Day card that Jonathon had made for me after the loss of Patty and Patrick, which read:

Mother,
I love you very much. Hope you have a good day. If you feel bad,
remember me and you will feel good. Thank you for all the
things you do for me. Thank you for your love for me.
Jonathon

Throughout this preparation for the custody hearing, all of my efforts regarding Jonathon were centered on my overriding concern to ensure his well-being and happiness in the future. For months after the crash, Jonathon had remained under the watchful eye of a psychologist, assuring that he was coping, grieving, and carrying on with life as well as could be expected. The doctor recommended that Jonathon live with our family, because he felt Jonathon would feel more comfortable in an environment that most resembled his life before the crash.

I was perplexed as to why Frank never attended a session, or at least talked with the doctor about his son. Finding it difficult to understand why he wouldn't do everything possible to help Jonathon through such critical times, I remembered that his seemingly distant nature was consistent with what I had noticed during his marriage to Patty. I also recalled a conversation I had with Patty prior to her divorce, in which I discussed the lack of parental guidance that I observed in Frank, and therefore requested that my children no longer visit her house unless she was present.

Following the crash, Frank had commented to me that he felt Jonathon seemed to be doing well, due to the fact that he never cried during the occasional time they spent together. I responded by mentioning the emotional openness between Jonathon and myself, and suggested that Frank be concerned with achieving the same freedom of expression with his son, instead of basing his opinions solely on outward appearances.

In any event, I decided to give Frank the benefit of the doubt, and expected him to see his son and be available for him on a regular basis. As it turned out, Frank would often arrive hours late or fail to show up at all for scheduled visits, and we would often go for weeks without even hearing from him, which was accordant with the way Patty used to remorsefully describe his behavior. I often thought back to Patty's phone conversations with Frank, in which she would practically beg him to at least contact the children, since he had declined to utilize his rights to visitation. I had been continually disheartened by Patty's disappointment, and found Frank's inconsistent presence in the children's lives quite disturbing.

Frank's persistent apathy towards his son seemed to frequently hurl Jonathon into a state of regression. In my mind, his withdrawal ensuing from the long periods of waiting for his father seemed comparable to the long periods of waiting he went through at the airport, expecting to meet up with his mother and brother, only to learn of the horrific tragedy. Once this was triggered in Jonathon, there was nothing that could help him to override those deeply anchored feelings of trauma and loss.

As the court date drew near, Frank began to show more diligence in his visitations with Jonathon, and his once infrequent calls and appearances became fairly regular, all of which left me suspicious of his motives for this sudden interest.

Meanwhile, I continued building a case that would guarantee securing guardianship of Jonathon. On the day of the custody hearing, Mom and I headed to the court house. We brought with us written documentation testifying to conversations Patty had with friends and neighbors regarding her concerns about Frank's parenting style. The attorney representing us was from a small law firm that we used for business matters at work, and it was also the law firm I initially chose to represent Jonathon in his suit against the airline, although I had wound up using a different firm specializing in such cases.

We sat on a bench in the courtroom and waited for the judge to make his appearance. The attorney we had initially worked with was not able to appear in court, and instead we were accompanied by a partner from his firm. During our wait, I watched as our "fill-in attorney" laughed and joked with Frank's attorney. When the hearing began, I listened to testimony that seemed to be one contradiction after another, as it presented an argument that upheld Frank's fatherly devotion not only to Jonathon, but also to his daughter from his first marriage. As I continued to pay close attention to the development of Frank's case, I recalled Patty's frustration about the lack of time (which, according to Patty, had only been a handful of instances each year) Frank spent with his daughter. And yet somehow, his attorney managed to conjure up a portrait of Frank that upheld his "extensive involvement" in his children's lives.

When it was time for my attorney to present our case, he informed the judge that Patty died in an airplane crash, and that Jonathon had been living with me since that time. He stated that I was Jonathon's aunt, and that I had been providing for him since the time of Patty's death. With only those words spoken, he was done presenting my argument.

The judge made his decision as quickly as my attorney had begun and concluded his presentation. He ruled that Jonathon would be allowed to stay with me through the duration of the school year, and to go on our already scheduled family vacation immediately after school ended. After that, Frank would have sole custody.

While Mom and I were shocked and devastated over this ruling, it was apparent the outcome did not affect my attorney one way or the other, as he managed to get in a couple more chuckles with Frank's attorney before leaving.

I wondered how this attorney could so nonchalantly disregard Jonathon's future. Was he that inadequate at practicing law, or was our case just another opportunity for him to submit a bill? Maybe it was a combination of both. I had been forced to watch this attorney, as if starring in his own sit-com, portray most eloquently a perfected mockery of expertise and integrity in the field of law. His execution of ineptness, along with his lack of ethics, were most compelling in what appeared to be a stellar performance.

I hadn't even stood a chance. The attorney did not mention my relationship with Jonathon, or the amount of time he had spent at my house prior to the crash. Not once did he refer to the close bond between me and Patty, or that Jonathon referred to me as "Mom." He did not bring up the recommendations from doctors, teachers, and friends, nor did he mention the benefit of Jonathon remaining in a familiar family environment. He also neglected to produce the written statements in his possession that addressed Frank's questionable parenting skills. Although I was angry over the judge's decision, I was also aware that he was presented with extremely distorted facts on one side, and no evidence to counteract this misleading testimony regarding Frank's parental capacities on the other side. It was no wonder he ruled the way he did. I left the courtroom feeling as though I had somehow let down Patty, myself, and Jonathon.

I was emotionally and physically drained by the entire situation. I had already been functioning on very little sleep, and this coupled with the court preparations had consumed more energy than I ever could have imagined. Even at this state of exhaustion, I was still considering disputing the judge's decision. However, I was promptly advised I would most likely only lose once again, as Patty had not yet changed her will before she died to indicate her wishes that I take custody of Jonathon, and Frank had no legal record indicating him as an unfit father. Therefore, I begrudgingly accepted the outcome of this hearing.

All who knew of the situation questioned Frank's authenticity regarding his sudden involvement in parenting, and many speculated that his true interest lay in the money Jonathon would be awarded as a result of the crash settlement. He had been unemployed for some time while he and Patty were married, and it appeared as though he was quite comfortable depending on her as the main breadwinner. In a roundabout way, it appeared that he could continue to do so.

❧ 16 ❧

While I was struggling to come to terms with what had transpired at the custody hearing, as well as mentally preparing myself for the fact that Jonathon would no longer be living with me after the school year ended, my attorney was making some headway with the airline. He called to inform me that he had received my husband's roll of film, which the state trooper had confiscated at the crash site many months earlier. The attorney also said a check had arrived for me from the airline, which I had been expecting for quite some time.

Shortly after the crash, the Care Team representatives apprised us that a camera had been found at the crash site. During a question-and-answer session, I was able to inform them that the camera was part of the business equipment Patty had taken with her on the trip. The women had assured us that we would be reimbursed for the camera, providing we could substantiate our claim with the serial number and a receipt. We did, and the airline had given us a check for $1,219.99, the full cost of the camera. Even though this had occurred in the immediate wake of the tragedy when I had still been numbed by the shock of my loss, I had considered the airline's promptness in attending to matters admirable....until I happened to turn the check over and read the back side, where to my astonishment, I saw a clause freeing the airline of all responsibility regarding the crash. The check I had nearly signed included a statement that indicated "by endorsing this check the undersigned releases and discharges American Airlines, Inc. and all others from all claims and damages arising from an incident that occurred on October 31, 1994."

I had read and re-read these words to assure myself that I understood correctly. What appeared to be the airline's sneaky attempt to acquire my signature on this release starkly contrasted with the Care Team's promises to assist us through the aftermath of the tragedy. I had decided to call the airline's insurance company in order to question the purpose for the fine print on the back of the check. Their response was even more amazing than the release clause itself, as I was told that "it doesn't mean what it says" and was then directed to sign and cash the check regardless of the inscription. Despite their assurances, I was willing to bet that had I signed the check, I would have skewed the situation in their favor. As the airline's response to my question about the release on the check was unacceptable, I requested that a second check be issued without this disclaimer of liability. Thus, my attorney's phone call that day was regarding this reissued check, which had taken about six months to receive, and like everything else, had required legal intervention.

A couple of weeks after acquiring the airline's check, I received a second call from my attorney that finally brought the news I had waited so long to hear, informing me that he had received Patty's personal belongings (Patrick's were legally to be returned to his father). Upon receiving this news, I was both glad and afraid all at the same time, as I had no idea what condition the items would be in, or what my reaction would be upon seeing her effects. All I knew for sure was that I wanted them.

I left the more lighthearted track of family life and headed downtown to my attorney's office. I wondered what clothes and shoes Patty had taken to Indianapolis, as well as which pieces of luggage she had carried. I thought that her clothes would probably be some of the more likely items to be returned, and I tried to mentally scan her wardrobe, speculating on what outfits she might have brought on her trip. It was as if these particular belongings, the last in her possession, somehow carried a piece of her life force. Although the airline had sent me a check for the work camera, and although I knew that the damage it had suffered was not repairable, I still expected that what was left of it would be returned, and I was eager to obtain anything of hers that was found. However, as much as I looked forward to finally having these possessions, I feared that seeing the damage to them might trigger a reaction for which I was unprepared. As I got closer to the attorney's office, I began to feel quite apprehensive and could barely wait to get inside the doors.

Upon entering, I was escorted to an empty conference room, where I waited to be seen. Unable to contain my anxiety, I began pacing back and forth next to a window ledge overlooking downtown Chicago. To calm myself, I replayed several songs in my head that Patty and I had deemed as "ours" over the years. One of the songs, "Who Put the Bomp," a Barry Mann song from 1961, had a catchy tune that seemed to forever stick in our minds, along with the Drifters' "Under the Boardwalk," which had always brightened up our days. However, our favorite song was definitely The Beatles' "Birthday," as Patty and I would be reminded each time it played that we held the designation of Irish Twins, and therefore hearing it was always uplifting. Whenever either one of us would hear one of "our songs" on the radio, it would often wind up recorded in a message on the other's answering machine. It was always heartwarming to come home to one of these songs, and as I moved restlessly in front of the window in the attorney's office, my sudden recollection of "our songs" calmed me down by reminding me of Patty's playful and loving nature, and the bond we had shared.

The conference room door opened, instantly jolting me out of these pleasant thoughts and back to reality. I was then handed a large box. The door closed again as the attorney exited, showing consideration for my privacy.

It felt like my moment of truth. I wondered if having Patty's personal possessions in hand would somehow afford me a sense of peace. I meticulously cut the tape on the box, taking care not to damage any of its contents. Holding my breath, I pulled back the flaps of the box.

As I leaned over to look inside, to my astonishment, what I saw did not include anything that I had imagined on my way downtown. Instead, sitting at the bottom of this large box under a lot of loose paper was another box. This one was quite small in size—very small, in fact. I reached inside and picked it up. Holding this feather-weight box in the palm of my hand, I slowly removed the lid, revealing Patty's driver's license and a small pouch.

The clarity of Patty's picture on her license easily revealed the twinkle typically seen in her baby blue eyes. Looking at her photo, I pictured Patty's appearance over the years, from her baby white hair as a child, to what eventually became beautiful, long, blonde locks. She came to be quite stunning with her blue eyes, blonde hair, and tall figure, making her graceful walk appear more like she was flowing. Whether it was her casual attire or effortless smile framed by the dimples on both sides of her face, Patty seemed to naturally emanate a warmth that made people of all ages feel comfortable. As I stared at the license, I cherished the familiarity of her signature, as I did all my recollections of Patty. The other item in the box was a multicolored pouch made out of silky fabric, about the size of a large wallet, inside which the license had been found.

I had difficulty believing there weren't more personal effects, especially seeing that these were in perfect condition. It's not that I expected to receive everything that she had brought with her, but I would have hoped for the airline to go through enough trouble to at least return a few belongings that did not contain a photograph or some identifying inscription. I would have been happy to provide them with photographs of Patty wearing various outfits, or some information that may have assisted with the identification process, but my input had not been sought in any way beyond the initial request by the Care Team to provide a list of what Patty had taken with her on the trip, which I could not do as I had not helped her pack. Suddenly, the words spoken during my conversation with the woman I met during the preliminary hearing echoed in my head as I recalled her sadness when she learned that, up to that point, the families had not obtained the vast number of personal items that she and the other workers had so painstakingly recovered. This recollection heightened my confusion as to how I had only received two possessions, as I was sure that had they allowed me to participate in the identification process, I would have been able to find more things that had belonged to Patty. I questioned my attorney about the lack of belongings returned. He was as surprised as I was, and assured me that he had already done all that was legally possible by filing the protective order to prevent further destruction of the personal effects.

This moment of truth did not deliver a way to find greater connectedness with my sister, but rather revealed what appeared to be the airline's emphasis on cutting their losses, and then quickly and efficiently continuing on with business, regardless of the emotional cost to the families. I suddenly became aware that to some extent I needed to let go of my reliance on the ability of these belongings to provide me with a sense of closure, as this was partially responsible for my feelings of helplessness and disappointment; however, I simultaneously believed that the airline should have recognized these objects' value as a means by which the victims' families might find a way of feeling connected with their loved ones in the absence of bodies, and therefore should have gone to greater lengths during the identification process in order to return as many of these items as possible.

I left the attorney's office with these possessions, as well as a set of interrogatories. This series of questions provided by the airline's insurance company were designed to gain detailed information about Patty, as well as her role as a caretaker, in order to arrive at a settlement amount for Jonathon. The inquiries covered issues regarding Patty's physical health, her work history, and her estate affairs. I was also asked details about the amount and type of support Patty had provided for Jonathon.

The insurance company was also looking for specifics concerning the grief and mental distress suffered by Jonathon. They wanted to know where Jonathon was at the time of the crash, and how he learned of the death of his mother and brother. Also, I was asked to provide a list of every person who had witnessed Jonathon's grief.

The interrogatories continued with inquiries about our relatives, concerning who had died, causes of deaths, any diseases and illnesses from the past five years, and our family's history of medical treatment. They requested a five-year history of all personal consumption by Patty—in other words, a listing of every expenditure including food, clothing, hobbies, education, medical expenses, retirement savings, and everything else in between. The airline's insurance company also requested knowledge of any alcohol habits Patty may have had.

These were among the questions that allowed the airline to formulate the work-life expectancy and life expectancy of my sister. Strangely enough, the Care Team representatives that came into our house right after the crash had asked many of these same questions, and yet I found myself having to restate information that I had already supplied.

As I walked to the train station, I felt completely overwhelmed by the detail of what I was expected to provide. I was unsure how I would get through this task of responding to questions used to calculate a mathematical sum equivalent to the value of my sister's life.

❧ ❧ ❧

While part of me remained torn apart and unnerved by the inconsiderate actions of the airline, I had to manage to keep the rest of myself as collected as possible, for on the home front, life was as busy as ever. The usual motherly obligations of caring for four children served as a reprieve from the more highly charged days spent addressing airline concerns.

While the kids' diverse daily activities had me constantly on the move, there were times when I was able to sit back and watch with pride as they demonstrated the knowledge they acquired from their various commitments, such as when Nikki and Jonathon made their First Communion. Jonathon looked handsome in his dress clothes and tie, while Nikki looked like a little bride in her white lace dress. Sad feelings accompanied us during this memorable event, as Patty was not there to witness her son growing up, and Patrick was not by his brother's side to help celebrate his accomplishment. Throughout the day I had to force myself to ignore the gaping holes left by their absences.

The time had also come for our family's annual piano recital, during which Jimmy, Andy, and Nikki each performed their individual solo piece. When the children were younger, it was common for me to also play a duet with each of them. However, as the children got older, instead of my featuring three separate duets, we began performing songs that were written for four individuals playing at two pianos. I was never quite sure how, but each year, in spite of all the fooling around that went on during our practice sessions, we would still manage to pull everything together and perfectly execute the pieces.

This year, our usual foursome had a new addition, for Jonathon had jumped at the chance to take piano lessons with my children, and was ready for his first recital. Jonathon was to play his own solo piece, and rather than me engaging in a duet with him, he was to participate in the performance with my children and me at the two pianos. It was nice to see how easily Jonathon incorporated himself into our family rituals.

Outside of the momentous occasions, most of my days were spent trying to balance my life with the children's hectic schedules. On one such afternoon, I returned home and checked my phone messages. I found myself listening to an enthusiastic message from my friend, Amy, as she chronicled something that had happened to her and her husband earlier that day; they had looked through their large sliding-glass door, where they saw a wolf on the lawn just beyond their backyard, which was an extremely uncommon sight living in a residential neighborhood. At first they both thought that they were just seeing things, but after a moment they confirmed that they were beholding the strongest, healthiest wolf either one of them had ever cast their eyes upon. As Amy described it, the wolf just sat there, as though deliberately posed, with a very comfortable and contemplative sense about it, gazing directly at their house. And then, as mysteriously as it had appeared, the majestic creature suddenly got up and trotted off.

Patty knew I loved wolves, and the clay wolf that she bought for me (and had asked Amy to paint) was meant as an expression of her love, which was why I was so devastated when I realized it had been shattered. Therefore, I couldn't help wondering whether this sighting was some kind of sign, reminding me that material items really don't matter—that there is much more to life. The clay wolf, or any other object for that matter, cannot assure longevity, good health, or happiness, nor can it promise life-long sisterhood and friendship. And, most importantly, no physical possession will ever guarantee stability or prevent change. I also considered the possibility of this occurrence symbolizing the idea that no matter how shattered our lives may seem here on Earth, beyond the confines of our physical experience is a world consisting only of wholeness and perfection. While it was feasible that the wolf's appearance had only been a coincidence, I chose to instead dwell on the idea of the universe being ordered by some balancing force, which deliberately placed this wolf in the realm of my existence so as to remind me that even though Patty's gift had been taken away, her lasting presence in my life had not.

Thinking about these inexplicable concepts made me recall another bewildering scenario that Amy had relayed to me, this one having occurred on the exact day of the crash. Amy had wanted to take her two young sons, two-and-a-half-year-old Ben and eighteen-month-old Nathan, to the hardware store in the middle of the afternoon, because they both loved helium balloons. Amy dressed her boys in Jonathon's and Patrick's outgrown raingear that Patty had given her, and away they went in the terrible storm.

In the past, whenever Nathan and Ben had been given balloons, they held onto them as though their lives depended on it, and if for some reason their balloons had escaped, their ensuing cries were deafening. But that Halloween day had been different. In the unusually severe weather, Ben had peered up into the icy rain pounding on his little face, purposely released his balloon, and then reached over and grabbed his little brother's balloon so that he could let it go as well. Nathan was not pleased, but Ben, who was the more quiet and reserved child, then spoke in what had seemed to be volumes for him, explaining, "It's a gift to the angels." As later discovered, Ben's "gift to the angels" roughly corresponded with the time of the crash of Flight 4184, which was documented at 3:57:56.7 p.m.

Sometimes, such unexplainable and unlikely phenomena offered the only form of comfort in a situation that was in and of itself impossible to articulate and seemed inconceivable to have occurred; by maintaining my belief that everything is guided by some higher purpose, even if it is unknowable during our lifetime, I was able to find order in chaos, detect glimmers of hope through all the devastation, and keep Patty and Patrick alive inside of myself. It was moments such as these that took me away from the trials of daily life, and back to the comforting yet painful thoughts of my sister.

❧ 17 ❧

The more I grasped for some sense of inner peace, the more my life became inundated with the many issues spawning from the loss of my sister and nephew, and this pandemonium seemed to increase with each passing day. As much as I tried to ignore my memories of the hearing, I could not erase the sense of shared experience I had felt from listening to the stories of the other families.

The comfort I had always found in my conception of home had been compromised by the hounding mental images manifesting from the inescapable reality of what I had learned at the NTSB's hearing. Before long, it became clear to me that my life could no longer be about my family and myself alone, for the alarming circumstances that had intruded into my life eventually compelled me to reach out beyond these once-safe haven walls to the outside world. I simply refused to sit by quietly and watch as we continued to be treated as if we didn't count. Having left the hearing equipped with phone numbers and addresses of new acquaintances, I placed a call to Jenny, as we had decided to stay in touch.

The first thing we decided to do was compile the most complete list we could of all the family members for the purpose of networking. A few families did not share our desire to network, so of course we honored their privacy.

Our plan was to distribute newsletters to keep the families apprised of all new information that came our way. After having experienced firsthand the anguish arising from dishonesty and the withholding of information, we attempted to provide what the airline had chosen not to make available. It was truth we sought; it was honesty, sensitivity, and respect that we deserved, along with the ability to make our own decisions for our families and their belongings. We felt that this consideration was paramount, for in its absence the healing process was unnecessarily prolonged and our intense pain and anger did not have the opportunity to subside over time.

With everyone's permission, the newsletter also included a list of names, addresses, and phone numbers of the families signed up to receive it. The web of contacts quickly spread and strengthened, providing many with much-needed emotional support, as well as the means to connect with those who could truly empathize with their pain, while simultaneously offering encouragement to move forward. Amongst each other, we could count on total acceptance, which was something difficult to find from outsiders. Also, with the families working in collaboration, we stood a greater chance of having our concerns heard and understood by the many forces we were up against.

Around the same time that Jenny and I began forming ideas for the family newsletter, I received a phone call from the attorney handling Jonathon's case against the airline, inquiring as to whether he could pass my name on to another client of his named Doug, who had lost a daughter on the same flight. Shortly thereafter, Doug sent me a letter that expressed interest in addressing airline safety issues, generating national attention to these problems, and beginning lobbying activity that would bring about reform. He closed his letter with the resolute statement that he had dedicated himself to this cause so that his daughter would not have died in vain.

Doug and I began a frequent chain of correspondence, covering family concerns and proposed solutions. Whereas his primary focus seemed more technical in nature, I concentrated on the airline's treatment of the families, and offered unwavering encouragement for all of the families to join together in the healing process. Before long, our attention was directed not only to the issues surrounding Flight 4184, but to those from previous crashes as well.

Working with Doug and Jenny, I was able to incorporate into my agenda both the preventative measures and emotional considerations that I perceived as lacking in the airline industry. Finally, I felt like I was regaining a measure of control over my life, which was something I had been straining to attain throughout the months succeeding the crash.

After a couple of weeks of preparation, Jenny and I sent out our first newsletter, which we titled *Families of 4184, Roselawn*. In it, we voiced our intent to keep the families informed of all new developments in connection with the airline. Generally, we hoped for this publication to function as a forum in which the families could discuss the many issues pertaining to the tragedy, as well as a vehicle to share books and other material that would aide in the healing process.

In addition, we provided a description of an unclaimed personal item that Tom and I had found at the crash site, and gave details on a man's watch that the airline had returned to the wrong family, which was in seemingly perfect condition and still running on Central Time. We printed a list of unidentified jewelry that the airline continued to retain, a list that we had obtained only through legal intervention. We also disclosed the fact that the airline was requiring proof of purchase in order to view any pictures of the jewelry.

For those families that hadn't attended the hearing, we offered information about a condensed version of a book available through the NTSB, which detailed their investigation of the crash. News articles covering the events from the week of the hearing were replicated to supplement any gaps in families' understandings of the proceedings, and Doug's more technical concerns were voiced as well. This first newsletter also provided details of a meeting we were setting up in my hometown for the families. Seeing as how we were continuously encountering problematic situations with the airline, many of us felt it was a good idea to maintain a uniform stance amongst the families; thus, we decided to form a group, Families of 4184, and initially proposed that our meetings would take place monthly. In an attempt to encourage families to search for hope amid the upheaval of this tragedy, we concluded the newsletter with a poem about death, reminding us that our loved ones are not far, and to always speak their names as freely as when they were alive.

As April came to a close, the day designated for the first official gathering of Families of 4184 was rapidly approaching. Doug, myself, Tom, and Jenny worked on an agenda for the meeting. On the day of the gathering, approximately thirty family members, friends, and a representative of an Illinois Congressman joined us at a local hotel that graciously agreed to donate their meeting room and equipment in support of our cause, and to provide discounted room rates.

As the families gathered for the meeting, we exchanged greetings and stories, of which there was one in particular that held everyone's attention. The night before our meeting, a storm had passed over the Dallas-Fort Worth airport, which is the main hub of American Airlines. Reportedly, three to six inch diameter hail fell during the storm, damaging the planes of several different airline carriers. Fifteen airplanes belonging to Delta Air Lines were quickly repaired and returned to service. The remainder of the damaged aircraft belonged to American Airlines and American Eagle, constituting nearly nine percent of their fleet. The ensuing damage was so severe that American Airlines was forced to cancel 219 flights the next day. We acknowledged the irony of this occurrence coinciding with our first meeting, for the airline's negligence in handling post-crash issues, most notably their apparent preoccupation with sustaining the company's profitability instead of addressing the loss of human life, had instigated the intersection of the lives of everyone in the room; fittingly, as we all gathered in unification and newfound friendship, the airline was facing a substantial economic setback resulting from nature's fury. The families discussed the possibility of there being a system of checks and balances beyond the limits of human control that could override even the power of a multibillion dollar corporation.

Our meeting started mid-morning with my opening statements, which were followed by family introductions and a prayer. The issues covered were divided between long-term goals and the more immediate concerns of the families. Items on the future agenda were related to concerns about airline safety, along with the need to make legislative changes regarding the airlines' post-crash responsibilities. Additionally, we briefly conversed about the formation of a non-profit organization dedicated to finding solutions to problems that arise in the aftermath of airline tragedies.

Several points of immediate significance were then presented for the families to discuss. Following the on-site investigation, all handwritten logs documenting uncovered personal effects and remains, as well as the photographs of these findings, were given to the coroner, despite the fact that he was not responsible for the recovery or return of the belongings; therefore, he was the person families contacted to see these pictures. Even though the president of PWI had informed the coroner that personal effects were being destroyed, because the coroner was not in charge of their recovery, he would not have known which of the photographed items had been disposed of at the behest of the airline.

During my meeting with the coroner I had declined to view the pictures, not only because we had no way of determining the many items that had already been destroyed, but also because the thousands of photos of personal effects and remains were commingled, and I refused to put myself through so much trauma only to not obtain any additional items. The coroner's photographic record had been viewed by several families at the hearing, and those who had decided to go through this disturbing ordeal revealed that they had still only been given back at most two or three of their loved ones' belongings.

Families shared stories of having received only a credit card, or a picture torn out of a passport. One woman, unsuccessfully trying to fight back her tears, spoke about the book her son had been writing. He only had one hand-written copy of the manuscript, and in order to finish it he brought it with him on the trip. After the crash, an entire book's worth of pages were lost or destroyed. At this point in her story, the woman questioned whether the entire manuscript had really been irreparably damaged upon impact, or whether the airline had not determined that any recovered pages were meaningful enough to save. I was able to recognize that if the pages had not been obliterated from the immediate force of the crash, then they would have been scattered over an expansive area of land; however, I still found it hard to believe that not even one could have been returned. Weeping uncontrollably, the woman explained her longing for this reminder of her son's kind and loving spirit that he so easily conveyed through his writing. This was to be her son's first book, and she was eagerly anticipating the day when she would finally have the opportunity to read it, which was no longer a possibility.

In stark contrast, several Bibles were found in perfect condition amid the scene of one of the most destructive crashes ever witnessed by the NTSB. As I was told by several individuals that I met at the preliminary hearing who had worked at the site, all the Bibles were found opened on particular pages and passages that directly pertained to the situation at hand. Picking them up, the workers took turns reading different passages aloud in order to relay strength and courage to their coworkers amidst the intolerably grim conditions. Such stories relayed from workers held special relevance during our meeting, for they allowed us to have faith in the decency of human nature, which was so strikingly absent from all our discussions concerning the actions of the airline.

These accounts of findings in the field also directed our attention to the fact that the planting season was rapidly approaching, and while the airline had promised some families that the crash site would be set aside as hallowed ground, through discussions with the farmer, other families had learned that the airline was not going to purchase this land; not only was this a decision that directly contradicted the airline's purported stance on this issue, but they had also failed to update us of this new development. Thus, even though the families had been urgently seeking to keep the crash site from being farmed, at this point it had become clear that this was no longer a possibility.

I shared details that I had gathered during a conversation with the farmer, during which he informed me that he was opposed to any memorials being placed at the point of impact, although he and his landlady (the woman who owned the land) were receptive to the idea of situating a memorial along the country road that ran about 400 yards east of the crash site. I had also learned that a significant amount of human remains, personal effects, and plane wreckage had been uncovered during the clean-up efforts of the second environmental company hired by the airline (which had replaced PWI). During our discussion, the farmer mentioned that when it was time for him to till the land, one last search for any lingering personal effects and remains was to be conducted by the second environmental company, and he offered to give the families one or two days of notice so that we could be present at the site during the tilling.

While we were disappointed that we had not been able to protect the land as hallowed ground, we were appreciative of the farmer showing respect for our concerns. We all expressed a strong desire to be present at the tilling of the field, as we wanted to be able to collect any remains or objects that surfaced during this process, which would afford us peace of mind from knowing that we had not neglected our loved ones or their personal possessions.

After the farmer disclosed that substantial quantities of effects and remains had surfaced during the second clean-up effort, which had taken place at the state's direction right after the NTSB hearing, we went on to seek answers concerning the location, condition, and quantity of these findings. Our attempts proved futile, as we once again obtained no response from the airline, nor did we make any headway with the environmental company. Even though the order was in place prohibiting the airline from destroying any additional personal effects, we still had not been notified of what had been uncovered, nor had we received any additional items. This, along with the airline's requirement of the second environmental company to sign a confidentiality agreement, left us with growing suspicions regarding the airline's commitment to upholding the legal order protecting the unearthed items. I was particularly vexed by the fact that the airline sought a confidentiality agreement, as it insinuated that they intended to persist in veiling its actions in secrecy.

We were all so thoroughly engrossed in conversation that before we knew it, the day ended long before any of us were willing to part. It was a day filled with productivity as well as emotion, as this was the day we began to set change into motion so that others would not have to endure the same pain we had come to know. It was also the day we decided to help ourselves, as Families of 4184, as well as the future families and victims of airline tragedies. We were ready to begin the journey of making long-overdue changes to a system that seemed devoted to supporting only big business without holding corporations accountable for their own actions.

❧ 18 ❧

The discussions held during the first family meeting had been both con-
structive and rewarding, allowing us to collaborate and clearly formulate
our main grievances and requests directed at the airline. Everyone present had expressed strong support and gratitude for this opportunity to
connect with others while engaging in a forum where concerns could be
addressed. Collectively, we pinpointed the most pressing issues to be
the airline's mishandling of the recovered personal effects, the need for
the land at the crash site to be declared as hallowed ground, the desire
for a monument to be erected in the field to commemorate the tragedy,
and the airline's omissions regarding all aspects of the mass burial, including the location and marking of the gravesite. During the time immediately following our get-together, we made a concerted communal
effort to address these concerns, hoping that we could achieve more as a
group than we had been able to do individually.

The representative of the Illinois Congressman who had attended
our meeting returned home and composed a letter to the group convey-
ing a clear understanding of the problems we had raised, as well as her
willingness to provide us with assistance. A family member from another
crash who had heard about our gathering sent a letter congratulating us
on the great job we had done in organizing the group. It was reassuring
for us to have the support of one another, as well as others who had also
dealt with the repercussions of previous airline disasters.

Following our first family get-together, the airline sent out details
regarding the dedication they were planning to hold for the unidentified
remains, indicating that it would occur in mid-August. When the airline

had sent us a letter back in January disclosing the existence of the mass burial, they had also provided preliminary information about this dedication, during which a monument was to be erected at the mass gravesite. The families had termed this a "sterile" monument, because at that time the airline was refusing to inscribe it with the victims' names, ages, family relations, or the fact that they had died in an airplane crash. They also expressed no intention of engraving the name of the airline, the flight number, or the date the crash had occurred. Once again, this issue generated immense frustration amongst the families, because the airline not only maintained strict censorship over the plans surrounding the upcoming dedication by refusing any family input, but also because they had chosen a cemetery approximately twenty-five miles from the crash site without consulting the families as to where we wanted to bury our loved ones.

Our sense of aggravation was exacerbated by the fact that we had been placing phone calls for months to the cemetery where the mass interment had taken place, attempting to determine details withheld by the airline about the burial, any markings at the gravesite, the location of the burial plots, and any other clues that would assist us in determining where our family members had been laid to rest. We were unable to obtain any knowledge from the cemetery staff, and we eventually discovered that they had been instructed not to speak with us and therefore denied answering our inquiries due to fear of work-related ramifications. "Blackout" was the term issued by the cemetery staff in reference to the mass burial, so as to reinforce their orders not to release any specifics about the plots of land purchased by the airline.

Between the secrecy surrounding all aspects of the mass burial, and the control the airline was maintaining over the inscribing of the "sterile" monument, the families were left perplexed as to why the airline was so adamant about withholding information that was vitally important to us, for their concealment seemed to only further damage their position with the families. Since we saw no obvious benefit for the airline to maintain this level of confidentiality, we wondered if they were simply determined to avoid any actions that could possibly cause them public embarrassment, or if there was more behind the reason for this secrecy than we realized.

Then, several weeks into May, one of the family members notified me of having received a letter from the airline's insurance company stating that individual names would be put on the memorial stone at the gravesite, but only if the families of the victims gave written consent. This felt like a triumph, for it was the persistence of the families that had eventually convinced the airline to relinquish their original position. In addition to putting the names of the deceased on the memorial stone, the airline also agreed to inscribe a four-foot-high column housing a bronze sundial that would stand in front of the granite wall of engraved names. The inscription would read "In Memoriam—American Eagle Flight 4184—October 31, 1994."

In the letter, the insurance company stated that the airline claimed to have sent a message two months prior (back in March) asking if this family member wanted his wife's name on the memorial. Not only had he never obtained this earlier correspondence supposedly sent by the airline, but no one else had either. He was further informed that time was of the essence if he wanted the inscription put on the memorial. He sent out a certified response to the airline, as well as sending me a copy of the communication.

The airline's assertion of having mailed the letter two months earlier seemed convenient, especially in light of the fact that we had somehow all acquired the January letter indicating that a service was to take place, and yet none of us had received this notification concerning the inscriptions on the memorial stone. To me, the airline's words meant nothing at this point, for throughout this whole ordeal their promises had not remained consistent with their actions, and in this instance their actions appeared to be focused on maintaining a favorable reputation in the public sphere, while disregarding any consideration for the victims and their families in the more private and containable sector of their business trajectory.

An earlier letter from the airline's insurance company, dated December 1994, about five weeks after the crash, came to mind, as it highlighted this discrepancy between the airline's smooth, calculated words versus their actions. They had expressed their "sincere condolences" for our loss, offered to "attempt to place" themselves at our "disposal with respect to any inquiries" we may have had, and stated their plans to do everything possible "to ease the burden of this difficult time." They had also mentioned their intention to see that we "receive fair compensation" for our loss, and that they hoped we would "ultimately retain as much of the compensation as the applicable law provides for without an unnecessary diversion of large amounts to litigation expenses." The company then continued on for several paragraphs listing the downfalls of signing on with an attorney:

> You may find yourself under pressure to sign a contingent fee retainer with an attorney whereby his fee is a percentage of the final award. The rationale for such a percentage fee is that the lawyer risks getting no fee if there is no recovery. There is no such risk in this case. There is also nothing to be gained by a precipitous lawsuit. We do suggest that it would be in your best interest to obtain the help of your attorney to evaluate the offer which will be made to you based on a fee for the work involved rather than on a percentage of the amount which you ultimately receive.
>
> Immediate legal action is not essential to avoid permitting applicable time periods (i.e., statutes of limitations, etc.) to expire. Should discussions not result in an amicable resolution of your claim, we [will] provide a reasonable extension of any applicable time limitation based upon the facts and circumstances of your case. You will then have ample time to select counsel of your choice, the basis upon which he is paid or whether you wish to institute a lawsuit. You do not have to be rushed into limiting your alternatives or committing yourselves needlessly to an inordinate legal expense.

The letter closed with the assertion that we should not have to "wait for reimbursement" while "this investigation proceeds."

Even back in December, I had regarded receiving this correspondence as strange, because I had already found legal representation on behalf of Jonathon, and therefore the airline was lawfully bound to communicate with me through my attorney. Also, I found it even more suspicious that the airline was so adamant about settling before the results of the investigative process were known, for it seemed as though they were attempting to avoid any further legal hassles if blame was placed in their direction.

"In your best interest" was a phrase the airline often used, and appeared to be quite fond of exploiting when trying to persuade the families to follow a particular course of action or when justifying their unsavory actions. According to them, it was in our best interest not to take legal action against the airline, and it was in our best interest not to be informed of the mass burial of unidentified remains that had taken place. The airline's destruction of the families' personal belongings also seemed to fall into this self-serving method of decision making. No choices made by the airline in any way appeared to be in our best interest; rather, their seemingly premeditated maneuverings worked only to their advantage, while we were left feeling deceived and ineffectual.

After hearing of the letter sent to the family member regarding the monument at the gravesite, I immediately sent out a message to all families relaying this opportunity to have victims' names inscribed on the memorial stone. In doing so, an emphasis was placed on the urgency with which they needed to contact the airline, as well as the significance of registering the letter in some fashion so that the airline had no way of denying having received our requests.

In addition to addressing the issues of Flight 4184, it also seemed necessary to begin examining the common threads between all past airline disasters. We were concerned with what appeared to be the airlines' inhumane treatment of the families, and their haste in returning to day-to-day business affairs. Several of us had been working on an agenda for a meeting in Pittsburgh scheduled to take place early in June, which would discuss the joint concerns of seven airplane crashes, and the representatives would include family members of the victims along with survivors.

The purpose of the Pittsburgh meeting was to construct a workable structure for a national group comprised of survivors and victims' families of airplane crashes that would lobby for long-term issues of air safety. Another element of this meeting would include a more short-term goal dedicated to formulating the role of a family advocate, and we deliberated on ways to present the family advocate role for congressional consideration. The idea of a family advocate concerned implementing a group that would serve as a third-party correspondent between the airline and the families of victims of air disasters, in order to ensure family and survivor rights as well as provide support to all those affected by the tragedy.

Additionally, a selection of officers was scheduled to take place at the Pittsburgh meeting for this new national group, which would come to be called the National Air Disaster Alliance, and this non-profit organization would work for victims of all air catastrophes. The issues covered at the Pittsburgh meeting were then to be discussed at an upcoming conference in Washington, D.C., scheduled for June 20th, held by the NTSB in conjunction with the Department of Transportation (DOT) to discuss the concerns of families and survivors, as well as proposed recommendations for change.

❧ ❧ ❧

The second edition of our newsletter, *Families of 4184, Roselawn,* was mailed in May 1995. It recapped our first meeting and asked families to write letters addressing the problems they encountered with the airline so that an accurate list of grievances could be presented at the conference in Washington, D.C. We also requested that each family send a duplicate of their letter to their congressman, in order to assure state awareness of our objectives.

The newsletter went on to share the appointment of board positions for Families of 4184; these board positions would allow us to function as an efficient and organized entity, and the people holding these various posts would be responsible for getting the needs of the families heard. I was working on certifying the status of Families of 4184 as a non-profit organization; this group was different than that of the national organization, as our concerns would remain specific to those of Flight 4184. Tom and I were appointed co-chairpersons, while the positions of secretary, treasurer, federal legislation relations, and Indiana state government coordinator were also filled. One of the family members volunteered to write the mission statement for our group. In addition, we began seeking out an attorney that would volunteer some time to our cause.

We also made an announcement indicating the time and location of the next family meeting, as I had already made arrangements with the same hotel used during our last gathering. The meeting was to be held on a Sunday in early July, and we had a picnic planned on the day prior for family and friends, so that we could continue to encourage the bonds that had formed between the families. The picnic was to be held at our house, which backed up into a park, and was also only minutes from the hotel.

The aims established during the first meeting would be utilized as the working agenda, which was briefly delineated in the newsletter. Many of the topics needing to be discussed on a national level during the Pittsburgh meeting were also pertinent to Families of 4184. The outline for our longer-term goals involved the implementation of federal legislation that would remove the airline's control over matters relating to the families, the disposal of personal effects and unidentified remains, and the selection of a mass burial site; we hoped for these responsibilities to be transferred to the third-party advocacy group that we were trying to institute at a national level.

In our publication, we referenced two lists that we had obtained from an official who worked at the crash site; we did not print them, but offered that anyone interested would be able to see them at the next meeting. One was a list of the flight's seat assignments, and the other was a passenger fatality list. From the list of seat assignments, I learned that Patty and Patrick were assigned to seats 2C and 2D. The passenger/fatality list indicated everyone's full name, age, and hometown. The passengers comprising this computerized list were representative of twelve religions, eight nationalities, and four different languages spoken, which emphasized the large expanse of people affected by this tragedy.

Once again, in order to inspire families to move forward in the healing process, an inspirational poem from an unknown author about moving on with life after the death of a loved one concluded the newsletter.

Throughout the time following our first meeting, the airline had assisted in fueling our newfound pledge to expose their wrongdoings, to make necessary changes where needed, and to help others in whatever way possible. Never once did I waiver from my conviction that the airline's statements had become devoid of any truth, as I knew that we were not simply misunderstanding or misinterpreting actions that so fully negated all of their promises. Speaking with other families of victims of airline tragedies only reinforced my perception of the airline's mismanagement of the situation, as I began to realize that these problems facing the Families of 4184 were industry-wide, and there was no established system in place to ensure the proper treatment of victims of air disasters.

The corporate mentality with which the airline chose to proceed throughout the aftermath of this tragedy simply did not translate into appropriate handling of the emotionally-charged condition that the families had been abruptly thrust into, forcing us to endure unnecessary pain, suffering, and trauma. I felt like we had unwillingly been dragged into a game with unimaginably high stakes, and the airline had rigged it to ensure our perpetual defeat. I just could not accept the airline's early settlement offers on behalf of Jonathon, for they appeared to be a desperate attempt at a quick, quiet, and tidy clean-up. I felt that the airline needed to endure a greater expense than financial costs, for a settlement of any amount of money would only allow these enormous injustices to continue. In my mind, the time had come to challenge the corporate values that seemed to govern this country's ideology, overriding such concerns as human cost and sentiment, and allowing everything to function mechanically. While I had entered this situation by circumstance and not of my own volition, I decided that as long as I was responsible for overseeing Jonathon's settlement, I would use this position to help instate changes in the system, so as to assure a more humanitarian approach.

❧ 19 ❧

As June 1995 approached, I found myself in an extremely hectic state. I was struggling to prepare for the Pittsburgh meeting, our family vacation, the meeting in Washington, D.C., the next gathering of Families of 4184, and saying goodbye to Jonathon when Frank took custody.

I was unable to attend the Pittsburgh meeting due to family commitments, but felt well represented, having worked quite extensively with Doug and Jenny on preparing an agenda to voice the concerns of Families of 4184. Having arrived in Pittsburgh, Doug and Jenny kept me fully updated of all proceedings. The gathering was to act as a prelude to the upcoming conference in Washington, D.C., conducted through the NTSB and DOT.

As planned, the meeting concentrated on injustices common to each of the seven crashes represented, which were identified and critiqued so that a unified national front could be presented to the NTSB and DOT. The details of the family-advocate role were elaborated, designating that all communication between the surviving family members, the airline, the FAA, and the NTSB be channeled through this third-party family advocate representative following an air disaster. The hope was that the interjection of this third-party advocate would prevent any self-serving conflict of interest by the airline.

Two days after the Pittsburgh meeting ended, our family was set to fly to Oregon for vacation, which involved my first flight since the crash. I questioned whether I would be safe on this trip, as well as whether it was a good idea for everyone to fly together. As the day of our scheduled departure approached, I began to feel hesitant about how flying would affect me, and speculated as to how I would react upon boarding the aircraft, going so far as to even consider the possibility of my refusing to get on the plane at the last minute. To help counter any onslaught of latent emotions, I made sure to pay close attention to my feelings as I prepared for the trip. I seemed to feel fine as I packed the suitcases, and I retained a sense of control amidst all the anticipation on the way to the airport. I even managed to hold it together while checking our luggage and waiting to board the plane.

A sense of relief began to settle over me, as I realized I had made it past what I considered to be all the major hurdles. I walked down the ramp to the airplane, feeling confident and composed. But at the very moment my foot touched down inside the aircraft, it was as if an automatic faucet had been activated. I was not crying out of fear, but rather out of an encompassing sense of grief that had washed over me in an instant. It took some time before I managed to regain my composure.

By the time we arrived in Oregon, I had overcome the anguish I experienced on the flight, and reveled in the time I was able to spend wandering along the magnificent coastline, surrounded by the love of my children. This family vacation was more meaningful than usual, as it would be the last time Jonathon would be a part of our family unit. We spent most days on the beach riding sand bikes, hiking, climbing, exploring caves, and building campfires.

As much as I enjoyed my vacation, I was disappointed that the timing coincided with that of the meeting in Washington, D.C., for I had also missed the conference in Pittsburgh. Once again, Jenny and Doug were able to attend the meeting, along with individuals from three other airline crashes. Representatives from the NTSB and DOT, along with several other government officials, met with the families and listened to misgivings and proposed recommendations. A list was generated to reflect the common concerns of the families, a summary of which included:

Notification process by the airlines:
- Airlines' 800 numbers to obtain information about downed aircrafts are always busy.
- Notification by the airlines takes too long, is sometimes incorrect, information is often withheld, or the representatives have few details to offer.
- Notification is done by representatives that lack the proper training and therefore make the situation more difficult.

Airlines mishandling of post-crash issues:
- Press receives information before family members, and is also permitted to view the wreckage first.
- Families and survivors would like a copy of the manifest list (the contact information the airline has for the victims) to be able to contact each other.
- Those affected cannot get the passenger lists, but attorneys are somehow able to obtain them.
- Airlines' Care Team members may have an inherent conflict of interest, insomuch as they act according to the direction of the airline rather than the families. They often ask probing questions about the victims' health and financial states prior to the crash. There is concern that this information affects the final settlement.
- Lack of coordination among various Care Team members causes confusion.
- Possible conflict of interest with the airlines being involved with all aspects relating to post-crash activities.
- The airlines control and make decisions about personal articles and decide what they will return without consulting families' needs.
- The airlines' timing in releasing personal articles is not appropriate.
- Removal of remains from crash site is not thorough.
- Once the investigation is over, the airlines claim no responsibility for personal articles or remains recovered.

- The airlines are not truthful about identification of remains and contents of caskets.
- Families are not involved in considerations of burial process.

Following the meeting, these notes were transcribed by the government officials in attendance. This list was to be consulted at yet another conference scheduled to be held by the NTSB and DOT in August, where these issues would be discussed amongst officials from ten major airlines.

❧ ❧ ❧

Upon my return from Oregon, I set about packing Jonathon's belongings, for he was to be picked up by his father in a few days, as per the ruling of the court. I was still fuming over what I perceived as my lack of legal representation, and was struggling to accept the outcome of the custody case, as it prevented me from upholding the promise I had made to Patty. I couldn't help but wonder whether Frank's involvement in his daughter's life would have been more extensive had there been money at stake. If he had truly wanted Jonathon and not just the money that he would acquire from the settlement, then why hadn't he taken Jonathon right after the crash? At the time of Patty's death, she had been in the process of changing the beneficiary on her life insurance plan from Frank over to her children. I had shown Frank proof of her intentions, and yet through legal channels he still went on to claim this money. If he really sought custody out of concern for his son, then why would he have taken money that Patty wanted set aside for Jonathon's future? I was torn up in angst over the whole situation, but all that I could do was hold onto the fact that I had always done my best for Jonathon.

Mom and I struggled to dwell only on the time we had been able to spend with Jonathon as we gathered up his belongings. To make the moving process easier, we placed his stuff in the front yard, where the kids were playing together. Before Frank's expected arrival, I called

Jonathon inside.

We sat on my bed together one last time, where over the past few months I had told Jonathon many stories of Patty's and my childhood, and where we had laughed and cried together, always in the safety of love and acceptance. Today, there would be no more stories. There was, however, something I needed to tell Jonathon before I said goodbye. As always, he sat and listened attentively with a wide-eyed expression. I reminded him of how much I loved him, and reiterated that I would always be there for him. Whatever he needed, whether it was big or small, all he had to do was ask. I urged him to always cling to what he knew to be true, regardless of the words of others. I knew that my advice may have exceeded what Jonathon was capable of comprehending at his age, but I was compelled to say it anyway. As I embraced Jonathon, I told him once more how much I loved him, and how much he would be missed.

Jonathon then resumed playing with my children as he waited for Frank, while I prepared dinner. Shortly thereafter, Frank came and left without any acknowledgement, and then Jonathon and all of his belongings were gone.

The pain I felt over Jonathon's departure and my unfulfilled promise to Patty naturally motivated me to do everything possible for the people who had become the newest members of my extended family— the Families of 4184.

Through joint efforts, Jenny and I sent out the third newsletter detailing the purpose and successful proceedings of the Washington, D.C., meeting. We also displayed our new logo, acknowledging and expressing gratitude to Amy, who had worked to design the perfect symbol to represent both our goals and our loved ones. This logo was designed in a circle with its perimeter consisting of sixty-eight red hearts, each one personifying a family member who perished on the flight. Above each heart sat a halo atop a pair of wings, denoting the idea of our loved ones being guided by a spiritual guardian in their journey after death. Inside the circle of hearts, the words "FAMILIES OF 4184 ROSELAWN OCTOBER 31, 1994 TRUTH HONOR JUSTICE" were written in a circular pattern just inside of the border defined by the hearts. The words Truth, Honor, and Justice were carefully thought out and discussed in great detail prior to having been chosen to epitomize our cause. A map of the world was placed within the circle of words with a red rose designating the location of the plane crash in Roselawn, Indiana; this image acknowledged the various countries represented by the victims' different backgrounds, and the circular shape was symbolic of eternal life.

In our newsletter, we also regretfully reported that the tilling of the crash site had occurred without the farmer fulfilling his promise to contact the families a few days prior to the plowing, and before we had the chance to inspect the field one last time before it resumed functioning as a usable plot of farmland. We were all disappointed, and because it did not seem as though the farmer had any personal stake invested in whether or not the families were present at the tilling, many of us suspected that the airline may have persuaded the farmer to disregard his commitment to contact us before farming the field. Subsequent conversations with the farmer revealed that more plane wreckage, personal effects, and human remains had surfaced during his tilling. As before, the airline never notified the families of these findings, nor of their disposition.

Unfortunately, we also had to reluctantly announce the cancellation of the next family meeting due to a torn ligament in my knee that required surgery. Upon receiving this news, many family members expressed their disappointment, as everyone had been looking forward to reuniting at the meeting. We saw one another as little blessings that had emerged from the depths of unimaginable tragedy, and together we were able not only to honor the lives of our loved ones, but also to gradually begin to come to terms with our losses, and once again enjoy some of life's happier moments.

❧ 20 ❧

The day of my surgery, I checked in for what was termed a fairly routine procedure for a torn ligament. I was prepped and then wheeled into a large room filled with many other gurneys and patients. The next thing I knew the surgery was complete, and in no time at all my dad was driving me home. With a tightly bandaged knee, I rested the remainder of the day with my leg elevated, glad to have put this ordeal behind me.

Within only a few days of my surgery, my knee felt like it was beginning to heal, but I noticed an excruciating pain developing in my leg below the knee. I wanted to undo the bandage, but I was urged to wait until my follow up appointment four days after the surgery, as exposing the area could cause it to become infected. The pain had become so intense that the night before my appointment I spent a good part of the evening aggressively massaging my leg in an attempt to get some relief.

When I went to my appointment, the intolerable leg pain I described led the doctor to send me to the hospital for some tests. Before the examination was complete, a gurney was ordered for immediate delivery. It was sent over expeditiously, and the hospital staff instructed me to get on carefully so as not to jar my body. I followed their orders, but was convinced that there had been some sort of mistake—this emergency treatment must be for someone else, as my dad was waiting just outside the room to take me home. At this point, it was firmly explained to me that the only place I was going was to a room upstairs, because my leg was full of blood clots from the knee down, which created a potentially life-threatening condition. The nurses and doctors were afraid to even touch my leg; they could hardly believe it when I told them how vigorously I had rubbed it the previous night. After some more worthless balking, I was wheeled up to a room that would be my new place of residence for the next seven days.

I was hooked up to an IV and instructed to stay in bed for the entire week, bringing my life to an abrupt halt. After the initial shock wore off, I began to let go and accept the situation. In fact, there were times I actually enjoyed laying in bed doing absolutely nothing, as the serenity and silence sounded like music to my ears, especially after the seemingly incessant racket that had been reverberating in my mind and life since the crash. I was relieved to be free of all responsibilities, even if just for a short while.

Toward the end of the week, I was finally allowed out of bed and even given permission to take a shower, and after considerable pleading, I was allowed to wear my street clothes, as long as I remained hooked up to my IV stand. That same day, Tom and I decided to go down to the hospital cafeteria, and on the way back we took a detour back to my room through a new wing of the hospital, where I noticed an unusually large revolving door that led to the outside. I was summoned by the thought of being free of the confining walls of the hospital, and so I stepped through the revolving door and into the open air. My husband followed with the door's next revolution.

As I stood there basking in the warmth of the sun, I was overcome by the joy to be found in all of life's little details, and I began to think that this was what stepping into Heaven might feel like. I felt the tranquility associated with the beautiful music of the chirping birds, which was intensified by the perfection of the deep blue sky. The soft, gentle breeze seemed to flow through me, beckoning me to follow and wander in search of all of nature's secrets. I felt humbled by the surrounding majestic forces, and suddenly was convinced that these simple yet rare moments contained the best that life had to offer. Sitting on the curb with my IV stand towering over me, it was as if all was right with the world.

Tom and I began walking through a residential neighborhood, greeting homeowners as we passed by. A loud ruckus accompanied us as the wheels of the IV stand rolled over the sidewalk; at times this sound was muffled by the freshly fallen mulberries that littered the way, and then there was the silence that occurred when the IV stand had to be carried over more rugged terrain.

That afternoon, I was reminded of life's wonder and beauty, something I had thought ceased to exist since having to endure life without Patty. For just one instant, the world had seemed to be comprised only of gentleness and love. I considered all the goodness life has to offer if we choose to make it part of our experience. The gift of that magical afternoon immediately directed my thoughts toward my sister, as though I had been given a glimpse of the perfection that would eternally surround her and Patrick.

✣ 21 ✣

Following my return from the hospital in the beginning of July, I realized the stark division that existed between the harmonious contentment I had experienced during the last day of my stay and my feelings over the prior eight months. The same natural elements that were responsible for producing the radiance of such a picturesque landscape had been encircling me all along, but amidst the devastating shock and trauma I had suffered since the crash, it seemed inconceivable to ever again relish in and reflect upon life's more impeccable moments. And yet somehow, over the past eight months, I had gradually learned to re-open myself to the wonders and possibilities presented with the dawn of each new day. I left the hospital with a newfound appreciation of all that was good in my world.

After my tranquil and therapeutic recovery, I easily resumed the engagements that had been occupying my time prior to the surgery. Primarily, I was involved with arrangements pertaining to the August dedication that the airline had promised to hold at the mass gravesite. While I did not forget the sense of peace that I had found during my stay at the hospital, several infuriating pieces of correspondence sent by the airline in the middle of July regarding this service made it nearly impossible to remain calm. Upon reading these communications, I was repeatedly forced to again consider the abundance of inconsistencies that had divided the airline's words from their actions, and all of the ways in which the families had been let down.

In these letters, the airline officials addressed not only matters relating to the dedication, but also responded to concerns that had been raised by the families, which were both general and specific to this up-coming event. They firmly expressed their desire that the families "fully understand...the many difficult decisions" that had gone into the "planning and development" of the memorial dedication, although they failed to detail what those decisions had involved. My anger flared the moment that I read this remark, as the airline's choices thus far had not seemed to entail any type of overwhelming regard for the expressed wishes of the families; rather, their reaction to the issues arising in the aftermath of the tragedy had for the most part only served to generate immense upheaval in our lives, and yet they still somehow conjured up the audacity to imply that we should almost feel apologetic for the difficulties involved in organizing this dedication.

Immediately after this comment, my belief that the airline's decisions were based upon their own agenda rather than any consideration for the families was substantiated, as they admitted that one of the reasons behind their correspondence stemmed from their perception that their company had been "misrepresented in recent news articles." Therefore, in order to counter such misrepresentations, they used compelling and apparently misleading words to insinuate that their intent was compassionate, maintaining that this service was being conducted with the "hope that it will provide some sense of closure for the families." I found it ironic that the airline was claiming to be in tune with our need to move forward in the healing process, as nearly every decision they had made up to that point had served only to obstruct any chance we had for "closure." Given the fact that the dedication wasn't being held until nine and a half months after the crash, the event presented us not with an opportunity for "closure," but only with a cause for more resentment.

The airline's concern with their public image also brought them to the conclusion that the families "deserved to have the facts." I simply could not fathom how airline officials could even try to alter our conception of them at this point, given how often they appeared to have gone out of their way to ensure that certain details stayed hidden from the families. I was no longer shocked over the fact that nineteen caskets of unidentified remains had been transported in the dark cover of night to a cemetery, that the airline failed to notify us of what came to be known as this "secret burial," or that the airline had ordered what cemetery staff termed a "blackout," prohibiting them from giving out any information to family members. In light of their previous actions, the airline's choice to withhold the fact that the farmer had refused to allow the crash site to be declared hallowed ground was not surprising, nor was the fact they had still persisted in upholding their promises to the families asserting the contrary. Even though I understood that this company was not to blame for the farmer's decision, they were responsible for the shattering effect that their veiling of this information had upon many families. Additionally, I had eventually come to terms with the knowledge that my sister and nephew did not lie peacefully in the caskets that the airline had sent to us; rather, I accepted that their remains had most likely been dispersed and lay buried in the mass plot, caskets in other parts of the world, a biohazard dumpsite, and the field at the crash site.

While I no longer felt shocked by the airline obscuring these truths, what I did continue to feel was anger, stemming from what appeared to be the airline's many deceptive maneuverings that kept the families uninformed and in a constant state of upheaval—all of which was exacerbated by their most recent claim supporting their commitment to provide us with the "facts." The only time I could recall the airline actually offering us the "facts" was on October 31, when they confirmed that Patty and Patrick were on their plane and had died as a result of the crash. I had become all too aware of the contrast between the thoughtful and concerned words the airline expressed, and what appeared to be their actions of concealment, along with what legal documents referred to as "gross negligence and a conscious disregard of the substantial, obvious, and justifiable risk that harm and damage would be caused by their conduct."

Thus, when I read the airline's response to the families' complaints, which argued, "While these families are entitled to their opinions, many of the criticisms have their origin in rumor or false information," I almost laughed, for we had directly experienced these injustices, and yet the airline's statement seemed to be indicating that they were mere figments of our imaginations.

Despite the airline's conviction that our concerns had "their origin in rumor or false information," the company negated this claim themselves when they addressed their own wrongdoings; in one of the letters, the airline officials referenced the "small nondenominational service was held at the request of the Indiana Association of Funeral Directors for the burial of unidentifiable remains," asserting that they "knew about the burial, but not the service," and then continued on to apologize for their decision not to notify the families about the burial. The airline's contention not to have known about this service seemed to be a way of bypassing any blame for not notifying the families of the existence of a mass grave, for even though they were not involved in the service, they had orchestrated the burial, and yet chosen to keep the families uninformed. In addition, they emphasized that the ceremony for the unidentified remains had been only one of many services held, for along with the three they had organized immediately after the crash, the families had also conducted "emotional private ceremonies," and they had felt "it would have been entirely too painful" to ask us to return for "yet another service." Mentioning these initial ceremonies in conjunction with their failure to disclose the mass burial was clearly self-justifying on their part, indicating that we should not be upset over our lack of inclusion in this later funerary decision. The only road to healing was that of the grieving process, and the airline thinking it appropriate to dictate the number of services we needed to attend only served to eliminate steps towards our recovery, thus extending the time it took to heal.

In their correspondences, the airline also directed attention to the arrangements they had made regarding the upcoming dedication, maintaining that they had "struggled with how many members each family could invite to the dedication," and that they had "set the number at eight because of space limitations at the cemetery." While this was understandable, they also disclosed that they "intend[ed] to invite representatives of the various organizations who assisted in the recovery efforts and selected members of the AMR CARE team;" I was irritated that the airline was offering the families only a fixed number of seats so as to save room for their Care Team members. With the amount of trauma instilled by the Care Team, their presence alone would only stir up resentment and anger in many cases.

Again disputing concerns that had been expressed by family members, airline officials contended, "perhaps most distressing is the suggestion that the airline is somehow organizing the memorial as a media event." They went on to attempt to persuade us of the contrary, declaring that the memorial was being erected "out of a deep sense of loss and a genuine desire on our part to assist with the healing process," and defensively stating, "Any other suggestion is not only wrong, but is offensive to all of us who have grieved—and still grieve—along with you." For the airline to claim offense at the families' questioning their motives seemed like circular logic, because they found the ways in which we had been offended as "offensive," and yet, had their intentions truly been sincere in the first place, much of this hurt could have been avoided. The airline then admitted that media coverage was "inevitable, given all the circumstances surrounding the accident," but offered reassurances that they would prevent the press from having direct access to the cemetery. I wondered what "circumstances" they were referring to, since they claimed that the families' "criticisms had their origin in rumor and false information." Their sudden and seemingly overwhelming interest in keeping the families from the media appeared to be related to their desire to prevent us from exposing any of these "circumstances" that may have endangered the company's reputation.

After having expressed the many ways in which the families' comments had upset them, the airline claimed, "we hope you will join us and draw comfort from the memorial and those who will be there to share it with you. We will come together in dignity to share our loss and give each other strength for the future, and we will do this in a way that respects the feelings and differing backgrounds of everyone present." Again, in my mind, these words were devoid of meaning, for even though I knew that this dedication would take place, I would never be able to see it as sincere. We could not "come together in dignity" with the company that had treated us and our loved ones with none, and there was no way that they could conduct a ceremony that "respect[ed] the feelings and differing backgrounds of everyone present," because thus far their actions had shown virtually no respect for our feelings or wishes.

$\mathcal{S}^{\#}$ 22 $\mathcal{S}^{\#}$

Throughout the month preceding the dedication, I remained in daily contact with the other families, both to ensure everyone was kept updated on all developments, and to maintain our new friendships. Not only were these conversations productive in regards to the airline issues, but they were also valuable on a personal level.

Even though we were still encountering major hurdles in dealing with issues specific to our crash, all the work done by Families of 4184, along with the families and survivors of other air disasters, was finally beginning to pay off at the national level of our agenda. The events that had transpired at the Pittsburgh meeting led to the official formation of the National Air Disaster Alliance, which was designed to challenge the airlines' misguided post-crash operations with the aim of enacting changes that benefited the families. Doug was appointed president of this newly formed entity, which on August 1, 1995, was incorporated as a nonprofit organization. Its mission statement pledged efforts to ensure the flying public and their families of the highest standards in aviation safety, and to implement post-crash emergency planning and comprehensive family/survivor advocacy support for all victims of air disasters.

The second Washington meeting conducted through the NTSB and DOT had been scheduled for August and was to involve senior executives from ten major airline carriers; the conference was intended to work toward solutions to the issues raised by the families of airline crash victims. Doug and three family members from other crashes were asked to attend the meeting to represent the National Air Disaster Alliance, and voice the concerns of passengers and families of airline disasters, talk about their experiences, and propose recommendations for change.

In addition to keeping the families posted on these progressions occurring on the legislative front, Jenny and I had decided that we would use the upcoming memorial dedication as an opportunity for a private gathering of the families. We chose to extend the invitation to the volunteers and officials who had worked at the crash site, since the families were so appreciative of their steadfast and painstaking efforts in the most unimaginable work conditions. We contacted all the workers we knew and asked for their help in spreading the word. I then called the hotel in Merrillville, Indiana, where a large number of families would be staying for the dedication ceremony. The gracious hotel manager agreed to give us a large banquet room free of charge, along with enough snacks and refreshments to last throughout the duration of the evening. I had buttons made up with our new logo, which would be handed out at the get-together with cards to explain its meaning. The event was scheduled to take place the night before the memorial dedication.

The week before the ceremony, Tom and I decided that we wanted to go to Indiana with the children on Wednesday, a couple of days before anything was planned to begin, because I wanted to re-visit the crash site to pay my respects to my sister and nephew, as I was drawn to this place where so much lay unresolved. During my last visit, I saw that a handful of crosses and flowers had been arranged off the county road located just east of the field, and I sought to plant crosses there for Patty and Patrick as well. While mechanically going through the motions to fashion a larger cross for Patty and a slightly smaller one for Patrick, I kept thinking of how surreal this process seemed, as I never imagined having to make crosses for my sister and nephew. I then gathered pictures of them to decorate the crosses, as I felt erecting two plain white crosses would have been an extreme misrepresentation of their vivacious spirits in life. It was important to me that these pictures portrayed Patrick's youthful exuberance, as well as Patty's zest for living and love of family. I laminated the several pictures chosen to represent them and mounted them on each cross running perpendicular to their names. I also wrote a brief memorial paying tribute to my sister's life that was to accompany her cross:

My sister, Patty, and I were both born on January 12, just one year apart, giving us the label of Irish Twins, although we were often told that we just as well could have been twins. We easily communicated without many words, as we knew one another as well as we knew ourselves. We also never backed away from trying to accomplish the impossible, and everyone knew that when Patty and I got together that the sky was the limit. Nothing was too big for the two of us. Patty was not only my sister; she was also my very best friend.

Patty's professional achievements were no small feat. She was a licensed investigator and president of a national investigative agency, and also volunteered her time coaching competitive and beginning swimming.

Patty's work accomplishments in life, great as they were, seemed almost small in comparison to the size and warmth of her heart. Her true achievements were defined by her personality and her generous smile, both of which seemed to always make others feel at ease around her. Patty's success lay in the values she placed on family; those values had been instilled in her by our parents, and she worked hard at teaching them to her two boys, Jonathon, age seven, and Patrick, age four.

One of Patty's most notable qualities was her laid-back demeanor, which attracted others because of her ability to make them feel comfortable. This laid-back demeanor, however, in no way interfered with her enthusiastic way of making or finding the fun in any situation, as she was always coming up with ideas that were both subtle and outrageous. Practical jokes were not uncommon when Patty was around.

I will miss raising our children together. I will miss going to Patty when I'm at my wit's end with my children, and having her put everything into perspective by listening, laughing, and then reminding me that it is their job to act in such a way since

*they are children. Then she would usually throw in a story
about our own childhood to make the point.*

*I will miss all of the things that we will never be able to do. I
will miss growing old together. I will miss planning and
attending our children's graduations and weddings, and
becoming Grandmas with one another.*

*I will miss the comfort of being able to talk with Patty about
anything. She would always listen to every word I said, and
then give me her honest opinion whether I liked it or not. And I
will miss laughing together—so hard that at times it seemed as
though we could not stop. She would do anything for me, as I
would do the same for her.*

*There is a gaping hole inside of me from my sister having
been taken away. But even though it hurts so terribly, I feel like
the luckiest person alive to have had Patty as my only sibling for
thirty-seven years.*

On our way down to Indiana, I shared a story with Tom and the kids recently relayed to me by Jenny, who had also decided to visit the crash site before the scheduled dedication, because she had previously erected a cross there in memory of her brother and wanted to maintain the surrounding area. Upon her arrival, she came to where she had placed the cross amid three others that stood nearby. Bordering the east side of the site, Jenny attempted to clear the terrain around her brother's cross of the overgrown weeds and grass. Her efforts to maintain her brother's cross and the few others around his had been difficult, as she did not live close by, making it nearly impossible to stay ahead of the rapid growth that encompassed the area.

Jenny had called me on that day immediately after returning from the site, and I had been startled by the enthusiasm in her voice as she proceeded to tell me her story. While diligently attending to the patch of land surrounding the crosses, a car had driven by, and upon spotting her had slowed and eventually come to a stop. As it turned out, the three occupants of the vehicle had debated about whether to leave this young woman alone to mourn privately, or to offer their assistance. After some discussion, the latter won out.

They had walked over to Jenny and introduced themselves; a woman named Helen and her two grown children, Julie and Chuck, lived in a small town not far from the crash site. Helen and Julie were emergency medical technicians, while Chuck worked for the Red Cross. They proceeded to recall their own experiences on October 31, 1994; while they typically did not listen to their scanner at home, that night they had decided to turn it on because of the extremely foul weather. The first call that had come in stated that two planes had collided in mid air, but soon afterward, this initial statement was amended to affirm that the crash had involved only one commercial aircraft, and it was announced that recovery efforts would be postponed until the next morning. Helen, Julie, and Chuck had felt compelled to respond to the call, and even though they were unable to offer medical assistance because they did not have the proper immunizations, the following day, they instead began canvassing a widespread area for food donations for those who worked at the site. For the duration of the clean up efforts, they had delivered contributions to a local kitchen, hauled cooked food to the crash site, washed dishes, or mopped floors—basically, they had assisted in any way possible.

Jenny had proceeded to tell me how after Helen, Julie, and Chuck had approached her, they offered to clean and maintain the area around the crosses. Jenny had been touched by the gentleness and kindness this family extended to her, and for me, her talk of their good intentions was like a breath of fresh air. I shared the excitement evident in Jenny's voice as I was communicating this story to Tom and the kids, for I couldn't believe how thoughtful and giving it was of these people that we didn't even know to reach out and help.

Just days before the American Airlines dedication, Jenny had informed Helen, Julie, and Chuck that most of the families attending the service would also be visiting the crash site. Helen had then presented an idea to create a more fitting memorial for the families. With no time to waste, the three of them, along with their neighbor, immediately got to work building sixty-eight crosses representing each passenger and the flight crew. They also obtained permission from the County Commissioner to erect this temporary memorial just off the main county road, in the wide drainage ditch edging along the east side of the farmer's field. Jenny spoke of the drive of Helen and her children to help the families, which was accompanied by their keen sense of awareness, leaving them ever mindful of the families' pain and conscientious of avoiding the infliction of more unnecessary suffering.

Thus, upon our arrival in Indiana, Tom, the children, and I were to meet up with Jenny so that we could be introduced to Helen, Julie, and Chuck. In mid-afternoon, we pulled up near the crash site, and the moment we stepped out of our vehicle, we were instantly confronted by the stares of reporters documenting every move we made. I was surprised at their presence, as I was unsure as to how they knew we would be visiting the site. I also spotted several other individuals, and began walking toward a woman I had never met, and yet somehow felt as though I had known for my entire life. Our paces slowed as we approached one another, and then, without so much as an introduction, we both reached out and hugged. A witness to our meeting later reported that time seemed frozen as all eyes and cameras focused only on the two of us. The woman turned out to be Helen.

Helen then introduced me to Julie and Chuck. Julie was my age, while Chuck was a few years younger. A warm, good-natured essence emanated from all of them. I then directed my gaze to where a pick-up truck sat, containing sixty-eight white crosses. I was in awe of this family's effort, not only in having made the crosses in such a short time, but also in having mowed and cleaned the entire area. I was deeply moved by their sensitivity to what was important to us, and their generosity in having accomplished such a massive task so quickly. They were such a godsend, especially in light of the fact that their benevolence contrasted so sharply with the questionable motives of the airline.

Before beginning the installation of the sixty-eight crosses, Tom and I unloaded the two crosses that we had made from our car and walked over to the small grouping of crosses already in place. I carefully looked around, scouting the perfect place for Patty's and Patrick's crosses. Contrary to the surreal state I had experienced while constructing the crosses, I was suddenly acutely aware of the reality they symbolized; this process of erecting my own personal memorial for my sister and nephew was in no way mechanical, for I stood only a couple hundred yards away from the last place they had existed in the physical world. My proximity to the crash site stirred undesirable images of Patty's and Patrick's final moments that hampered my constant struggle to retain some sense of peace.

As my children and husband looked on, I methodically struck the top of Patty's cross with a mallet. I struck it a second, then a third time; with each blow, I was reminded of the past nine and a half months, and the reality behind each movement penetrated me so deeply that it seemed as if I was also being slowly anchored to the earth. Through a blur of tears I watched as the images of my sister's smiling face sank deeper and deeper toward the hot, dry land. I finally had to turn the mallet over to my husband, as I was fighting to maintain my composure. After finishing with Patty's cross, we placed Patrick's next to hers.

Following this personal tribute, Tom and I joined Jenny, Helen, Julie, and Chuck, and, together with my three children, we all began pounding the sixty-eight crosses into the extremely dry, cracked earth. The sheer number of crosses so vividly personifying the many lives lost on the plane permeated the air with a sense of eeriness. We all worked hard, and for the most part, we all worked in silence.

After completing our new memorial, Jenny and I walked out into the field. The land appeared much different in August than it had six months earlier during the cold, barren setting of midwinter. The crops this year looked healthy and had already been growing for several months. I had learned that each planting season the crop was rotated between corn and soybeans; although it was a cornfield we were presently moving through, it had been a soybean field into which the plane crashed the previous October. As we made our way through the thick growth, we came across two areas where no crops grew at all. One was substantially larger than the other, measuring approximately twenty-two by fifty-seven feet. The smaller of the two measured roughly nine by twenty-nine feet. We could distinctly see that truckloads of new soil had been dumped over a vast area of the farmland, and yet these two areas displayed no signs of growth.

Later, we learned that the larger of the two barren areas marked the parameters at the main point of impact, and the other patch was situated at the smaller impact crater. In some ways, it seemed like we were still looking at the immediate aftermath of the destruction, even though no wreckage was visible.

Just nine and a half months earlier, an emergency call had alerted the local volunteer fire department of a downed aircraft in this exact location. That night, the fire fighters had struggled to make their way out into this field, only to be cut off by the two drainage ditches lining its sides, and they were stuck trying to contend with the marsh-like sludge created by the heavy rains. After they had eventually found their way through the mud, their initial suppositions of a small plane crash had been instantly shaken upon seeing a large airplane tire in the area where we now stood. This was also where the County Hazardous Material Coordinator had encountered an overwhelming number of scattered human remains while making his way to the main debris site, and consequently had declared the site a biohazard. After rescue workers had caught sight of the extensive destruction throughout this field, the search and rescue was called off approximately forty-five minutes after the initial alarm had been sounded. And it was adjacent to this site that the county highway department had spent the whole night building an access road so that the operation could resume at the break of dawn.

My exact location was where the only two recognizable pieces of the aircraft had been found, raising questions as to the whereabouts of the remainder of the fuselage and the seats. The investigators had concluded that the majority of the wreckage, along with most of the passengers, would most likely be found at the bottom of the large crater; thus, two days after the crash, equipment was brought in to pump the water from both craters. And this particular area was where the severity of the tragedy had finally become evident, for when the eight-to-ten-feet-deep crater was fully pumped of water, no fuselage, no seats, no bodies, and no other plane wreckage had been seen. The crater's emptiness gripped everyone, for it had magnified the grim reality that the fragmented debris littering the field was all that was left of what had once been a commercial plane and its sixty-eight occupants.

For whatever reason, it was clear that life was still not ready to resume in these areas where the craters lay underneath the tons of new soil. It was as if the Earth, like the families, needed more time to heal, and nothing was going to force this process to be expedited.

Before leaving the crash site that day, I thanked Helen and Chuck for all they had done. When I approached Julie to do the same, she asked if there was anything else her family could do for any of us. Without hesitation, I then went on to say that I would like a service to be held for the families at the roadside where the crosses had just been erected. Without the slightest pause, Julie's response was, "If that's what you want, then that's what you'll have." Although it was already late Wednesday afternoon, I didn't doubt the integrity of her words, and so we scheduled the service for 11:00 Friday morning. The only job Jenny and I had was to inform as many of the families as possible that in addition to the airline's dedication, there would be a service near the crash site. Meanwhile, Helen, Julie, and Chuck set out to accomplish yet another miraculous feat.

Besides notifying families of the roadside service, Jenny and I began distributing the buttons with our new logo to the families and news reporters. We also gave buttons to the hotel employees who worked the check-in desk. Their support helped counter our feelings of discomfort from the influx of American Airlines personnel staying at the hotel.

The airline paid for most of the expenses for the dedication ceremony; however, the unaccommodating flight arrangements they made for some of the families showed a frustrating lack of consideration. Several families were offered plane changes with long layovers as opposed to direct flights. Others booked and paid their own way to avoid these extended layovers, while some, in spite of their aggravation, decided to endure the inconvenience of the airline's arrangements. One family was so appalled by the thoughtless planning that they simply decided not to attend the dedication.

On Thursday night, we held a private gathering of families, friends, rescue workers, and anyone else who had contributed to assisting with the aftermath of the crash. We were cautious not to let the media or airline personnel get word of it, since it was a very private meeting that allowed us both to share stories about the lives of our loved ones, as well as to talk with those who had come to know them only in death. During the meeting, we displayed several unclaimed personal belongings that had been found in the field, and we also had a listing of the passenger seat assignments for those interested. This record generated conversation about the possible interactions among passengers seated near one another.

Throughout the meeting, families thanked those who had worked with their loved ones, while the workers talked about the care and love they put into doing their job. They reached out to learn more about the crash victims that they had only become familiar with through pictures, other identifying factors, and whatever images they loosely formed in their own thoughts. These workers seemed to crave the ability to imagine the life and spirit that the remains had once contained, just as we, the families, craved assurances that our loved ones had actually been cared for and honored in death.

Regardless of how big or brave the workers tried to appear, sincere emotions surfaced that night. Those who needed to do so were able to talk about their experiences and be truly heard, while those who needed to be silent were given the freedom to do so as well. Everyone freely expressed sensitivity, support, and even humor, all of which allowed many of us to take one more step forward in the healing process.

The following morning, we headed to the crash site well before our service was planned to take place. Helen, Julie, and Chuck were to bring sixty-eight pots of flowers donated by a local florist, with which Jimmy, Andy, and Nikki were to help decorate the site.

As we approached, we could see the road lined with TV cameras and crews. The road leading into the field had been barricaded with a barbed-wire fence, preventing families from accessing the crash site. Reinforcing this blockade were local police officers hired by American Airlines. Officials from the company had been present earlier in the week, and had tried to prevent Helen, Julie, and Chuck from cleaning the area. It was only when Helen produced written documentation from the county commissioners granting temporary permission for this service that they had been allowed to resume their preparations.

In hiring the local police, American Airlines did not seem to take into account the prevailing goodness of human nature, for in spite of the presence of these officers twenty-four hours a day, the land was cleared, the memorial was set up, and the barbed-wire fence was moved so that those who needed to could walk down the access road and out into the field. Indeed, the officers even extended their blessing, stating, "Do whatever you want to do" and "This needs to be done, so good luck with it." The policemen on duty even asked for and proudly wore the family buttons.

We were never able to understand why the airline was so adamant about guarding the area, but in spite of their attempt to prevent us from accessing the crash site, as well as to stop the service by not allowing Helen to make the preparations, my parents, along with approximately fifty other family members and friends, gathered there on Friday morning. Many families walked out into the field to pay their respects, despite the hot sun, temperatures over ninety degrees, and high humidity. After everyone returned, we stood along the roadside easement, just several hundred yards from the point of impact, with our sights fixed upon the large drainage ditch where sixty-eight crosses stood commemorating the life of each individual on the plane. Only occasionally did I glance over to where my personal memorial for my sister and nephew was situated, just a few feet away from the sixty-eight crosses, because it was simply too painful to look at.

Three local clergy spoke words that paid homage to all those who perished. This simple, no-frills service was beautiful, as it had sprung only from sincerity and the best of intentions. Helen, Julie, and Chuck oversaw all the details, making sure that the service started only after all had returned from paying their respects in the field, and providing tissues and drinking water to help counter the effects of the heat.

The peaceful, loving feeling of our service, however, was soon undermined by the anxiety of not knowing what to expect from the airline's upcoming dedication ceremony. Following our roadside service, we went back to the hotel, where we were to be picked up for the dedication; the airline was providing transportation to the event since there was not enough parking available on the cemetery grounds to accommodate everyone. Some families were bused, while others were transported by limo. Upon arriving, we were escorted to a large outdoor canopy under which were many tables, all decorated with white linen and floral arrangements. The servers were formally dressed as if working at a black-tie event. While a violinist played in the background, the families were wined and dined.

To an outsider, it must have appeared to be the perfect reception in the perfect setting, although nothing could have been further from the truth. The drawn, sad expressions worn by many of the guests dramatically contrasted the elegant atmosphere, and spoke to pain that could not be masked with the finest food or the most soothing music.

When lunch was over, everyone made their way to another large white canopy near the gravesite, where the service was to take place. The enclosed area was large enough to seat five hundred people; the rest would stand outside the perimeter of the tent.

The airline had security posts stationed throughout the cemetery to keep out those who were not invited, including the media. Before the ceremony started, Jenny and I, along with other family members, spoke with reporters standing outside the security ropes and held what would later be referred to as an impromptu press conference. The cameras then moved to an airline spokesman, who emphasized that American had worked with the families every step of the way, and had gone to great lengths to accommodate everyone.

As I began walking toward the tent, I noticed Helen, Julie, and Chuck standing outside the ropes along with the media. They said airline personnel had made it clear that their presence was not welcome at the service. Right in front of the security guards, I pulled up the rope to allow this family to enter. As far as I was concerned, the service could not be inundated with airline personnel while simultaneously excluding these special people who had become so important in all of our lives.

We all took our seats just before the dedication commenced. For the next forty minutes or so I sat and listened to the airline's "politically correct" service. I saw no sincerity in the ceremony, nor was I in any way moved. While those officiating the service were honoring those who perished, several family relations were mentioned, such as mother, father, aunt, and uncle, but somehow the title of brother and sister was excluded in every instance, which many saw as a glaring oversight.

After the dedication, we were directed to the memorial, which consisted of a column approximately four-foot-high that was topped with a sundial, and which stood in front of an inscribed granite wall. The airline had buckets of white roses available for the families to place in front of the wall. Since the sixty-eight names were randomly inscribed, it took me a bit of time to locate Patty's and Patrick's names. When I finally spotted them, I slowly ran my fingers across the inscriptions and placed two flowers down.

Reporters later commented on the vast difference between the service at the crash site and the dedication at the cemetery. They described the events as having two contradicting themes: the one that "had love in it" versus "the cold one"; the reports went on to indicate that the division between the ceremonies was "symbolic of the chasm" between the airline and the families.

The day had been full of exhausting emotions, and everyone could have easily retired after a quiet meal, but instead, approximately ten of us met for dinner at the hotel. There, we temporarily let go of our sadness and anger to laugh and have some much-needed fun. After dinner, we moved to the open lounge near the lobby, where we were joined by several others. A casual onlooker probably could not have guessed the sad occasion for our gathering by the way we were enjoying one another's company.

The morning after the ceremonies, it was time to head home, or so I thought. The previous night, I had been informed that a governor's picnic was being held in downstate Indiana the day I was due to depart, which would offer one more way to bring public recognition to the safety concerns surrounding the ATR aircraft. Just moments before I was ready to hop in my car to go home, Jenny and two other friends appeared, insisting that I attend the picnic with them. After a brief conversation with Tom, I grabbed a few items, said good-bye to my family, and jumped into Jenny's car.

Prior to leaving for the picnic, we drove to the cemetery, where we again made our way up the brick path that led to the granite wall of engraved names. A few of us stood there solemnly and in silence. This time we were not preoccupied with airline personnel, reporters, or the hundreds of others that had been present the day before, and the painful emotions I had stuffed away finally surfaced.

Weeks after the dedication, I was on the phone with my good friend, Karen, describing the installation of the crosses and the airline's dedication. At that time, she had not known that I went down to the crash site a few days early to erect my personal memorial for Patty and Patrick, but upon my revealing this information, she proceeded to tell me about her own experience on that same day. Since the day we had arrived in Indiana was a workday, that morning Karen had arisen early, and for some inexplicable reason had begun sobbing uncontrollably. The busyness of getting ready for work and sending her children off to school did not distract her from this outburst of sentiment, nor did her work as a dental hygienist. She had cried the entire day, not knowing how to respond to the puzzled looks of her patients, and told me that the only other time she had ever carried on that way was the day she had received the news that Patty and Patrick were killed. Hearing her story caused me to realize how amazing it was that I could have endured something as painful as erecting Patty's and Patrick's crosses without falling to pieces, and we questioned why she would have been simultaneously overcome with such intense emotions without even knowing the reason. Could it be that she had somehow helped to carry my grief, allowing me to move through the day's events without becoming emotionally paralyzed? Could there actually be connections in life beyond what we can explain or physically prove? Or could something this strange just be considered a coincidence?

As I listened to Karen's account, these and many other thoughts traveled through my mind, and I reflected upon all the ways that other people, even those that were perfect strangers, had helped the families and me throughout the time we spent in Indiana. The actions and words of Helen and her family, as well as all of the workers, had helped to ease the difficulty of the circumstances under which I had made the trip, and had provided me with the support I needed to make it through the occasion. Thinking about how trying this experience had been for me, I began to consider the idea of where strength comes from, and how it is that we can endure such distressing moments. I decided that maybe it was possible that the day I had planted Patty's and Patrick's crosses, Karen had somehow unknowingly channeled all her strength into me, so that I could keep standing beyond the pain that arose from that symbolic gesture of once again laying my family to rest.

❦ 23 ❦

Following the airline's dedication service, it seemed as if all the hurt and anger that I had been pushing past in order to resolve the many different issues with which I was confronted was once again steadily rising. On top of my ongoing grieving process, the added pressure of organizing the family gathering, preparing for the family service, and attending the airline's dedication had proved to slowly erode what was left of my composure, leaving me feeling like a slow pressure cooker with its top ready to explode. I had never experienced anything like this before, and was alarmed by the disconcerting state in which I found myself. I thought that this sudden surge of emotions was odd, considering that so much time had passed, and I had already been through so much, but nonetheless, I found myself inexplicably consumed by this unexpected angst. Regardless of this unsettled state, I still had to attend to typical family responsibilities, along with airline matters. I also remained intent on staying available to help the families of Flight 4184 in whatever way possible, as they too must have been enduring their own grief.

In the midst of my personal turmoil, I had to begin preparing for the upcoming deposition required for Jonathon's case against the airline, during which I was to support answers I had previously supplied in the interrogatories. My attorney's discussions with the airline regarding Jonathon's eventual settlement had not yielded any satisfactory results, and so we continued to move ahead with the lawsuit. The deposition afforded the airline's insurance company the opportunity to gather any supplementary information that they felt would be pertinent to their case. I was apprehensive about these proceedings, for this time I wouldn't be able to respond on paper in the comfort of my own home.

However, I was able to find some momentary relief from these stressful circumstances through my dreams, in which Patty would appear from time to time, usually seeming playful and happy. One night she emerged surrounded by tall pillars; I watched as she ran behind one pillar and then the next, peeking out with a big smile on her face, just like when we played games of hide-and-seek as children. Another time, I had the impression that she was standing only inches from me, so close that I could see the radiance of her skin and "our" distinct ridges on her front teeth. She looked whole and perfect, and her mere presence was able to fill me with comfort and love.

On another night I awoke from sleep with the distinct perception that my entire bedroom was jammed with the people that had been on Flight 4184, which was nearly the same sensation I had felt in the hotel room during the preliminary NTSB hearing in Indianapolis. At times I questioned the validity of these impressions, but then I would remember that Tom had felt visited by someone from the plane in our hotel room, and other family members had also encountered similar phenomena. For me, these feelings were akin to instances in which someone correctly senses danger, or has a premonition that something will happen before it actually plays out. I could never prove the truth in these feelings, but could only accept them as part of my own reality.

Unusual incidents that occasionally occurred in my home would also cause me to wonder about the connection between this life and the afterlife. There were several times during the afternoon when I saw one light bulb after another flickering at different times, and yet none of them needed to be replaced. One day, after a series of such bizarre events, I found myself saying out loud, "Ok, Patty, if you are the one causing these inexplicable things, please clearly let me know." A couple days later, I was spending the morning at home alone in the family room, folding laundry. The guest on the TV show I was watching claimed to be getting in touch with those from "the other side" who had passed on. Halfway through the program, our security alarm began to sound. Startled by the blaring siren, I jumped up and hurried to the keypad to deactivate the alarm. I wondered why the system was even operating, as it was never turned on during the daytime, and furthermore, I had no idea who would have activated it, given that I was home by myself. Moreover, even if the alarm had somehow been switched on, then why hadn't it already sounded during the several times I had gone outside and come back in that day? We had had this system for quite some time, and it had never given us any problems before.

Oddly enough, when I arrived at the key pad, I immediately noticed that the alarm system was not even in the "on" mode, making it quite difficult to turn it off. I tried switching it into the "on" mode to see if that would allow the alarm to be deactivated, but the siren just kept on blaring. Next I entered the code a second time to turn the alarm off, but to my surprise, the siren still continued to sound. I repeated those same steps several times to no avail. Completely perplexed, I reached for the keypad once more. But an instant before my fingers started to punch in the code again, I froze.

Suddenly, it occurred to me that this might be Patty's definitive response to the request I had made only days prior. I laughed, assuring her that I had received her message loud and clear, and thanked her, marveling at her endless enthusiasm for finding the fun in situations. I resumed watching the fitting TV show with a big smile on my face, even though I was unable to hear a single word of the program. The alarm sounded for several more minutes before it finally stopped...on its own.

In such curious instances, and during the times I would see Patty in my dreams, I felt reassured that she was still somehow part of my life. My faith in her presence offered me sporadic reprieves from the hectic nature of my life.

❧ ❧ ❧

These moments that allowed me to feel so in tune with Patty motivated me to contact some of her closest friends, whose relationships with her accumulatively spanned from the time of our grammar school days through the time of the crash. On Patty's behalf, I felt compelled to reach out to these individuals who had held a piece of her heart, and offer them some way to say goodbye. But accomplishing this task was not without setbacks, as I was challenged by marital name changes, relocations, and simply trying to remember the names of those I wanted to contact. However, through creative measures (involving police assistance, a little luck, and some patience), I was able to get in touch with everyone on my list.

In the process of acknowledging my sister's past relationships, I discovered that Chris, Patty's best friend from high school, had married and moved away. In the midst of trying to figure out how to locate her, she sent my parents a letter. Chris had recalled reading the name of my parents' church in Patty's obituary in the newspaper, and seeking to express her condolences, she forwarded a letter through the church to my parents. A short while later, Chris and I met for breakfast and talked for hours. Chris told me that she and Patty had run into each other earlier that same year, which I had already known from a previous conversation with my sister. They hadn't seen each other since high school, and were both excited at the prospect of catching up. But time got away, as did the chance for this reconnection. Through our sharing of many fond memories, we were able to bring their relationship to what felt like full circle.

Another sympathy card to my parents enabled me to get in touch with Phil, another close friend of Patty's. When we met, I sat and thoroughly enjoyed the many stories he relayed about my sister. He brought up one instance when he and Patty were on the phone while she was driving with the radio playing in the background. The moment a particular song came on, in mid-sentence Patty told Phil that she had to hang up and call her sister's answering machine to record the song, and before he knew it, their conversation was over. Phil marveled at Patty's constant and spontaneous impulses to brighten up the days of those that she loved. He was also awed by the similarity of my mannerisms to what he recalled of Patty's. Listening to Phil celebrate all the characteristics that Patty and I shared prompted me to reminisce about the unique ways my sister and I would communicate. There were times when our conversations consisted of only partially spoken sentences and words, and we had perfected the ability to clearly understand one another without saying anything at all. These linguistic shortcuts allowed us to get more covered in a much shorter time span, and we had eventually learned to ignore the questionable looks we would get from outsiders watching and listening to our interactions. At times, people expressed observing our communications as "an experience," because they were left entirely clueless as to what had taken place, and before they knew what had happened, Patty and I had already moved on to the next subject. Even as I was sharing these recollections with Phil while exiting the restaurant, he was grinning at the similarity of my walk to Patty's.

It was fulfilling to have the opportunity to connect with Patty's past, while simultaneously finding small ways to help myself heal and move forward with my future.

❧ 24 ❧

When the day to give Jonathon's deposition arrived, I maneuvered my way through the crowded streets to a high-rise building in downtown Chicago. I felt as prepared as possible, yet at the same time I was nervous about having to testify to the "loss of society and loss of support" sustained by Jonathon as a result of his mother's death.

Upon entering my lawyer's office, while waiting for the attorney who would accompany me to the deposition, I met with the firm's director of litigation, with whom I had spoken with quite frequently. He had been keeping me informed of the progress being made regarding the pending lawsuit, as well as helping me to organize last-minute details for the deposition. In coming to know many of the other families, as well as some of the crash-site workers, I had gathered information that I thought might prove useful to our case. As I passed such knowledge on to the director of litigation, he would often shake his head in disbelief that I had somehow acquired these details. I explained that I could not just sit idle during this process, as it was vitally important to me to ensure that the outcome benefit Jonathon.

The director of litigation then advised me of a report recently completed by an expert witness his firm hired, which contained the results of an investigation into both weather conditions and the level of pilot responsibility as causal factors in the crash. He was surprised when I asked the name of the investigator, as he thought it an unusual request, but he was even more amazed that I recognized the name. I had known the investigator from our life-guarding days in high school, and had recently become reacquainted with him, which was good, because it gave me the opportunity to call him with any questions I had upon reading the report.

When the attorney was ready, we walked several blocks to another high rise occupied by the airline's insurance company, where the deposition was to take place. We took the elevator to one of the top floors, and then followed the path of marble flooring to a large conference room, which was furnished with an oversized cherry-wood conference table surrounded by many comfortable-looking chairs. Directly across from the doorway, an entire wall of picture windows overlooked Lake Michigan, which would serve as the backdrop during the next several hours of questioning.

Upon entering the room, we were met by two attorneys representing the airline's insurance company, and one court stenographer responsible for recording the proceedings. The deposition began by asking for my personal information, including my full name, date of birth, and address. The attorney conducting this part of the proceeding was a soft-spoken and seemingly compassionate woman, and her unassuming demeanor greatly conflicted with my understanding of the purpose of this meeting. I wondered if the airline had chosen her to conduct my deposition because they hoped her approachable nature might soften my awareness of the fact that the company was seeking to dismantle the integrity of my statements and prove the existence of even one scrap of evidence compromising Patty's worth as a mother. Did they truly think that for one minute I would believe this woman was on my side?

The insurance company's attorney went on to ask about our immediate and extended family's health history, paying extra attention to that of Patty and Jonathon. Her questions mimicked those of the two Care Team women who had been assigned to assist our family "in any way possible" immediately following the crash. I also remembered the words of a friend who had lost his brother over Lockerbie, Scotland, during the terrorist bombing of Pan Am 103; all along, he had warned me to be careful of what I said to airline personnel, as they would use any information against me that would help to influence the outcome of the case in their favor.

At this point, I realized that there was a good chance that these attorneys were directly comparing the answers I had given to the Care Team women with my statements at this deposition in order to determine any discrepancies. Did they actually think that I hadn't been aware of what I was saying right after the crash, or that I would jeopardize the validity of my statements by giving conflicting information? I could feel my anger building from what I felt was a legal game being played against me.

As my mind continued to race with suspicion, the attorney began making inquiries into my employment, as well as into the ways my outside activities had changed since the crash. I was also asked about Patty's life, from infancy through adulthood, with particular consideration shown to her employment and health history. Throughout the interrogation, I was cautious of this attorney's strategies, most notably her frequent tactic of returning to previous questions and asking them in a different fashion. I felt as if she was somehow trying to trip me up in order to discredit my previous responses, and so each time I found her doing so I stated that her question had already been answered.

I was subsequently requested to describe Patty's personality, which shifted the deposition from needing facts to wanting my opinions and feelings, making the process much more trying. I instantly searched for the right words to portray Patty's vibrant spirit, which was so easily reflected in the fun-loving way she enjoyed life. After a brief pause, I stated that Patty was an exceptionally calm, open, and comfortable person to be around, and that she was also remarkably loving.

This more personal line of questioning moved on to include whether I had ever observed Patty expressing any fear or anxiety when she flew. The attorney was seeking for me to elaborate on a statement I made in the interrogatories regarding the terror I speculated my sister had suffered prior to impact. She asked what I believed Patty had experienced on the plane, and how long I thought she had been aware that the plane was going down, explaining that she was specifically looking to estimate the amount of time Patty had endured such a panic-stricken state. By the time the attorney shot out this last question, I could no longer force myself to imagine my sister only moments prior to her death. I just could not tolerate this incessant badgering, and desperately wondered whether she would ever have the sensitivity to stop.

By the end of these investigative inquiries, I had long since lost the battle to fight back my tears, and was struggling just to formulate even a single-word answer with any clarity. Recognizing the toll these scrutinies had taken on me, my attorney suggested a break.

After several minutes of attempting to compose myself, I returned to the conference room not only distraught, but also furious over having been prodded to the point of becoming emotionally vulnerable in front of these people representing the airline. Mostly, I was enraged over the attorney relentlessly prompting me to conjure up the most unbearably distressing images of my sister that I could form.

Since I had not been capable of responding just before the break, I was again asked whether there was anything else I believed my sister suffered, or if I wanted to elaborate upon the trauma I thought she had experienced.

I carefully and deliberately explained that during the horrifying gyrations of the airplane, my sister would have been frantic for her own safety, but even more so for that of her four-year-old son. I said I assumed that from the onset of the bad weather Patty might have felt some anxiety, which upon the first roll of the plane would have changed to sheer terror. As I spoke, I desperately tried to ignore the picture of Patty attempting to overcome her own panic in order to comfort Patrick that so clearly manifested from what I was being forced to consider. When I finished explaining what I supposed Patty had undergone, the attorney posed the most egregious question of all: "Do you have any evidence of any of these claims?"

How could I possibly have any evidence, given that I had not been there to bear witness to what Patty had gone through? This request was cold, cunning, and ridiculous, and I couldn't even begin to fathom the ways in which they sought to interpret my reply to serve their own agenda.

When I eventually managed to regain my capacity to speak, I reminded the attorney that she had asked me only what I *thought* had occurred, and I had provided her with my speculation; however, I also firmly stressed that I could not know anything with certainty, for I had no way of obtaining any evidence. The attorney replied that she had merely asked if I had any.

After this frustrating discussion, I was hoping that the deposition was coming to a close, but the inquiries continued. This round focused on events that occurred in the period of time immediately before and after the crash, including the last time I saw Patty, as well as where she had bought her airline ticket. I was asked to describe how I first learned of the air disaster, which led to me relaying the details my dad had provided at the time that he had first told me of the tragedy. Images of Patty and Patrick plummeting to their death were replaced with those of my father sitting at my kitchen table clutching his head, looking like I had never seen him before. I could still vividly see his anguish as he desperately sought the whereabouts of his youngest daughter and grandson.

Again my attorney intervened, stating that this line of questioning was troublesome for me, and asked for the airline's attorney to be more sensitive. She acknowledged this request, and went on to re-examine what information my dad had given me about the crash; additionally, she launched an examination into how my dad had received news of a downed aircraft, and what actions I had taken following our conversation.

As I spoke, I clearly visualized a picture of myself on that night sitting at my kitchen table on the telephone, and I saw myself dialing the Indianapolis airport and being transferred from one person to the next, reliving my mounting distress from my unsuccessful attempts to locate Patty. I glimpsed the image of enthusiastic children engaging in their year-long anticipation of Halloween festivities that drastically contrasted with Dad's expression reflecting the looming likelihood his youngest daughter had boarded an ill-fated airplane. And I could almost hear the screams I had let out upon receiving Dad's phone call confirming the worst, forcing myself to fight back tears as I revisited that horrific night detail by detail, emotion by emotion. The attorney required that I expand on these efforts to have my sister contacted in the airport, as well as to provide more details about the phone call I made to the American Airlines' 800 number that was listed at the bottom of the TV screen, during which I had been on hold for hours.

Additionally, I was instructed to specify Jonathon's exact whereabouts during this time, who he had been with, and how he had found out about the crash. When I told her that Jonathon found out about his mother's and brother's death from the television, she was obviously jolted, for she instantly repeated my words. I went on to explain that by the time Mom and Dad had gone to Jonathon's house upon receiving confirmation of Patty's and Patrick's deaths, he had already fallen asleep in his mother's bed, exhausted by the overwhelming magnitude of the news he had just heard.

I proceeded to describe what happened the following morning when Mom and Dad had gone to pick up Jonathon from his house. The attorney wanted to know how Jonathon reacted to the news about his mother and brother, which Mom had delivered so gently upon waking him. She inquired as to Jonathon's reaction when he was brought to my house, and whether he had been able to talk about his feelings.

The attorney progressively focused on the time Jonathon had lived with me, and what kinds of things we had discussed. She explicitly sought to determine whether he had been willing to talk about his mother and brother with me and with my children. The attorney investigated into how the loss of his mother and brother had emotionally affected Jonathon, and the ways in which the symptoms of his grief had manifested. She then interrogated me about the custody issues, including how I had prepared Jonathon to move in with his father, and whether or not he had accepted my explanation as to why he was leaving my house.

Just when I thought my level of aggravation had reached its pinnacle, the attorney raised the issue of the concerns surrounding my notification of Patty's remains, along with the many subsequent problems that emerged in relation to the disposition of unidentified body parts. This generated memories of the apprehension I had felt during our private funerary service, along with the emotional upheaval that I had experienced while standing before the two caskets, unsure of their contents—desiring to know the truth, and yet simultaneously fearing what that truth held. Images resurfaced of hauled truckloads of dirt still containing parts of our families, and of the human remains my husband and I had found months after the crash. Ultimately, the attorney's question brought back my ongoing concern about the actual resting place of my sister and nephew.

Following this grueling testimony, we took a brief break. Afterward, the second attorney representing the airline took over from the female attorney with another series of inquiries about Jonathon's feelings and reactions at the memorial service, and about how long Jonathon was out of school following the crash. He required additional details regarding custody issues, and had me reiterate what had transpired on the day Jonathon departed with his father.

The deposition finally came to a close after hours of questioning, which had only been broken up by lunch and two short breaks. Even though I felt emotionally wrung out, I had somehow made it through the grueling deposition. I wasn't sure how my testimony would impact Jonathon's settlement, and I doubted whether or not my words had sufficiently conveyed the enormous devastation that this tragedy had thrust upon our family. The brutality of this entire legal process made me realize why some families had settled early to avoid a drawn-out battle with the airline; however, I refused to give in to tactics that would allow for an easy and tidy resolution, and remained intent on fighting for some justice and recognition of the lives that had been lost.

❦ 25 ❧

As October 31, 1995, drew near, preparations were underway to commemorate the first anniversary of the crash. Every cell within my being
was triggered by this upcoming date and seemed to be in a heightened
state of awareness. It seemed as though I had an internal alarm clock set
to go off at this time of year that instinctively awakened me to my unresolved feelings associated with the crash, much in the same way that hi-
bernating animals annually awaken at the onset of spring.

Without wanting to do so, I would suddenly find myself reliving
many of the events that had occurred as a result of the tragedy. The
memories seemed to have a life of their own, coming and going without
warning, and I would fight back tears as thoughts came to mind of the
enormous transformation in all our lives over the past year.

I couldn't help but lament the drastic loss that Jonathon had been
forced to endure. I recalled moments that spoke to the innocence of a
seven-year-old, like the time about a month after the crash when
Jonathon had called me over to the hall closet just inside the front doors
of my house. Not knowing what to expect, I had watched as he slipped
into the closet and disappeared behind all the coats. Upon his reemer-
gence, he surprised me with a decorative penguin that was approximately a foot-and-a half high, wobbling on its stand from having been
moved. Jonathon had dutifully presented the penguin to me, stating
that it was a Christmas gift Patty had bought for me earlier in the year
and stored in my closet (which might as well have been hers, for she
would never hesitate to define things collectively as "ours"). As I accepted the largest penguin to be added to our lifelong collection, I

smiled through the tears streaming down my face, remembering the comfort I gained from my life having always been so intertwined with Patty's.

*** *** ***

I was not the only one who was deeply affected by the nearing date of the anniversary; all the families, as well as those who had volunteered at the site, in different ways expressed their cognizance of the monumental and difficult nature of this event. Helen and her family were back at work, again lobbying before the county commissioners. The temporary permission granted in August had allowed the sixty-eight crosses and baskets of flowers near the crash site to remain for only five days. Many had voiced their unhappiness about this state of affairs, especially given the families' general desire to have a permanent memorial at the site. This time, Helen requested consent from the commissioners to establish a permanent roadside memorial. The unwavering drive of these three people to fulfill our wishes eventually won unanimous support for our cause. Additionally, the county commissioners demonstrated their encouragement by hand-selecting one of the largest and most perfect field-stones to be centrally placed at the roadside memorial; this stone was to be mounted with an inscribed plaque they were also donating, which read: "In memory of passengers and crew of Flight 4184, October 31, 1994."

It was during this time that Helen, Julie, and Chuck came to be collectively known as "Mission Un-Impossible," as nothing seemed to prevent whatever it was they set out to do or provide for the families. Helen and her children, with the assistance of friends, went on to re-instate the sixty-eight crosses, handwriting the names on each individual cross. While making all other preparations for the upcoming first anniversary service, Helen repeatedly asked Jenny and me what the families specifically wanted. But to us the details never seemed important; rather, it was simply the coming together of the families at this site that was meaningful. However, a few days before the ceremony, I realized that I really wanted Eric Clapton's song "Tears in Heaven" sung during the service. I called Helen with a sense of hesitation, since I had told her that whatever she chose would be perfect. Apologetically, I began to request that this song be performed, but before I even had a chance to finish my sentence, Helen replied that it had already been chosen for the program. This was just one of the many occurrences over the years that illustrated the strong connection and like-mindedness between Helen and me.

Building a relationship with Helen had allowed me to feel as though I had somehow acquired a second mother, probably much in the same way Jonathon felt when he said he had two moms. Every so often, I would worry that my mom might feel slighted by the closeness between Helen and me, but these fears were put to rest when Mom and Helen met for the first time. During their conversation, Mom actually thanked Helen for loving her daughter. I felt privileged to again be able to witness my family's ability to extend grace and love to all who touched our lives.

❧ ❧ ❧

The morning of Halloween, my thoughts recurrently flashed back to this day exactly one year before, when my sister and my nephew had still been alive. After school, the children had raced home to get ready for trick-or-treating. Patty, Jonathon, and Patrick were to have arrived shortly thereafter to join in the yearly tradition. All had been right with the world.

This year, instead of planning for the holiday, we were preparing with apprehension and sadness to drive to what had once been an unknown town to me: Roselawn, Indiana. This was where we were to pay our respects to those who had perished in the field the previous year. We were to attend two memorial services, one that had been arranged by Helen's family, and the other to be held by the local firefighters. Despite the kind efforts made by the community to honor our commemoration of our loved ones, I was still filled with a deep sense of pain and loss.

Grey weather had moved in, misting the area with a light rain, adding to the already gloomy nature of the day.

We arrived prior to the start of the first memorial service, which had been arranged by the local firefighters who responded to the initial call about a downed aircraft. A press conference had been scheduled to be held before the service. Inside a large hall at the fire department, five of us, including myself, three other family members, and one former American Eagle pilot, sat before a row of tables filled with microphones. As we waited for the press conference to begin, people continued to gather in the hall until it was almost full.

The longer I lingered in anticipation, the more uncomfortable I became. A part of me felt like leaving, but just moments before I was about to walk away, my thoughts turned to Patty, and I was reminded that I was there to honor her memory. In my mind, I could almost hear Patty insisting that she would have done the same for me, and so with a slight huff of an attitude, I silently replied, "Fine. I'll stay."

A few minutes later, the press conference began. The first interview topic concerned the farmer's planting of the crash site, which took place despite some family members' offers to financially reimburse the farmer for at least one year of profits. Photographs showed the location of the impact craters where the corn had attempted to grow, but had instead ended up as stubby sprouts. It was almost fitting that this lack of growth occurred in the same shape as the impact craters, while the corn grew abundantly throughout the rest of the field. Concerns about the crash site not having been thoroughly cleaned were also discussed, along with the ongoing findings of wreckage, personal effects, and even human remains.

The next topic was the NTSB's final hearing, which was supposed to have been held one year from the date of the crash at the latest; however, the hearing continued to be postponed because the French manufacturer of the plane and the French government maintained that there were errors in the NTSB's final report, thus preventing its approval and release. Reports from the FAA indicated that all ATR turboprops were suspected of having vulnerability in icing conditions. Although improved deicing equipment allowed the aircraft to resume full operation, many still saw a necessity for restrictions to be placed on this aircraft.

I spoke of the vast number of personal effects that had been collected and documented, and yet only a strikingly small number of items had been returned to the families. As I relayed this information, those present in the hall were noticeably stirred, and gasps could be heard.

We also mentioned to the press the August formation of the National Air Disaster Alliance, and gave a brief overview of its goals. The inaugural meeting of the newly formed National Air Disaster Alliance was announced to be taking place in November, at which time the issues specific to our crash would be merged with those of six other air disasters.

When the conference was over, several people in the audience came to me expressing feelings of disbelief and sadness that the personal effects hadn't been returned to their rightful owners. Individuals who had personally collected the items talked about the care with which they had handled them. It was like a déjà vu, as I was hearing the same story I had heard at the preliminary hearing. One volunteer told about an intact college jacket with only a slight rip on the sleeve, which the airline had earmarked to discard; thankfully, this man took it upon himself to remove and eventually return it to the owner's family.

The service at the local fire station following the press conference was attended by families, friends, and a significant number of people from the community. The families were presented with a brass plaque engraved with the names of those who perished, and a separate stone was revealed containing the inscription, "Sincere thanks to all who responded to the crash of Flight 4184." Family members, local firefighters, and other volunteers gave speeches. Community members read two poems; one of the family members read a letter referring to us all as representatives for those who had lost their lives; and the local high school chorus sang "Amazing Grace."

Upon the completion of the first service, we drove to the roadside memorial. On the way, we passed a house with a large oak tree on the front lawn decorated with sixty-eight yellow ribbons, a gesture I found to be quite touching.

When we arrived at the roadside candlelight vigil, I was struck by the number of families that had turned out for the memorial. Many locals were also in attendance, along with volunteers and workers who were involved with some aspect of the crash's aftermath.

The area had been prearranged for the service; our lovely new memorial stone and plaque from the commissioners were displayed, flowers were interspersed among the sixty-eight crosses lodged into the ground, and white candles sat in front of every cross waiting to be lit. Additionally, each cross was adorned with a yellow ribbon bearing the date, "October 31, 1994" across the top of all the bows, and the ties were decorated with the following prayer:

Now I lay me down to sleep;
I pray the Lord my soul to keep.
If I should die before I wake,
I pray the Lord my soul to take.

The words, "God Bless Flight 4184" were added at the end of the prayer. I learned that two thoughtful young women in no way associated with the crash had felt compelled to make these sixty-eight ribbons for each victim on the plane, and had tied the ribbons around the crosses in the bitter cold at 2:00 a.m. that morning.

As each family found their loved one's cross, they would light the candle that had been placed in front. Helen, Julie, and Chuck oversaw all activities and continued attending to details, assuring that matches and tissues were provided, and holding umbrellas over those who knelt to pray before the personally inscribed crosses.

The weather worsened throughout the day, and by the time our first-year anniversary service was underway, the dark, dreary skies opened up, releasing large, icy raindrops—conditions that seemed to nearly replicate the cold, driving rain of the previous year.

Local clergy led the service, which included guitar playing and songs wonderfully performed. At the exact time of impact a moment of silence was observed, while approximately one mile away, a local church sounded its bells sixty-eight times.

Over the past couple of months, my anticipation of this moment of silence had detonated bursts of anxiety, as it was the instant of not only Patty's and Patrick's death, but what I felt was my partial death as well. Part of me wanted to scream out and crumble to the ground, as I had exactly one year before upon receiving confirmation of the tragedy.

But I didn't fall; I just stood there in pain as a flood of hot tears mingled with the ice-cold raindrops splashing onto my face. The silence was broken only by the sound of freezing rain pounding on umbrellas, as though the heavens were crying and suffering right along with us.

As I faced the point of impact in the open field, I struggled not to visualize the plane plummeting from the sky at over 425 mph, and I fought not to picture the plane as it hit the ground, redefining everyone and everything on it.

After what seemed like an eternity, the clergyman resumed speaking, snapping me out of that dark place and into the realization that I had made it through that moment that I had so feared. Miraculously, all sixty-eight candles had stayed lit and continued to burn brightly through the duration of the ceremony in spite of the downpour. The entire event was more than any of us had hoped for, and helped to ease some of the emotional turbulence we all felt on this day.

Before leaving, many of us made our way down the gravel road that led into the field to once again stand in the place that had been forever seared into our memories, but we encountered a barrier in the form of the farmer himself, who stood guard at the barbed wire fence he had put up precisely to keep people away. Family members, crash-site workers, and police officers gathered around as some of the men set out to remove the blockade. In the midst of the commotion, the police and firemen pulled the fence aside and kept the farmer at bay so that I could slip through the opening and avoid the explosive situation; many others soon followed. The farmer eventually relinquished his stance, agreeing to allow only relatives to walk out to the field and pay their respects. Several questioned his odd behavior, and as before, when the farmer had been so adamant about planting his crops, some thought the airline might have prompted his actions in their attempt to prevent any additional discoveries in the field.

A short time later, those who attended the memorial service gathered at a small church a couple miles up the road, where we all ate and socialized in the activity room. Helen, along with the female parishioners of the church, had beautifully set up the room and prepared the food. Laughter and peace dominated the atmosphere, as we all sat in friendship and appreciated the love and integrity with which the service was put together.

At the end of the evening, Helen, Julie, and Chuck drove back to the memorial site before heading home. They found one last family member kneeling before his loved one's cross in the solitude of the night, amid the unrelenting wind and rain; somehow, even hours after the service, the sixty-eight candles continued to burn around him as brightly as they had upon first being lit.

At times like these, it was uplifting to see the unbearable pain and grief caused by the tragedy offset by such small miracles, for being privy to these little gifts continued to give us hope for the future.

❧ 26 ❧

One way or another, I had somehow made it past an entire year of firsts—first birthdays, holidays, anniversaries—basically, my first key moments in life without Patty. While this year had been filled with stress and exhaustion from my ongoing struggle with the airline, there were deeper, more complex feelings gnawing at me that did not have anything to do with outside factors, but were rather a product of a gaping hole that existed in my personal life, which had only magnified in scope since the crash. My parents, Tom, Patty, and I had built up a successful business over the years, and as a result I had all I could hope for materially. Basically, I had everything I thought would make me fulfilled and happy, but in some ways I was neither. I came to realize that I was in a marriage void of emotional connection, and I felt as though I continually gave support, partnership, and loyalty to my husband without him reciprocating any of these efforts. Tom had repeatedly broken the sacred vows of marriage that in my eyes bound us together, and I felt that he had failed to uphold his commitment to treat me with love and respect. There was nothing I could count on him for, and I began to question my purpose in staying with him. His family upbringing was substantially different than mine, and our views on parenthood greatly conflicted.

What was I teaching my children by staying in an unhealthy relationship? I felt like I was setting a bad example for them about the importance of pursuing their own happiness and passion in life, as I had settled for a man that did not share my drive to approach every day with an abundance of zealous energy, and who was not someone that shared my values, dreams, and passions. These feelings of dissatisfaction were not new, but had been easier to overlook when Patty had been alive, as I had always thought of her as my soul-mate, and it was therefore easier to accept the emotional incompleteness of my marriage. The death of my sister and nephew had taught me to fully appreciate each day as a gift, and had reinforced my cognizance of my own mortality. If my life were soon to end, could I look back and be fulfilled with how I had lived? Or would I wish I had done things differently?

Distraught over these looming concerns, one evening I drove to a college campus about thirty minutes from my house where I was to meet a friend for an exercise class. I strolled through the campus among the old buildings and well-established landscape, unable to find the class or my friend. Outwardly, the clear night's sky enhanced the beauty that surrounded me. Inwardly, however, I was consumed by turmoil that directly opposed the tranquility of the warm, pleasant evening.

As I wandered the campus, I came across one of the largest trees in the area, probably at least a couple hundred years old. I sat under it, leaned against its trunk, and began to cry. I cried for my sister, for the life that I no longer recognized, and for all the stresses and sorrows that I had endured over the past year. After the crash, I had forged ahead out of love for my children and parents, but had somehow lost sight of what I needed to do for myself.

Where was I to go, and what was I to do with my life? In the midst of searching for answers, I saw an image. Through tightly shut eyes, I saw one tiny glimmer, like the flicker of a single candle or the sparkle of one small star many light-years away. The instant I saw this one little sparkle of light among all the blackness, I felt hope that somehow there could be a purpose beyond all this pain. I came to realize that I should not be focusing on how and why things had happened in my life, but rather I had to learn to accept the changes. Eventually I stopped crying, collected myself, and headed for home.

Throughout the next several weeks, I began to adjust my priorities in a way that would reflect how my life had transformed, and that would allow me to more effectively care for my own needs. I decided that it was no longer good enough for me to be in a marriage lacking love, passion, sincerity, honesty, acceptance, and the many other qualities that were important to me, which all seemed to be so readily available in my close friendships. At that instant I knew I wanted and needed to divorce Tom. Immediately I drove to the office to share this realization with my mom. She comfortingly responded that she knew I had been unhappy for a long time, and that she was glad I was taking steps to remedy the situation. I was relieved to have finally come to this conclusion, and I knew I could always count on Mom's gentleness and support.

Part of this commitment to better my life also involved beginning the process of at least partially removing myself from the more overwhelming demands arising from the airline issues that had exhausted me over the past year. While there were engagements to which I had already dedicated myself, I wanted to try and refrain from becoming overloaded with additional obligations, for I needed to make room in my life to address the situation at home.

Even though the difficulties I had endured because of the airline had created great distress within me, I began to understand that the strength I had found in myself while going through that ordeal was what had allowed me to come to this conclusion regarding my marriage. Having survived the year of firsts, I was ready to initiate a transformation in my life and regain some control. I knew it wouldn't be easy, but I felt well on my way, having taken the initial and most difficult step by making the decision.

27

Although I had decided to make changes in my personal life, I refrained from taking immediate action, because pressing events to which I was already committed were approaching that took precedence over these more lasting adjustments. I had to make final preparations for my November trip to the inaugural meeting of the National Air Disaster Alliance held in Pittsburgh just a week and a half after the anniversary memorial service.

I felt anxious the day I was to leave town, as I knew I would be flying in foul weather. Waiting to board the aircraft, I found myself evaluating each of the other passengers, trying to assess which ones could be counted on in the event of an emergency. Once on the plane, I also made a mental note of where these passengers were seated.

During the short flight, rain pounded the aircraft, and at times the wind tossed it around, almost as if it were a toy. The storm worsened as we neared Pittsburgh. I gripped the armrests, praying that I would be safe and hoping that God would not take another member of our family. Just as we were about to touch down, one more gust of wind hurled us off the center of the runway. I held my breath. A moment later the wheels met the ground, jerking as they struggled to grip the runway. After I exited from the aircraft, a fellow passenger commented, "I'm surprised we landed safely. It seemed like we should have been cartwheeling down the runway." Grateful that I was securely inside the airport, I responded, "I felt the same way, and I'm very thankful to be having this conversation with you."

I arrived at my hotel, where the inaugural meeting was to take place, which was scheduled to last for two full days. After settling in, I joined the few others from Families of 4184 that were present, along with representatives from other air disasters. During our initial discussions, by-laws, membership status, and a five-year goal were addressed. In order to satisfy legal requirements for the formal establishment of the organization, election protocol was instituted for officers, a board of directors, administrators, and volunteers, along with policies regarding dissemination of information to the media. Additionally, a business plan was formulated that covered the current financial status of the organization, budget projections, fundraising goals, organizational structure, and the location of headquarters.

Throughout the course of the meeting, we examined air safety standards involving pilot and flight-attendant training, mechanics, air-traffic control, and other safety issues. Along with these more technical considerations, we also deliberated upon problems concerning families and survivors, delving into topics regarding post-crash emergency measures, which included airline preparedness, emergency-care plan implementation, and coordination with local authorities. Also pertaining to this was the idea for a third-party family advocate.

Adhering to the previously determined comprehensive agenda resulted in a most productive meeting. Upon leaving Pittsburgh, the workings of this new national organization that would help amend some of the wrongs in the airline industry were underway, and I felt some satisfaction in having played a part in igniting these calls for reform.

※ ※ ※

I had been home again for some time when the producers of the "Geraldo Talk Show" asked Jenny and me to appear on a program they were putting together on how airline disasters have changed lives. I declined the initial request, as I had begun preparing for divorce proceedings, and I was also occupied with business matters and everyday life. As usual, my hesitation was a product of my discomfort with publicity, especially regarding this sensitive subject; however, once again, my trepidation was overruled by remembering the steadfast efforts of Families of 4184 and the National Air Disaster Alliance, knowing that the more exposure we got for our cause, the greater our chances would be of transforming the flaws of the airline industry. Four days later I was on a plane to New York.

The day after our arrival, the limo driver picked Jenny and me up early in the morning. We met him dressed for the show, but had been specifically instructed not to fix our hair or put on any make-up. On our way to the television studio, we stopped at a beauty salon, where our hair was cut and styled. When we pulled up to the studio, a line of people waiting to get seats had already formed outside. After Jenny and I were escorted into the building, we entered the room where the make-up was done, and I was immediately directed to a table with a dozen roses sitting on top. When I read the attached card, I discovered that the flowers were an expression of love and well-wishes from my son, Jimmy, which filled me with gratitude on being so lucky as to have such thoughtful and supportive children.

Several of us sat around and chatted as we were called one by one to have our make-up done. Soon it was my turn, and the make-up artist breezed through her creation. When she handed me the mirror, I took one look at myself and gasped—the make-up was so thickly caked-on that I felt like I was no longer in my own skin. The make-up artist assured me I looked fine, claiming that such a look was necessary for television and the lighting. Personally, I didn't really care what look they wanted me to have, because I was not willing to compromise my own image and values just for television, and so I excused myself and went to the restroom, where I removed as much of the make-up as possible.

With our looks complete, we were led onto the stage and seated with several representatives of two other airline disasters; two of the women were survivors of a plane crash, while the other two had lost a loved one in a more recent tragedy. Just off the stage, in the front row of the audience, former NTSB Chairman Jim Burnett, former American Eagle pilot Stephen Fredrick, a relationship and behavioral expert, and a certified counselor of crash victims were in attendance to offer their expert opinions.

A few minutes later, Geraldo introduced the title of the show, "The Flight to Heartbreak," and with solemn music playing in the background, he went on to say that the show was about "heartbreak, loss, and lives that might have been;" it was about the pain carried by people whose lives have been forever changed by an air disaster.

Geraldo began with the most recent crash. As personal stories were shared, clips of air crashes and pictures of the loved ones being honored were projected on a large screen. During a commercial break, the producers said they were looking for us to display heightened emotions and relay our stories dramatically, but my emotions were the last thing I wanted to reveal on national television. After the other participants delivered their individual accounts, Geraldo then turned his attention to me, specifically asking for elaboration upon the circumstances of Patty and Patrick having taken that flight, and how I was notified that they had been victims of the crash.

As I began to speak, the screen exhibited what seemed to be larger-than-life pictures of Patty with her two boys. At one point Geraldo interjected, stating how much Patty and I looked alike. Pictures of the crash were then shown, detailing a field littered with airplane wreckage, personal effects, and an extraordinary number of stakes, and all the while, somber background music continued to play. Seeing oversized pictures of my sister and nephew in which they radiated with health and vitality made it difficult to remain composed while recounting my experiences.

Geraldo also inquired about the airline's nondisclosure of the burial of unidentified remains, as well as about the findings Tom and I made during the week of the preliminary hearing. I fought to tell the story without falling apart, knowing that the producers would have loved nothing more. In order to maintain my composure, I tried to build my response toward our recent progress in addressing the airlines' mishandling of post-crash concerns, both those specific to Flight 4184 and those pertaining to the national agenda; in my discussion, I briefly mentioned the Pittsburgh meeting as exemplifying the positive developments we were hoping to enact in the industry.

In order to supplement the more technical and professional aspects of the issues raised, the panel seated in the front row then gave a segment on airline safety and the counseling of victims' families. Jim Burnett, the former NTSB chairman, supported my dedicated stance toward the victims' families with the remark, "If more people in the aviation industry were intensively exposed to accident investigations and the experience of victims, perhaps we would have a different cultural attitude toward these events." I was thrilled to see another government official in such a high position assume a viewpoint of compassion and awareness rather than indifference, for such people are the vehicles that allow for the possibility of change.

The former chairman's statement was followed by the opinions of the counselor of crash victims, who insinuated that her role in alleviating the damage inflicted upon victims' families by the airlines was of greater importance than reforms in the industry. I responded to her position, arguing that if the airlines handled these situations in a manner that prevented additional trauma, then there would be a lesser need for the presence of counselors in the first place. Geraldo supported my comment, and with a burst of applause from the audience, the show concluded.

When I returned home, I didn't talk much about the show, because I didn't want to expose myself to public commentary. I hoped that when the production aired several weeks after filming, it would only be viewed by a handful of people I knew. What I didn't count on was that the day before this segment was to air, I was repeatedly featured in the advertising previews, which, of course, cancelled out any possibility for anonymity.

Not long after my televised appearance, I was asked to be included on a training tape to be used in the airline industry. Dr. Carolyn Coarsey was conducting interviews at a university production studio in Indiana that were to include approximately thirty individuals connected to at least a half-dozen airline crashes, in order to relay our experiences in facing such a crisis. The film was produced to aid airline personnel in responding more effectively to victims' families, in order to help eliminate the compounding emotional trauma of insensitive responses.

The filming session was certainly less dramatic than the one associated with network TV. Thankfully, such extravagances as the hair salons, make-up artists, and limo drivers required for the Geraldo show were not part of this production.

The taping went well; however, I still found it difficult to talk about the impact of the tragedy. Sometimes my grief felt as raw as when the crash had first occurred, and other times I could talk without emotional attachment. Despite the formidable nature of testifying to my experiences, I did not have the same qualms about partaking in this project that I had regarding my appearance on the Geraldo show, because I knew that sharing my story would help to advance the industry's progress in bettering their treatment of families.

All of my recent engagements had briefly taken me away from my personal concerns, but I felt that the delay had been worthwhile, for I was able to advocate for public awareness and support of the reforms that the other families and I had been struggling to enact. Following my return from Indiana, I felt like I was ready to resume tackling the changes I needed to institute in my own life, in order to secure a better life for my children and myself.

❦ 28 ❦

Before I knew it, another January was upon me, and that meant facing the prospect of enduring another birthday without Patty; this year, however, I was determined to adopt the joyous spirit with which Patty and I had always celebrated together in the past. At this time, I also saw my personal life entering a stage of transition, as I was in the midst of moving ahead with my intent to pursue a divorce, striving to maintain a positive outlook for the future, and preparing for my parents' departure.

Mom and Dad had decided to move to a new residence, about a three-and-a-half-hour drive away, in a small town in the northwest corner of Illinois. They had decided that a different location, scenery, and daily routine could only help ease their ongoing heartache. I would always support any decision my parents made; however, the timing rattled me, since I would have no family around to support me while I moved ahead with plans for my long-overdue divorce.

One afternoon, in order to take my mind off these upcoming and significant life-changes, I drove to a shopping mall to run a quick errand. Since I was in a hurry to get home, while in the department store I felt proud of myself for maintaining my focus and not allowing my eyes to drift off to the rows of tempting merchandise. But halfway to the escalator, I began to notice yet another strange phenomenon taking place, as though someone were standing behind me with their hands on my shoulders.

Then, as if someone were actually guiding me, I proceeded to weave in and out of several aisles until I arrived at a specific display within the jewelry department. A moment later, my hand found a particular area of the earring display, where amazingly, out of all the turn-stiles filled with hundreds of pairs of earrings, my fingers took hold of the most beautiful pair of penguin earrings I had ever seen. They were silver with a gorgeous, colorful stone in the middle. I was in awe.

Back when I had gotten my ears pierced, I had been at the mall with Patty and the kids, and had immediately known that I wanted a pair of penguin earrings, for this seemed to be an appropriate addition to our penguin collection. However, we encountered one obstacle after another, for no matter where Patty or I looked, we had not been able to find this particular design of jewelry. We searched for years to no avail, and I had eventually accepted that it would be pierced ears for me with no penguins.

Therefore, I could not believe that I had finally stumbled upon such an exquisite pair of penguin earrings. I figured that the earrings were surely quite expensive, and I worried that I didn't have enough money with me to buy them. Afraid to look, I slowly turned them over, only to see that the price had been marked down several times. I laughed out loud, suspecting that Patty had played a role in my find, as she had always been known to discover the best deals. I had spent approximately five years fruitlessly hunting for penguin earrings, and yet suddenly here they were, just one pair amongst the thousands displayed in the store. It was also only three days before our shared birthday, and so I laughed again, thinking, "Leave it to you, Patty, to make me buy my own birth-day gift!" With a huge smile on my face, I proudly presented this price-less treasure to the cashier. When I got home, I gingerly placed the earrings on a shelf because I wanted to wait the three days until January 12 to wear the earrings for the first time.

The morning of my birthday, I woke up and instantly rushed to put on the earrings. Remembering the lighthearted way in which I had been led to my gift made me realize how privileged I was to have a sister who had always surprised me with such thoughtful expressions of love over the years, and who somehow seemed to be continuing this practice, even in death. I recalled one particular occasion when I had returned home after a long, relaxing walk to find the largest and most beautiful bouquet of flowers I had ever seen—so wide that it extended far beyond the opening of the doorway to my house. Patty had unexpectedly come across the discarded flowers at our church/school complex, and thought of me when she saw them. Somehow, she had managed to squeeze this enormous bouquet into her car along with our five children before driving back to my house. She had gone through all this because I had been feeling low, and she thought that this gesture would cheer me up— which it did, but no more than the consideration and will behind her accomplishment in delivering me the flowers.

I smiled reminiscing about that day, and decided that this year I would celebrate our birthday by filling my thoughts only with the stories that spoke to Patty's loving and giving nature, and all the ways we had been able to complete one another's lives.

Following our birthday, the remainder of the month was spent moving forward with the details of my divorce, as well as packing up Mom and Dad's house. By the beginning of the next month, Mom and Dad had sold their house and relocated to their new residence. I was happy for them, but felt sad over their departure. However, I could not allow these emotions to get the best of me, since I had to figure out how to close the door on my old life, so that a new one could be opened.

༄ 29 ༄

I spent what was left of the winter months consumed in attending to my personal agenda, but I had still managed to keep up on the developments taking place within the airline industry. By the beginning of July 1996, I was on my way to Washington for a public meeting explaining the contents of the long-awaited NTSB final report revealing the probable cause of the crash of Flight 4184. The report's release had been repeatedly delayed until this time, twenty months after the crash, again due to the ongoing pressure from the French manufacturer ATR, as well as discrepancies between the opinions of the French government and the NTSB, all of which had caused this publication to be revised several times.

According to news articles, a suspected cause had been revealed within days of the crash, and was included in the first version of the final report completed nearly one year prior, but had not been publicly released due to arguments with the French government. Many family members were angry going into this final hearing, as the numerous postponements had resulted in what some referred to as a state of "emotional limbo." This sense of aggravation was exacerbated by the fact that much of the information disclosed during this meeting had also been briefly addressed during the preliminary hearing back in February 1995, although no conclusive determinations had been formed at that date. Thus, many family members felt that there was no reason that they should have been denied a timely resolution, seeing as how the evidence for the cause of the crash had been known for so long.

Regardless, the NSTB presented the results of the investigation, reporting that the factor playing the largest role in the probable cause of the crash was the "loss of control that occurred after a ridge of ice" built up on the wings. U.S. investigators placed the majority of the blame on the French manufacturer, ATR, while the French government accused the FAA of contributing to the crash by failing to uphold regulations consistent with the manufacturer's aircraft manual. This discrepancy resulted in the release of two volumes of the NTSB's final report, one reflecting the views of the NTSB, and the other containing the response of the French government.

In Volume I, the NTSB argued that despite France's aviation administration having been aware of the control problems, they had "failed completely to disclose" to U.S. regulators the known dangers of operating ATRs in freezing rain or drizzle. The report determined that the manufacturer, ATR, had been alert to the aircraft's control issues from five incidents prior to the crash of Flight 4184, including one fatal crash in which ice buildup also initiated the sudden roll of an ATR plane. It also maintained that the company had sufficient cause to modify the airplane and to provide pilots with adequate information about such dangers, but did not do so. The "All-Weather Operations" brochure for the aircraft was critiqued as being misleading and minimizing the known catastrophic potential of operating ATR planes in freezing rain. In addition, the NTSB criticized the FAA for their negligence in evaluating the aircraft as adhering to U.S. flight requirements. The NTSB ruled that the FAA had not properly monitored the airworthiness of ATR planes, and had taken insufficient measures to ensure that the aircraft-design standards for flying in icy weather were satisfactory. The report also concluded that the FAA contributed to the crash by failing to mandate that U.S. flight guidelines be updated to alert pilots about the potential hazards of operating in freezing rain, and by not requiring the manufacturer to remedy these problems. As the summary stated: "If the FAA had acted more positively upon the safety board's aircraft-icing recommendations issued in 1981, this accident may never have occurred."

The NTSB once again absolved the plane's pilots and air-traffic controllers, maintaining that given their lack of adequate warning about the dangers of flying ATR planes in freezing rain, the pilots had handled the plane properly. Investigators said the crew had no reason to expect loss of control.

Volume II of the report was comprised of responses from the manufacturer, ATR, and the French government to the NTSB's findings in Volume I, with which they strongly disagreed, maintaining that the NTSB's report was inaccurate and one-sided. The manufacturer told investigators it had provided the FAA with icing information regarding the aircraft, although the FAA claimed to the NTSB that they never received such warnings.

While many of the facts revealed during the proceedings merely expanded upon what we had previously been aware of, the NTSB also presented thirty-six new safety recommendations to the FAA, which included consistency in pilot training, modifying the ice-related safety features of ATR aircrafts, and outlining precautionary measures for ATRs in certain weather conditions. However, many family members remained skeptical, as these changes were merely recommendations that the FAA might or might not implement after considering the economic effect of its decisions on the airlines.

While the NTSB is considered an advocate for the traveling public, they only have the authority to propose safety recommendations, without the power to enforce compliance. The FAA is the organization responsible for regulating aviation safety, which includes choosing whether or not to implement the reforms suggested by the NTSB; however, the FAA is also known as the governmental body accountable for the commercial advancement of the aviation industry, creating a built-in conflict of interest.

Ultimately, no changes recommended by the NTSB could be enforced without the FAA fully supporting these proposals; thus, many families were left feeling frustrated at the ambiguous outcome of the final report, as there was no way to determine whether or not these proceedings would be successfully incorporated into FAA guidelines. To me, it seemed like these organizations, which were supposed to function as checks and balances to one another, had instead somehow wound up

clashing with one another, and as I sat listening to the recommendations, I wondered if the cycles of blame surrounding the circumstances
of this disaster would prevent these suggestions from being enforced.

❧ 30 ❧

After I returned home from the final NTSB hearing in Washington, instead of waiting for my divorce paperwork to be finalized, I decided to get a jumpstart on the inevitable and began preparing to move out of my house. Tom did not share my concerns about our marriage; he was content with staying in this partnership that I saw as unhealthy and emotionally incomplete, and to me, even his outlook on the situation reflected these problems. Knowing that nothing between us would ever really change, I refused to allow myself to become preoccupied with his perspective, and simply focused on moving ahead with my plans.

Thankfully, the legalities involved in my divorce went relatively smoothly, which was a nice break from the complicated and drawn-out struggles with the airline. I felt relieved that I had finally summoned the courage to act upon what I knew would be best for me and my children, and while I was aware that my choice came with added struggles, I was willing to accept these hurdles as a small price to pay for the prospect of one day leading a happier, more fulfilling life. Upon finding a new place to live, I walked out of my house for the last time, leaving behind almost sixteen years of a marriage defined by shattered dreams and broken promises.

I quickly settled into a small, two-bedroom apartment with my three children, which I found to be a much more appealing setting despite the lack of living space. I shared a room with my daughter, Nikki, while my two boys shared the other. Nikki was thrilled with our new surroundings, for she suddenly found herself in a situation that was akin to nightly "sleep-overs." Every evening, Nikki's excitement was apparent in the enthusiasm in her voice as she chattered away in the pitch-blackness of our room after the time for "lights out."

Meanwhile, Mom and Dad quickly became busy with their changed lives. The congestion of their former suburban lifestyle was replaced with a serene country setting of rolling hills and wooded areas densely populated with wildlife. Mom became treasurer of a charity group, while Dad became commander of the Veterans of Foreign War (VFW) association, and they both got involved in the church choir. Somehow they still always had time to be there for their daughter, even amongst the many different interests this more laid-back setting afforded them.

As the beginning of the school year approached in their small town, Dad fulfilled a dream of Patty's to teach religious classes at the local church, and he derived a great sense of pride from realizing one of Patty's wishes. While teaching, Dad told stories as subtle ways to impart important lessons to the children, similar to those he used to tell me and Patty when we were young.

It seemed as though my family had finally begun traveling down the path to peace; while we would never again be the same, we were all moving somewhere different than where we had been before the crash, creating new lives for ourselves that cherished the memory of what we had left behind. As time went on, there were more and more moments when I actually felt free of deeply rooted pain. While I felt like I was mostly progressing, there were still instances when I would again experience rushes of grief that would come on suddenly and without warning; any experience of blissfulness could be snatched away by a certain song on the radio, a specific thought or memory, or someone simply inquiring as to how I was doing. Not being able to predict what would trigger such reactions was quite disconcerting.

In general, the whole healing process was surprising to me, because I wasn't expecting to have what felt like these sudden surges propelling me backwards, and I wondered when they would stop, when I would be able to again feel "normal." As much as I wanted a life free of painful associations, a part of me refused to let myself forget—even though I

208

knew that I could never forget. I wanted so badly to continue moving forward, but sometimes I would have difficulty even defining what that meant; it seemed like I was stuck in limbo, having come too far to go back to where I had been, yet feeling uncertain as to the direction in which I should proceed. It took me some time to realize that even if I was moving aimlessly, I was still moving, and that regardless of the direction I chose to go, I was moving forward in the sense that I never allowed myself to lay down and accept defeat.

❧ 31 ❧

The oscillating emotions that I experienced throughout my struggle to find some lasting sense of peace were complicated by the fact that I still had to face daily reminders of the tragedy in order to continue pursuing Jonathon's case against the airline. Throughout the months following the deposition, both the airline and my attorney had been compiling information that would assist in reaching a settlement either through negotiations or a trial. In September 1996, I received a copy of the third amended complaint (as my original complaint had been revised several times throughout the legal process), as well as a duplicate of an order entered by the judge assigned to this case, indicating that particular issues of litigation would be governed by the law of the state in which each victim had lived, as opposed to the state where the crash had occurred.

Indiana law had already been applied to five settled cases pertaining to the crash of Flight 4184, as it had been home to those victims. Apparently, certain laws in Indiana were known to be quite restrictive in a way that would benefit the airline during litigation, and the outcomes of these five cases had led the airline to seek a ruling mandating that Indiana law govern claims made by the remaining thirty-three non-Indiana plaintiffs. Thus, the judge's ruling denied the airline's request by upholding the law of domicile, and was viewed as a victory for plaintiffs not living in Indiana. At the time I obtained the amended complaint and a copy of the judge's order, I was also informed of the judge's decision to choose only four to six cases to prepare for trial; these ensuing settlements would then be used as a guideline for settling the other cases.

In building Jonathon's case, my attorneys drafted a "Pretrial Settlement Memorandum," a fourteen-page document comprised of an introduction, the analysis of damages, and the settlement offer, all to be used for the sole purpose of facilitating pretrial settlement discussions. Upon completing the report, my attorneys sent it to me for review. The introduction stated that Patty and Patrick had boarded American Eagle Flight 4184 from Indianapolis to Chicago on October 31, 1994; additionally, it revealed that while in its holding pattern, the aircraft had suffered an uncommanded roll that resulted in the plane's impact with the ground, all of which caused my sister and nephew to suffer fatal injuries.

The analysis of damages began by citing the judge's recent ruling that the law of domicile would control the calculation of damages from trauma inflicted upon the victims just prior to their deaths, referred to as "pre-death damages." Throughout the memorandum, many previously settled cases were cited supporting the stance established by the judge's decision. The document went on to itemize the losses Jonathon had suffered as a result of Patty's death, and also included a detailed report from an outside service calculating the predictable age to which Patty would have lived. Having died at 37.8 years of age, the experts estimated a life expectancy of another 43.2 years, seeing as how Patty had always been in good health. Suggested figures for her loss of wages and employee benefits as the president of our company were figured, along with the loss of household services, and a projection of personal consumption was also indicated. Ten pages of numbers and dollar signs revealed the estimated deficits in each category from October 31, 1994, to the remainder of her expected life span.

The document went on to mention how Patty had loved her children unconditionally, and had a wonderful and exemplary relationship with them that extended far beyond what one would consider average. It disclosed that she was the primary source of behavioral instruction, entertainment, love, and moral and religious guidance for her children, and argued that the discovery deposition had merely touched upon the strength of these relationships.

The circumstances leading to Jonathon having to take a separate flight from his mother and brother were detailed, naming the airline agent who issued Patty's and Patrick's boarding passes, as well as the ramp agent who assisted them onto the plane. That agent had recalled that Patty and Patrick were the last two passengers to board, and that they had sat near the rear of the plane, which differed from the information in the Passenger Seating Manifest that listed their seats as 2C and 2D.

The memorandum reviewed the chain of events leading up to the crash, giving a slightly more detailed account than I had heard at the preliminary hearing. The plane had departed the gate at 2:14 p.m. but did not actually take off until 2:56 p.m. central standard time, forty-six minutes later than scheduled. After taking off, the plane ascended to approximately 16,000 feet, which it reached by 3:12 p.m. At that time, it began a descent to 10,000 feet, which was reached at 3:18 p.m., and was then maintained as the plane circled in the assigned holding pattern. At approximately 3:46 p.m., the last announcement heard by Patty and Patrick came from the captain apologizing for the delays, giving an update on the hold, and reassuring passengers that there still might be time for them to make their connections, since most flights were probably delayed. The plane then continued circling at 10,000 feet until approximately 3:56 p.m., at which time Chicago Air Traffic Control instructed Flight 4184 to descend to and maintain an altitude of 8,000 feet.

The crash sequence was then overviewed, documenting its start at 3:57:29 p.m., when, according to the Digital Flight Data Recorder (DFDR), the airplane's autopilot disconnected, instantly causing an uncommanded roll; the plane then dove for about twenty-seven seconds prior to impact. The memorandum documented the DFDR's last recording of all available parameters as occurring four seconds before impact; the DFDR indicated that "the aircraft was at an altitude of 3,303 feet" with a pitch of "61 degrees down" and "traveling at a speed of 351 knots." Partial parameters were recorded within these last four seconds, which designated "airspeeds up to 373 knots and g-forces accelerating up to 5.2009 prior to impact." One knot is equivalent to approximately one-and-one-eighth miles per hour, which translates to a speed of approximately 425 miles per hour. A g-force is a unit of force;

one G is equal to the force of gravity exerted upon a body at rest on the Earth's surface, of which the force pulling down the plane was over five times more powerful.

These descriptions of the horrific final moments before the crash, emphasizing the power with which the plane had blasted into the field, immediately led into an analysis of Patty's distress levels throughout the duration of the crash sequence. The report asserted that her panic would have been compounded by the fact that she had to consider not only herself, but also the welfare of her young son. It acknowledged that while we would never know exactly what Patty did in those final twenty-seven seconds of her life, we could be sure that she was well aware of imminent death.

Adding to the gut-wrenching details contained in the document was the transcription of the cockpit voice recorder, which revealed a period of four-tenths of a second between the initial crunching sounds of the crash and the loss of electrical power. The mere fact that the voice recorder continued documenting sounds during this brief interval allowed for the conclusion that the nose-first impact would have resulted in over half a second delay for people like Patty and Patrick seated in the rear of the aircraft, which led to the inference that they had suffered an awareness of disfigurement prior to death. Even though a fraction of a second seemed logically inconsequential, this description forced me to keenly visualize the horrific scene that had ensued during this flash of time that in my mind seemed like an eternity. Consequently, I forbade myself from looking any further into the record of this haunting and traumatic imagery.

After a night's rest, I hesitantly resumed reading with a section that gave a brief synopsis of the efforts of the agencies involved in the removal of human remains and personal effects at the site, which had begun at sunrise on November 2. On November 9, government investigators had turned the site over to the airline for decontamination and removal of several inches of topsoil.

On November 14, the FBI removed their personnel from the crash site, relinquishing to the airline control of their inventories and computer database. Subsequently, on November 15 and 16, the airline had conducted a mass burial of unidentified remains without notifying family members. The report argued that the airline's burial was a premeditated action, and that their shipment of the remains to the cemetery was conducted at night to conceal detection. It also mentioned that personal effects and human remains had existed at the crash site as late as February 1995, which was when my husband and I had made our discoveries during the week of the preliminary hearing.

Based on all the enclosed information and analyses, my attorneys concluded the memorandum with a recommended final settlement amount for the airline to provide for Jonathon.

With my review of the document having been completed, my attorneys requested a picture of Patty and her two boys to use as the cover page for the pretrial document. I gave them a color photograph showing Patty happily smiling with her arms wrapped around her two vivacious boys. This external placement of a portrait so full of love and life severely contradicted the internal contents detailing descriptions of death and destruction.

Not long after the final changes were made to the memorandum, the law firm informed me that in order to prepare for the trial as effectively as possible, a video reenactment of the flight from the moment the plane made its initial roll to the point of impact was going to be created. I had already seen a video simulation during the week of the preliminary hearing, and so at least I knew what to expect; what I was not anticipating to hear was that this video reenactment, through computerized animation, would include the perspective not only from outside the plane, but also from the point of view of what the passengers inside may have experienced.

All at once I formed a mental picture of the atmosphere inside the cabin. I saw it all quite vividly—the panic, the fear, the time distortion. Patty's natural instincts to fight for her own life and that of her child must have kicked in, but what would she have fought against? The unforeseeable conditions causing the plane's roll and subsequent dive? The unimaginable and inescapable power of the G-forces?

I could not rid myself of these impressions, and the more I tried, the sharper they became. About an hour later, I called the director of litigation at the law firm, requesting that if a video reenactment was to be made, for it to include a mother attempting to care for her young child. If this case went to trial, I wanted the jury to see for themselves the sheer terror and helplessness my sister would have experienced, an especially crucial point given that the airline had attempted to minimize the possibility of suffering prior to the crash.

My continued engagement with the legal process in many ways seemed like a double-edge sword, for in my eyes, settling early with the airline would have contributed to perpetuating an unjust system that allowed corporations to defy moral and written standards, but settling early may have also allowed me to put the tragedy behind me sooner. Regardless of what may have helped me most, my pain and anger over the crash, as well as what seemed to be the airline's many injustices, had compelled me to seek truth in the face of inconsistencies. Even though I may have chosen the more grueling path, I knew that it would have been far more difficult for me to have done nothing at all.

❦ 32 ❧

The joining together of families of crash victims and survivors had led to the creation of the National Air Disaster Alliance back in August of 1995, and the efforts of this organization, along with various governmental agencies, had finally resulted in the passing of the Aviation Disaster Family Assistance Act of 1996. On October 9, 1996, many families gathered in Washington, D.C., to witness the signing of this document by President Bill Clinton, and to celebrate our goals having finally come to fruition.

The endorsement of this Act initiated the process of eliminating the airlines' control over situations arising in the immediate aftermath of air disasters by broadening the power of the NTSB. The changes mandated by the Act were divided into several sections, the first of which covered the NTSB's newly acquired responsibilities for providing assistance to families of air disaster victims; the NTSB was to designate an organization to assume the position of family advocate, become the coordinator for communication between families and governmental agencies, and act as a mediator between the families and the airlines.

The next section of the Act required all major airlines to formulate plans and submit them to the DOT and the NTSB within six months of the date the Act was passed. Specifically, these plans were to act as guidelines for airlines following a crash; at minimum, they were to include policies to assure that families are promptly notified of the tragedy by the assigned family advocate or other appropriately trained individuals, passenger lists are provided to the NTSB and family advocate, families are consulted about the disposition of all remains and personal effects, all unclaimed possessions are retained for at least eighteen months, families have knowledge of the construction and inscription of all monuments to passengers, and assistance is provided to families traveling to the location of a crash. This section of the Act was concluded with the mandate that the airlines pledge ample resources to assure the enactment of the provisions outlined in their plans.

The last major stipulation contained within the Act included the establishment of a task force comprised of family members, airline representatives, and members of various governmental organizations in order to develop a model plan for handling the aftermath of air disasters, which was to then be drafted into a report and presented to Congress within one year of the passing of this legislation.

Back when Jenny, Doug, and I were listing the concerns of Families of 4184 so that they could be incorporated into the larger national agenda during the Pittsburgh meeting, I had never imagined that one piece of legislation would address not only the problems specific to our crash, but also those that were raised by the mishandling of other post-crash situations. As I read through the Act, I noticed that each and every one of the issues that we had drafted for the Washington meeting the previous year was covered, almost as though our preliminary outline had simply been expanded upon, with not one of our concerns being dismissed. At that moment, I realized that all the difficulties I had encountered throughout this whole process had not been in vain, for even though I still faced my legal battle with the airline, this piece of legislation would ensure that, in the future, others would not have to endure such trying and traumatic struggles. Although I knew that this Act could not change the reality of what had transpired, in an inexplicable way I felt like I had managed to find some form of justice for Patty and Patrick. This whole process had made me aware of my own strength, because I knew that regardless of my unrelenting pain I had never stopped fighting for what I believed to be right. This knowledge helped me to live beyond the sudden end to all that I had once understood my life to be.

The passing of the Act quickly initiated the process of reform. The following month, I flew to Washington, where the NTSB had invited family members and survivors of air disasters to a breakfast meeting in order to help them determine how to best assess the needs of families in the wake of an air tragedy. After breakfast, Vice President Al Gore joined families in a formal session to discuss the new legislation, with a heightened focus on generating ideas for the new task force mandated by the Act.

Later that day, a separate hearing initiated by the White House Commission on Safety and Security, and overseen by the chairman of the NTSB, afforded families the opportunity to present either written or oral testimony to the Commission. This Commission was created by President Clinton and led by Vice President Gore, and had been established just prior to the signing of the Family Assistance Act. The Commission was responsible for addressing a milieu of issues in the aviation industry, amongst them the concern that more compassionate and effective assistance to the families of victims would be provided, which supplemented what had already been mandated by the Act. During testimony, survivors and families of victims from numerous air disasters addressed areas of concern ranging from safety to more personal issues.

Even amid states of grief and personal struggles, the unification of so many families to demand provisions for a better future had a profound effect. Not only had our courage been the catalyst to enacting change, but our efforts had also opened the door for meaningful progress to occur in the industry, and I felt privileged to have been afforded the opportunity to witness the continued movement toward reform.

❧ 33 ❧

A short time after my return from Washington, Jenny and I sent out a final newsletter to the families of Flight 4184. Our smaller group had become incorporated into the national organization, and from then on those interested in aligning themselves with this cause became active participants in the National Air Disaster Alliance, which continued to promote airline safety, ensure family and survivor rights, and provide support to all victims of air disasters. Our last newsletter gave an overview of the past two years, and extended blessings to everyone in their ongoing road to healing.

I decided that this was the point at which I could finally disengage from my formal involvement with airline issues, for not only was the national organization effectively and efficiently organized, but my main concerns had also been addressed by the passing of the new legislation. While Families of 4184 was no longer a formal entity, we had all promised to keep in touch and maintain the friendships that had developed. Each and every one of the people I had come to know through my involvement with our group had become integral parts of my life, in that we had all helped one another through the bleakest of times, and I knew that they had been indispensable to my ability to move beyond my trauma and despair.

Even though I had chosen not to actively participate in any official organization, I still devoted a part of my life to the memory of the tragedy, frequently corresponding with outsiders who had either been directly involved with the crash or touched by it in some way. Those of all ages came to Patty's and Patrick's crosses to honor their lives. One young boy, not much older than Patrick, asked his mother to help him pick out the perfect pumpkin, which they then brought to the memorial site on Halloween, placing it next to Patrick's cross. The little boy had his mother write Patrick a letter expressing what he wanted to say, being too young to do so himself. Notes were also left at Patty's cross extending sympathies and prayers; many of these people disclosed that for inexplicable and unknown reasons, they had felt drawn to Patty's memorial, and had been compelled to reach out to her family.

The number of messages was almost overwhelming, but I was touched by each and every outreach of support. In addition, such correspondences often offered valuable details concerning events that had transpired in the immediate aftermath of the tragedy. Just as the woman had come forward at the preliminary hearing in Indianapolis to describe the injustices she felt the airline had committed, either in person or through letters, many other workers also began to voice what they had witnessed after the crash, feeling they could no longer abide by their employers' demands of secrecy. Their perception of the wrongs that had been inflicted upon the families prompted them to convey the reality of their experiences.

I met with many of these individuals, which led to my acquisition of confidential documents from different agencies associated with the clean-up and identification process. I passed on to my attorney what I thought was the most pertinent information. These documents contained facts that completely contradicted what the airline had initially presented to us as truth.

Several of the people who contacted me were employed by the National Guard; this organization was intricately involved in handling the tragedy's aftermath, and the report of their daily efforts at the crash site was filled with haunting and gruesome testimonies. The National Guard report documented numerous instances that illuminated the extent to which the lives of these men and women had been irreversibly changed from their participation in the recovery attempts for Flight 4184. Originally trained as medics, the men and women who were assigned to or volunteered for this job would have typically provided medical care;

however, seeing as how the crash left no survivors, these individuals had then assumed that they would be responsible for the personal possessions prior to their return to the families, or for securing the crash site. None of them had been prepared for their assigned role as "trackers," which basically meant that they were in charge of recording and washing everything that had been removed from the field, including both personal effects and human remains.

Early in the clean-up process, headquarters for the various agencies working the site had been moved from the local high school to the National Guard Armory, not far from where the crash had occurred. It was there that airline personnel had set up their station, along with the State Emergency Management Agency (SEMA), the Federal Emergency Management Agency (FEMA), the Federal Bureau of Investigation (FBI), the Indiana State Police, the United States Armed Forces Institute of Pathology (which assisted the coroner), the Cook County Medical Examiners Office, the Indiana National Guard, and the Indiana Funeral Directors Association.

By the third day after the crash, the drill floor of the National Guard Armory had been turned into a morgue. Any debris suspected to contain human remains had been placed in red bags at the crash site, kept in refrigerated storage trucks, and eventually hauled to the morgue to be retrieved by a National Guard tracker. After obtaining a bag, the tracker's first task had been to open it and spread out the contents to be photographed. Sifting through these loads required a lot of caution, as there was no way to predict what might be encountered; sharp pieces of the airplane structure had often been mixed in with personal effects and human remains, creating a potentially dangerous situation for the tracker. To assist the coroner in discovering the identity of the passengers, trackers were required to move victims' remains through a number of stations, including photography, dental, pathology, x-ray, and finger printing. Trackers had also regulated all collected data by cataloging everything recovered from the crash site, assuring that it was done with detailed accuracy.

All personal items, including handwritten notes, schedules, family pictures, and jewelry, were isolated and delivered to a separate cleaning area. The trackers responsible for the personal effects had become back-logged each day due to the time and precision they devoted to cleaning each item. Many of them later told me that they had worked as though for their own loved ones, hoping to convey their empathy for the fami-lies through the thoroughness of their efforts.

At the National Guard Armory, the room assigned to airline per-sonnel had displayed walls lined with rolls of brown paper where each victim's name was written; substantial space was left underneath for their physical description, along with any personal items family members in-dicated the victim may have had in their possession at the time of the crash. Everyone I spoke to easily recalled Patrick's name written on the large sheets of paper as "Master Patrick Henry"—"master" being the title used to refer to young children. In a strikingly similar account to that of the man with whom I had spoken at the preliminary hearing, who had found Patrick's Ninja Turtle shoes and workbook in the field, the guardsman who cleaned Patrick's shoes revealed that he had also broken down and cried when handling the small shoes, as they were a very real reminder of his own young son.

A Guardsman I spoke with mentioned that within the walls of the armory, it had been easy to see the individual journeys made throughout the lives of the sixty-eight individuals that had simultaneously perished in the Indiana farm field. Many of the passengers' future plans were found at the crash site, recorded on what had become torn and muddy pieces of paper from schedule books outlining activities for the following day, the following week, and the following year.

Compounding the harrowing nature of the trackers' assignment was the constant risk of infection, as microbes from around the world could have been present, given the diverse backgrounds of the passen-gers on board the plane. Initially, the site had not been fully understood or taken seriously as a biohazard. Many of the workers had not been aware that biohazardous conditions were not solely a product of people carrying communicable diseases; rather, when human tissue is exposed to open air, bacteria can grow independently and be easily transferred by flies or the touching of items. As a result of this lack of understanding, many workers had been contaminated and had spread the infectious bacteria because of the lack of proper decontamination procedures.

Moreover, each day the workers were faced with decaying human remains and airplane fuel, which not only brought a risk of infection, but also carried a smell different from anything they had ever encountered. They put Vicks or oil of wintergreen on their protective facemasks to help diminish the intensity of the odors; but many revealed that thereafter, those previously pleasant scents served to remind them only of death and decay.

These extreme conditions required an inordinate amount of supplies and equipment. The recovery efforts lasted over two weeks, and some of the items used in a one-week period alone included 6,500 pairs of gloves, 3,795 boot/shoe covers, 2,241 coveralls, 1,700 masks, 74 respirators, and 51 pairs of goggles.

Throughout the fourteen days that the National Guard trackers were handling the remains and items cleared from the field, several different agencies had assumed and then relinquished control of the recovery process. This constant shift in administrative management led to frequent changes in protocol, often mandating that already completed work be redone; this added stress, exacerbated by the rapid rate at which the human remains began to decompose, inflicted additional depression and agitation upon the National Guardsmen. Most of the trackers at one time or another experienced emotional breakdowns from having to process approximately 200 to 250 individual human remains each day. To make matters worse, the National Guard soldiers had been prohibited from discussing the details of their duties with anyone, not even family or friends. They had been afforded sleeping arrangements with orders not to go home. Some slept from exhaustion at the end of their twelve-hour shifts, while others were afraid to sleep because of recurrent nightmares. In order to help ease some of these adverse psychological effects, two chaplains, along with Red Cross counselors, were made available to the trackers.

Even with these support measures in place, by the ninth day of the clean-up process each of the trackers had removed themselves from the morgue at one time or another out of complete distress, and all original personnel were eventually replaced due to extreme mental strain.

In the National Guard's report, trackers were referred to as having become both victims and survivors — a description that I had also become familiar with, as it was often used to characterize the families. The magnitude of the entire project deeply impacted all those present during the efforts; the Guardsmen I spoke with assured me that they had all worked to the best of their abilities, which included keeping the identified remains of family members together, and they specifically mentioned being exceptionally careful to keep Patty alongside Patrick at all times. The distress endured by the workers led them to seek some type of closure, the general consensus amongst them being that the opportunity to meet with the families might allow them to regain some peace. Individuals had come forward at the preliminary hearing to reveal their stories, and since that time I had crossed paths with many others, whether by chance or deliberately, and had listened to their grief-stricken accounts. Such benevolent and considerate feelings were voiced in a letter sent to me by one of the workers I met during the week of the preliminary hearing:

> *I am not very good at expressing myself but just want you to know that I care very much and it meant a lot to be able to meet you and the other family members.*
>
> *I felt as if I became very close to Patty and Patrick and all the other people from the plane. I am glad my friends and I were there to help care for them. I wouldn't have wanted strangers to be there if it had been my family. I know I really am a stranger and I can't even begin to imagine your pain, but somehow those people became like family to me and I didn't feel like a stranger. That might not make sense to you; it doesn't to many of the people around me. But my friends and I became very protective and nurturing toward your loved ones. I wanted to talk to their family members, but I was afraid because of*

*everything those in charge told us. I would like to be on the
mailing list for your newsletter.*

*As tragic as the whole thing is, I am a strong believer that
the crash victims are in a better place now, and I do take comfort that they live on and I will meet them face to face one day.*

*My thoughts and prayers have always been with you,
Terri. I am not very eloquent but I hope your pain can be less-
ened by knowing how much I and all the others really did care
for your loved ones.*

While there were workers such as this one who had come forward
shortly after the crash to express their condolences, others initially remained in obscurity and silence due to hard feelings they had developed
toward the families as a result of misleading information dispensed by
the airline. Apparently, many of them had inquired about the memorial
services the airline held only days after the crash. The services were open
to the families, public, airline personnel, and news media; yet, airline officials had told the workers not to attend the services, claiming that the
families would view their presence as an intrusion. Of course, this statement could not have been further from the truth—the airline had come
to this conclusion without consulting or informing the families. In actuality, we appreciated the opportunity to meet those who had cared for
our family members; however, as we had not been aware that the airline
had discouraged them from reaching out to us, we had no way of coun-
tering the false implications of the message at that time.

Almost two weeks after the crash, caskets had arrived at the armory
and the embalming process was started. Not long after, the identified remains had been shipped to the families for burial. This was another
emotional time for those who had come to know our loved ones in
death, as these workers, having seen the first of the caskets upon their arrival, also watched as the last of the caskets were shipped out. A National
Guardsman told me that those in command had not allowed the workers to see Patrick's small casket, as they thought it would have just been
too traumatic.

When the time had come to collect all of the unidentified remains for the mass burial, many of the workers reported observing caskets so stuffed with body parts that it was difficult just to get them closed and locked. After the caskets of unidentified remains had been transported to a local cemetery, the workers again inquired about attending this mass burial service. For the second time, the airline maintained that the next of kin did not want any of the workers in attendance, despite the fact that the families had not even been notified of the burial. At this point, many workers began to hold a grudge against the families, as they had no reason to doubt the airline's claims. Meanwhile, the families had been oblivious to all that was transpiring—the small service held by the funeral directors at the local cemetery, the existence of the mass burial site, and the workers' desire to be involved with the closing ceremonies of the tragedy. By keeping the workers and families apart, the airline seemed to hope that the truth about the burial of unidentified remains and the destruction of personal effects would continue to be hidden from the families.

Of course, we eventually did uncover the truth of what had happened, and in spite of the airline's efforts to keep us apart, the families and the workers eventually made contact, largely due to the gathering we had held prior to the airline's memorial service for the unidentified remains, to which we had invited many of the workers. Any harbored tension between the two groups seemed to dissolve upon that first meeting. The spiraling web of lies that the airline seemed to have woven in order to obscure the reality of their actions in the end had only served to illuminate their own lack of integrity.

In addition to what I discovered from speaking with workers and reading the National Guard report, I gained further knowledge as to the extent of the devastation at the crash site from another account of the tragedy written by an emergency-room surgeon. He had also worked in hospital morgues, but reported that despite all of his experience, he had still been poorly prepared for what he had witnessed. Before reading his account, I had become accustomed to gruesome, yet generic, testimony, as none of the documents had contained details pertaining to any particular individual. Thus far, I had not been shocked by the contents of any of these stories; however, as soon as the doctor began describing his first observations upon entering the field, the next thing I knew I was reading about a four-year-old child's hand with an adult finger still clutched tightly in its fist. Instantly, I burst into tears, knowing Patrick had been the only child on the plane. Suddenly, it was confirmed in my mind that not only had Patty been aware of her imminent fate, but that Patrick had been as well.

Besides feeling physically ill, I again became furious at the airline for continually trying to minimize the impact of the crash on its victims. They had repeatedly insisted that no pain or suffering had occurred prior to impact, yet how tightly must little Patrick have held onto his mother's finger in order for his grip to withstand an impact at over 425 mph?

All of these stories demonstrated that the impact of this tragedy reached far and wide, well beyond the worlds of the families, and what had transpired throughout the process of handling its aftermath was a testament to both the best and worst sides of human nature. While the airline's behavior was oftentimes heinous and inexcusable, the actions of complete strangers would often help to fill my heart with hope and love. Ultimately, at least fifty-five organizations and individuals were involved with the recovery process, from firemen and other such responders that had the training needed to assist crash-site workers, to massage therapist associations that just wanted to help in whatever way possible. In particular, the Red Cross was indispensable to the relief efforts, for they provided psychological and medical support to the workers of the various agencies present, voluntarily dedicating their time and resources to assist those that were so deeply affected by what they experienced at the crash site. As I reflected upon the wide variety of people and organizations that had reached out to these workers, I was touched by the sense of community that presided over the process that involved my sister and nephew being laid to rest.

❧ 34 ❧

As the days, weeks, months, and years continued to pass by following the crash, I came to understand that there was quite a bit of truth behind the idea that the more things change, the more they stay the same. Throughout the year following my attorney's drafting of the Pretrial Settlement Memorandum, negotiations had been underway between my attorney and the airline to determine an appropriate amount of money to be awarded to Jonathon, but none of these discussions had resulted in a satisfactory conclusion. Thus, by July of 1997, I was *still* engrossed in such legalities, and my preparatory efforts were intensifying because a tentative trial date had been scheduled for September. The airline was beginning to make more serious offers to settle out of court; although substantially higher than their previous proposals, as far as I was concerned, these offers were still grossly inadequate compensations for my sister's life and the trauma Jonathon had sustained as a result of the airline's indiscretions throughout the aftermath of the tragedy. The judge assigned to our case even commented to my attorneys that he had heard my interviews on television, and that he thought there was more to the story than the airline seemed willing to acknowledge.

Around this time, the director of litigation at the law firm came to my apartment to discuss the case. During his visit, he perused the many photo albums I had put together over time journaling the memories of my family. For two and a half years he had heard about our family's closeness, witnessing how it sustained my drive to seek some form of justice, and yet he admitted he was surprised at the extent to which Patty and I had been integral parts of one another's lives, as well as how our two families had developed as a single unit.

As we discussed the final pretrial preparations, he handed me an additional set of interrogatories that I needed to fill out. The interrogatories were to be completed in anticipation of another deposition set for early August, only weeks away from the expected mid-September trial date. The questions again addressed the events that transpired following the crash, demanding more elaborate descriptions than I had offered during the first deposition, and I was required to provide supplementary details regarding the alleged "intentional, reckless or grossly negligent conduct" of the airline.

On the date of the deposition, my attorney and I arrived at the same office building where the previous deposition had taken place two years earlier. I was greeted by the female attorney who had first questioned me on behalf of the airline's insurance company. She was accompanied by a representative of the plane manufacturer, ATR. The publication of the NTSB's final report had indicated that ATR was at least partially accountable for the crash having taken place, and so ATR, along with the airline, was determined to be liable for damages ensuing from Patty's death. However, the airline was also charged as being responsible for the damages inflicted by their mishandling of circumstances throughout the aftermath of the crash.

As this second deposition began, I was asked to recap my experiences the night of the crash, as well as to re-explain what my parents and I had encountered in dealing with airline personnel. I substantiated my previous testimony with what I had subsequently learned from a discussion with a retired airline employee, who at the time of the crash had been instructed by airline management not to reveal any specifics to the families, and to keep our calls on hold for an indefinite period of time.

After I *again* testified to the sequence of events that transpired the night of the crash, I was requested to reiterate the details of the airline's deceptive treatment of the mass burial and unidentified remains; it almost seemed like someone had pushed the rewind button on a recording of the first deposition, as I was virtually repeating my testimony, except this time I was asked to provide further evidence of my allegations. With the hope of dismantling the airline's claim of not having had control over the handling of remains, and of not having been apprised of the mass burial service when it had occurred, I arrived prepared to prove that not only had they been cognizant of the day-to-day progressions concerning the tragedy's aftermath, but that they had also been instrumental in the planning and enactment of what had taken place. While speaking to various workers, families, and other personnel involved with the events ensuing after the crash, I had been advised of a person the airline had hired to appear before a judge in Indiana to obtain death certificates for the unidentified remains *prior* to the mass burial, and I relayed the name and payment information for this individual to the attorney conducting the deposition. I explained that he had also been hired by the airline to oversee the embalmment process, and I provided the date he had been contracted.

Additionally, I used the contradictory statements in the airline's letters to demonstrate the inaccuracy of their initial claim to have been ignorant of the mass burial's occurrence, and went on to reveal that upon discoveries made by several family members, the airline relinquished this position by admitting that it had taken place, but still maintained that they had not known at the time. I was able to further hinder the airline's case by identifying Care Team members assigned to several of the other families, who disclosed that once the airline had no longer been able to deny their involvement in the mass burial, management had blamed the cover-up on a miscommunication between them and their own Care Team. Ironically, the Care Team had been oblivious to all of this because the airline's management had lied to them about the mass burial's occurrence as well, proven by the fact that many of the Care Team members had contacted their assigned families extremely distraught upon finding out the truth.

Along with exposing the airline's deceitful treatment of the burial, I also addressed what I had learned about body parts being sent to the wrong families. When the attorney questioned whether we had viewed Patty's and Patrick's remains, I stated that at the time we had no motive to confirm that they were actually inside the caskets, as we could see no reason why the airline would lie about such a thing.

The subject of the deposition next moved to my perceptions of the airline's suspicious management of the crash site. I relayed information about the confidentiality agreement the airline had required of the second environmental company hired to clean the field. Just as I had two years prior, I found myself describing the discoveries that Tom and I had made at the crash site during the preliminary hearing, as well as how we had handled the return of those items, which were the first personal effects that the families had received. The attorney inquired as to my more recent visits to the site, which after two and a half years continued to produce plane wreckage, personal effects, and human remains. During my last trip, I found a significant portion of the plane with grooves that at one time seemed to have encased an interior window; this was the largest piece of wreckage I had come across thus far. Additionally, I listed the personal effects I recently discovered in the field, the largest being a leather belt with a buckle on the end of it. In response to a question about the several human bone fragments I saw still lying on the ground, I stated that I had picked up and examined what I found, but had subsequently laid the items back where I had found them.

Near the end of the deposition, the airline's lawyer returned her focus to the person who had gone before the judge to request death certificates for the unidentified remains, wondering if I had been aware of this person either before or during the time he went to see the judge. Instantly angry and offended, I felt as if the question was an attempt to pin some blame on me by insinuating that I had been aware of these occurrences at that time, which would have effectively undermined my complaints against the airline. I snapped that if I had known of the request for death certificates, then I would have also been informed of the upcoming burial, which I most certainly had not been. Fuming, I sat for some time in anticipation of the next question; a short while later, my attorney finally broke the silence by asking, "So your answer would be no?" I shot the airline's attorney one last look before firmly stating, "So my answer is no."

This deposition again involved several grueling hours of questioning before I was able to head home. In spite of having completed my testimony, the whole ordeal gnawed at my remaining stamina for reliving everything that had transpired with the airline. I just could not believe that after nearly three years the airline was still playing the same games that had aroused my anger in the first place. Throughout the weeks preceding the scheduled trial date, I could feel more and more of my energy depleting; ever since that day of the crash all that time ago, I had awoken each morning and attended to duties of motherhood and work, while simultaneously trying to find the will to continue battling the airline. With the end finally in sight, I was almost in awe of my own enduring ability to withstand the airline's ridiculous maneuvers.

Each time I felt my stamina fading, I would remember my unfulfilled promise to Patty to raise Jonathon, which would instantly reignite my determination to see this through to a satisfactory end. Despite the fact that the outcome of the custody hearing had limited my power to directly participate in Jonathon's upbringing, I was still intent on using all of my available resources to help him, and I felt as though I was at least partially honoring Patty's request by fighting to help provide him with a better future.

Thus, I remained in frequent contact with my attorney so that I would know of any changes or developments taking place with Jonathon's case. Just weeks before the trial was set to begin, I received a phone call bearing some important news. The judge had previously decided to choose only four to six cases to prepare for trial, allowing their outcomes to stand as representatives for all the other suits pertaining to the crash of Flight 4184. He had recently selected which cases to pursue, and Jonathon's was one of those chosen. This was partially because Patty had been the only passenger with a dependent on board to protect, and thus no other case could have served as a model for the specifics of Jonathon's claim. Additionally, my attorney informed me that our case was selected as a model because it covered nearly every issue addressed in the other claims, including the fact that Patty had been the main breadwinner of the family, and had been a single mother responsible for the welfare of two children. My attorney disclosed to me that when the judge announced our case as one of the selected four, the airline representatives had immediately asked the judge to reconsider, but he refused. My attorney assumed that their alarmed reactions arose out of fear of what evidence I might bring forth on the mishandling of the human remains and personal effects, as they knew that I had extensive knowledge on the topic based on responses I had made during the depositions, as well as statements I had previously made to the press.

My involvement with Jonathon's case forced me to perpetually reflect upon all the losses that my family and I had suffered because of Patty's and Patrick's deaths. The more I thought about everything that had happened the more I realized that, over the past three years, I had never gained enough distance from the situation to let go of the anger I had been harboring. In these moments just before the definitive close to my many years of battling the airline, I felt it necessary to retrace my motives for relentlessly pursuing Jonathon's case, so that after the outcome of the trial, I would be able to let go of the animosity I held toward the airline and finally release myself from the negativity that I had carried since the crash.

From the onset of the legal process, I had declined to settle with the airline, not only to acquire more money for Jonathon, but also to direct public attention to the many ways in which the families had been wronged by the airline, which had continuously compounded our agony and distress for years after the actual crash. In my mind, accepting any of the airline's earlier settlement offers would have effectively absolved them of all accountability for their actions, and would have denied my instinct that a monetary compensation, regardless of how large, would have still made it too easy for the airline to escape without ramifications for the trauma invoked by their mishandling of the tragedy's aftermath.

After the first anniversary of the crash, the concerns specific to Flight 4184 had largely disappeared from the public eye; yet my family's struggle with the airline had lasted for years, forcing us to face daily reminders of our loss. I saw the looming possibility of a trial as another means by which our story could be heard, and hoped that the airline might be urged into claiming some responsibility for what transpired. Thus, I decided that I was going to at least see this case through to the brink of trial, because I knew that would assure a substantial amount of media coverage of the issues, and I hoped that public awareness of these problems might prevent them from being repeated in the future.

My conviction to seek some justice, not only for Patty and Patrick, but also for the prolonged struggle endured by my family, afforded me a way to release the anger that had generated inside of me throughout the past three years. I knew that in order for such unhealthy feelings to subside, I needed to at least see my concerns acknowledged and feel as though my voice had been heard. I also recognized that in feeling resolved about my ability to confront the adversity thrust upon my family, I could fully transcend what had for so long been an all-encompassing ordeal without being plagued by lingering regrets.

꒰ 35 ꒱

The trial was due to start on Wednesday September 17, 1997. While the ultimate objective of the proceedings was to arrive at an appropriate settlement amount for Jonathon, it was first necessary to establish responsibility for the crash. Although the NTSB had held an investigative hearing, their findings, while important and influential, were not definitive indicators of guilt in the eyes of the law. Thus, it was ultimately up to the judge or jury to decide the degree to which the airline and the plane manufacturer, ATR, were legally accountable for the crash. Prior to issuing a settlement amount, the jury would also need to determine the extent to which the airline was liable for the damages inflicted by their mishandling of the tragedy's aftermath. I was told that it could take up to seven weeks before a verdict would be reached.

The morning of the scheduled trial date, I awoke with trepidation, not sure what the day would bring. Upon my arrival at the Federal Courthouse, I engaged in nervous small talk with many of the other families while we waited for the trial to begin. This day seemed to mark the beginning of the end of an unbelievable passage of time, from the first day of life without my sister to my attempts to honor her wishes for Jonathon.

After waiting a good part of the morning, we got word that one of the jurors had a medical emergency, and so the judge had postponed the trial. As soon as the lawyers acquired this information, they quickly resumed their negotiations. In an attempt to avoid the grueling process of trial, attorneys on both sides were rigorously working to reach a settlement prior to opening statements, which had been rescheduled for the upcoming Monday.

Throughout the intervening days, I reflected upon my conflicting thoughts over the prospect of going to trial. On one hand, I knew that a trial would assure that all the details of our experience would be revealed; on the other hand, I was also aware that this process would involve my family and friends, and I was hesitant about dragging them through yet another grueling ordeal. The more I considered all of this, the more I understood that both choices came with consequences; in reality, I knew that this situation offered no possibility for an ideal or perfect outcome.

I began the morning of Monday, September 22 quite early, with an inexplicable sense that the time for my interference was over. This decision in part arose out of my knowledge that ample media coverage had already been given to the contents of this trial during various preparatory stages, and from the figures proposed in the more recent settlement offers, I felt confident that Jonathon would be adequately provided for, regardless of whether the settlement was reached through negotiations or trial.

Somehow I wound up running late, and so to avoid missing my train downtown, I parked my car in the library parking lot next to the train station, despite the posted tow-away signs. I arrived before court started, and joined the families gathered in a large conference room, where we would not be bothered by the media and where we could easily be reached by our attorneys in the event they needed to consult us, as even just moments before trial, negations were still underway.

A few minutes prior to the time we were all going to head into the courtroom, my attorney called me out into the hallway and informed me that he had accepted the latest settlement offer for Jonathon, based on the extraordinary value to which the defendants (both American Airlines and ATR) had consented to pay.

So many thoughts ran through my head...I remained motionless in disbelief that the whole affair was finally over. There would not be a trial, and I would not have to involve my parents, friends, coworkers, and possibly even Jonathon, thus sparing them from also having to relive their horrific experiences. And as for the settlement, I could hardly even fathom the amount—it far surpassed all of our expectations.

I had come to the courthouse prepared to accept the fact that any outcome unavoidably came with certain downfalls, for the complexities involved in our case inherently denied even the concept of a fully satisfactory conclusion. Yet, a part of me still felt a little disappointed, as a trial would have exposed the entire truth as we had lived it, and would have demonstrated to the public just what we, the families, had been subjected to because of the money and power of a corporate giant. However, I reminded myself of the fact that changes had already begun to be made in the industry due in part to the families' efforts, and that I had accomplished my own objectives. In the midst of all these thoughts I heard, "Are you all right?" With a jolt, I realized that I had been standing frozen and silent in front of my attorney since hearing the news.

Before parting, my attorney asked me to remain quiet about the recent settlement, so that the judge could make the announcement in front of the courtroom. Even though I had already been informed of the results, I still proceeded with the others into the courtroom for the expected trial so that I could sit with the families and hear the triumphant end to what for us had been a nightmarish and seemingly endless ordeal.

The courtroom quickly filled with the families, interested bystanders, and so many media personnel that until I asked them to relocate, there was no room for the families to sit. The jury was also in place as we waited for what most assumed would be opening statements. Had the trial taken place, the jury would first have determined the airline's and the plane manufacturer's degree of liability, and then decided how much money was to be paid to the families of the five selected passengers. This determination would have then been the basis for the settlement of the twenty-seven other claims pending in federal court involving this crash.

When the judge finally appeared, we sat and listened to his declaration that intense mediation efforts had been underway since the previous week, and that a settlement had finally been reached. The jury was subsequently dismissed, but the families were asked to stay seated because attorneys representing the airline and the plane manufacturer would be speaking to us. The media also was allowed to remain present, so that they could cover the proceedings.

Silence again fell upon the packed courtroom as the attorney representing the airline stepped forward. He delivered an emotional and apologetic declaration on behalf of the airline, "We are terribly sorry this happened. Terribly sorry. We can never compensate for the losses you have suffered. I am sorry it has taken so long to get this resolution."

While surprised at what he said, I accepted this genuine attempt at reconciliation. His apology went a long way with me, as it was something I not only wanted to hear, but also *needed* to hear in order to help draw nearly three years of pain and resentment to a close. It didn't matter whether or not his words truly represented the sentiments of everyone at the airline, for at that moment it was his sincere conveyance of the apology that was meaningful.

In contrast, the subsequent statement made by the attorney representing the aircraft manufacturer ATR aggravated many family members, including me. Even though he apologized for the crash, he then went on to blame it on a weather phenomenon. He made matters worse by putting a positive spin on the situation with the comment that the crash had sparked an interest in better predicting particular weather conditions that could lead to such disasters.

I was beside myself with anger. I just could not believe he had the nerve to imply that this crash was necessary for progress to occur while standing in front of all of us that had lost so much because of it. Seven previous incidents had occurred with the ATR aircrafts, including a crash in Italy with no survivors. Not only had the manufacturer been aware of prior problems with these planes in icing conditions, but they had also kept quiet about a study that had been done on this subject supporting such concerns; thus, this attorney's insinuation that it was a fluke for Flight 4184 to have crashed was infuriating.

After the attorneys' address to the families, the judge dismissed everyone from the courtroom, and I headed straight for a telephone to call my good friends, Karen and Sandy, who had been watching my children. I became very emotional the moment I heard Sandy's familiar voice, as I attempted to relay the news that a settlement had finally been reached. It was Sandy who had first come to my house at the onset of this tragedy, and it was he with whom I was speaking at its conclusion, making it seem as though this whole process had come full circle. His soothing words sought to reassure me that everything would be alright, for it was all finally over.

Several of us then exited the doors of the courthouse, only to be rushed by dozens of reporters with cameras. I gave one interview after another, emphasizing my opinion that in this case there were no winners, for no amount of money could ever replace sisterhood, the love from a mother or brother, the daughter of proud parents, or the grandson of loving grandparents. I spoke briefly about the journey that we had all taken, and felt relieved by this opportunity to publicly bring our story to a close in a way that illuminated the power of individuals to enact change and bring about justice. It was also important for me to announce that with the settlement made, it was time to move forward with my life.

A short time later, only family members were asked back into the courtroom, where something unprecedented was to take place—the evidence was to be introduced as if the jury was present and court was in session, so that we could know every detail of what led to the crash. Everyone was surprised, but also expressed appreciation for the judge affording us this opportunity to put any lingering questions to rest. The evidence presented included all the information our attorneys had compiled, as well as an animated reenactment of the crash similar to the one displayed at the preliminary hearing, which was played in conjunction with the cockpit voice recorder. We listened to attorneys' statements revealing that investigators believed that ice on the wings had caused the aerodynamic disturbances and the plane's eventual roll. None of the evidence surprised me, because I had previously encountered all of this same information; however, this fact did not change the painful reality of what was being described, and I still found it difficult to hear. Thankfully, a video showing the possible perspective from inside the plane was not shown.

With the legalities having come to a close, a handful of family members, along with several of the attorneys, went out for dinner. Toward the end of the meal, a gentleman who knew some of the attorneys approached our table, and after a brief introduction turned to me and asked how I was getting home. I was alarmed by his forwardness, yet didn't want to be rude, and so I thanked him for his concern, but explained that I'd be taking the train back. Persisting, he went on to say that he had seen me on TV earlier that evening, and had wanted to help in some way. The attorneys I was with suggested I accept the ride, as it was quite late. Realizing that I had probably missed the last train, I accepted the gentleman's offer to arrange for my transportation home.

When I walked out of the restaurant, I gasped as I stood before my mode of transportation. On the day that marked the end to almost three long years of enduring a torturous journey through the legal system, moving to new residences after my divorce, a new job, and the quest to effect change in the airline industry, a car door was opened for me on a glistening white super-stretch limo. As I had never traveled in such luxury before, I stepped inside with appreciation, hoping that this was a sign of an end to all the bad experiences and of good things to come in the future. The man wished me a pleasant journey home, giving instructions to his driver to take extra care in transporting me.

After a nice chat with the driver, we finally arrived at the library parking lot in my town, where approximately fifteen hours earlier I had left my vehicle. But the lot was empty. While I was startled at first, I then focused on the posted tow-away signs directing me to the whereabouts of my vehicle. Once there, the driver maneuvered the limo, weaving in and out of the many rows of impounded cars and trucks, and stopped as close to my vehicle as he could.

While in some ways the events of the night could have been perceived as misfortunate, I was acutely aware that a blessing had been placed upon me that evening, for had I taken the train home as planned, my situation would have been much worse. If I had learned one thing from my experience, it was the importance of being grateful for every gift given, no matter how small or strange it may appear. In some ways, I saw the resolution of Jonathon's case against the airline as another small blessing, for even though it had come only after three exhausting years of struggle, I knew that I could live with the end result and feel no regrets. I stood there and thought about how unpredictable life can be, realizing that while it would be easy to be consumed with the fear of all that could go wrong, I was going to instead focus on all of the wonderful possibilities that might lay ahead in my future.

❧ 36 ❧

As all endings give rise to new beginnings, with the close of my involvement with American Airlines I was approaching the opening of a new chapter in my life. News articles the day after the resolution of our claim referred to the settlement as "unprecedented," citing it as the largest liability ever awarded in an air disaster case. The papers covered the emotional statement made by the airline's attorney, which was American Airlines' first public apology made to the families.

Despite the positive outcome, I felt completely depleted by all that had transpired, and so during my second day of work after the conclusion of the settlement, I took the advice of concerned coworkers to go home. There, when no one was watching, I cried harder than I ever had before. Afterward, I felt relieved, but I wondered how many more tears of grief were left inside of me. Even though I was logically aware of the fact that I had finally come to the end of a drawn-out and traumatic journey, I still found myself in a state of emotional turbulence that no amount of reason or rational thought seemed to be able to override. My healing seemed to be taking place in layers, for old layers would have to be peeled off before healthier ones could form, and sometimes the feelings left exposed would cause me to wonder whether I was moving forward or backwards. However, over time, I came to see that the recovery process was defined by a pattern of ebbing and flowing, because in order to truly come to terms with what had happened, I had to first face all that I had felt since the tragedy had transformed my life.

Thus, I persisted in allowing myself the room to heal, continuing to pay careful attention to my own needs. Before I knew it, October

31, 1997, the third anniversary of the crash, had come and gone; with the passing of each year, this day seemed to become easier to get through.

One month later, colored photographs of the remaining personal effects that the airline had retained were at last sent to the families, accompanied by a brief description of each item. There were fifty-eight photographs in all, displaying jewelry, keys, family pictures, and day planners, none of which had belonged to Patty. While I was thankful for this long-awaited opportunity to view these belongings, it seemed that had they been released three years prior, much of our resentment could have been prevented. At this point, seeing these images only stirred up hard feelings at a time when we were all looking to move on from the tragedy.

Several months after obtaining the photographs of the belongings, I received a phone call from Dr. Carolyn Coarsey, who had interviewed survivors and family members of victims of air crashes for her response-training video the previous year. She invited me to speak at one of her corporate training sessions for airline employees, which was an example of the training programs mandated by the Family Assistance Act, so as to detail my family's experiences, including how the airline had prolonged our struggle to move forward. Although I had mostly withdrawn from activities pertaining to the airline industry, I felt sharing my experience would expand the employees' understanding of what families encounter following a tragedy, and thus accepted her invitation. I was still willing to devote time to ensuring that what we had endured would never happen again.

A couple days before the training session was scheduled to begin, Carolyn called to say that while the class would be held at Delta Air Lines' headquarters in Atlanta, representatives from many other airlines would also be present, as it was common practice for the airlines to engage in reciprocal training. Just before we finished our conversation, Carolyn advised me that Russell, one of the people in American Airlines' command center during the time the crash had taken place, would also be attending the training session. Russell had been a Care Team Leader, and had been responsible for responding to the questions of the different agencies working the crash site. The airline had pulled all of their Care Team members a few months after the crash, at which point Russell had become the main point of contact for the families. Thus, the news that Russell would be at the training session startled me, as I still had unresolved feelings about the sudden disappearance of the Care Team members assigned to my family. Carolyn explained that she had thought it best if I knew beforehand that he would be attending the class, so that I could decide whether I would be alright with his presence. Even though I told her I was fine with it, she still suggested he and I talk on the phone prior to our actual meeting, which I thought was a good idea.

The next day, I received a phone call from Russell. He began the conversation tentatively, admitting that he also was also glad for this opportunity to talk beforehand, as he didn't want me to feel uncomfortable during the training session. I quickly assured him I wouldn't be the one to feel uncomfortable, given that any tension would have been a result of the problems his employer had created.

After this shaky start to the conversation, we delved right into the unavoidable.

I discussed what my family had endured because of the Care Team, as well as the experiences of several other families. I brought up how members of the Care Team had shown up at some families' doors inappropriately dressed, chewing bubble gum, blowing bubbles, and not really knowing what their jobs required. I described their inability to provide my family with information, their sudden disappearance, the cancellation of their phone numbers, and our powerlessness to reach someone at the airline who could provide us with much-needed answers. Russell seemed to be shocked by some of what I disclosed, and saddened by the rest.

After allowing me to air my concerns, Russell responded by explaining the airline's intentions in supplying families with Care Team representatives, which included the provision of compassionate responses and a personalized point of contact. I said that these beneficial objectives had in many cases never materialized, either due to insufficient employee training or conflicting aims of upper management. As for the unexpected disconnect with our Care Team members, he maintained that once a family signed on with a law firm, the airline was no longer legally allowed to be in direct contact with them. I countered this justification by pointing out the airline's inconsistent adherence to this policy; for one thing, the airline had contacted us directly on several occasions after we had procured legal representation, attempting to entice us into a settlement, and for another, the Care Team members assigned to other families had stayed on to help them even after legal representation had been obtained.

At the end of our conversation, Russell again expressed his sympathies, articulating how sorry he was for the added trauma we had suffered because of the airline's treatment. I thanked him for having the courage to call. I didn't blame him for the discrepancies or lack of ethics that seemed to characterize the behavior of the company with which he was employed, and I trusted the sincerity of his intentions.

A few days later I flew to Atlanta, where the two-day training session was to take place. Its purpose was to teach airline representatives the skills necessary to more effectively deal with survivors and family members after an air tragedy, so as to provide the best possible environment for healing. The response video that other family members and I had been interviewed for the previous year would be shown during the session in order to emphasize key points.

The training class included presentations, discussions, and role-playing. I was asked to share what I encountered throughout the aftermath of the tragedy, and the gruesome reality of my story prompted one of the airline managers to request that I "soften" the facts of my experience, which I found to be quite inappropriate. In contrast, during one of the breaks, an airline representative presented me with a poem he had written the night before entitled "The Message":

Someone like you brings a lot to the table.
It's remarkably exciting to see you so stable.
As we sit in training we learn and we hear

From your experience and uncomforted tear.
Its importance is something we all will learn,
From the past, airlines have taken such a turn . . .

Thank you for sharing and opening up our mind,
I know that will have an impact with our kind!

As he gave it to me, he apologized for its amateur construction, which I promised didn't matter, because it was the thought behind it that I most appreciated. Up to that point, I had no idea whether or not my words had made any kind of an impact, and so I was honored and reassured by the fact that this man had taken the time to write me the poem.

At the conclusion of the training session, I was further encouraged by the fact that nearly everyone attending the class thanked me for sharing my experiences, insisting that I had helped give a new and more realistic perspective to the events following a crash. I was grateful that they had not only attended this training session, but had also dedicated themselves to doing their jobs to the best of their abilities. One of the last trainees to come up to me revealed that she had been working at the gate where Patty and Patrick boarded the plane on the night of the crash. She distinctly remembered how they had run hand in hand to the gate to avoid being late for departure, as they had been the last passengers to board the plane, and recalled how cute Patrick looked dressed in his Ninja Turtle costume. As I stood before one of the last people to see Patty and Patrick alive, my mind raced with all the things I wanted to say and the questions I wanted to ask, but the need to avoid such an emotionally taxing discussion overrode such impulses. Through tears, I thanked the compassionate woman for disclosing that information to me, trying to appease her fears of having upset me by assuring her of my appreciation.

I left for home glad that I had attended the training session, but surprised by my ongoing sensitivity to many of the issues raised. Following the class, Russell and I stayed in touch and eventually became friends. He later admitted that when he found out I would be attending Carolyn's seminar, he wanted nothing more than to back out, but could not find a way to do so without it looking obvious. Even though it was difficult at times to meet the people that had been intricately involved with one aspect of the crash or another, I was thankful for my enduring ability to stay open to living life in spite of its hardships, for in this instance it had afforded me the gift of friendship.

My new life was once again leading me into unexpected places, and putting me in contact with people I never would have imagined myself knowing. Regardless, it was uplifting to see the sympathetic faces of individuals associated with the airline, as it made me realize that while I had been wronged by a corporation, people existed within it that wanted to make things better for the future. I was beginning to look forward to the new adventures that my life held for me, all the while holding the memory of my sister and nephew in my heart, taking them with me wherever I was to go.

༜ 37 ༜

With one of the greatest constancies life offers, time continued to flow by, propelling me forward in various directions. Almost four years after the crash, the pendulum had begun to swing toward a life more full of joy and happiness, and away from one that had been predominantly full of sorrow and pain.

With some order and peace having been restored to my life, I was finally able to give some thought as to finding a permanent residence after renting three different apartments over the course of only two years. One day I had a hunch to make some phone calls to inquire about homes for sale by their owners. I was only able to reach one of the families, but surprisingly, they described a house that seemed like a perfect fit for my family. As soon as I stepped inside the front door, I knew without a doubt that I was standing inside of our new home.

Our move was as swift and effortless as my decision to buy the house, which was unusual considering that I was doing all of this with three children. Following a long day of moving, I turned off the lights in what I had designated as my room and climbed into bed, where I noticed something glowing on the ceiling directly overhead. Looking closely, I recognized two glow-in-the-dark stars, which I instantly saw as symbolic of Patty and Patrick watching over me. A huge smile came onto my face as I reflected upon the idea that perhaps the ease with which I had found and moved into my house was attributable not merely to good luck, but rather to the good fortune bestowed upon me by my very own angels.

After settling in, I was immersed in the bustling activity that two teenage boys and a daughter who thought she was a teenager brought into the household. In an atmosphere so filled with life, it was easy to keep myself in a state of contentment. Not long after our move, the fourth anniversary of the crash arrived, with families, friends, and volunteers once again gathering at the crash site. That year, I even managed to mostly hold onto pleasant feelings throughout the service commemorating the tragedy by recalling my many fond memories of Patty and Patrick.

As opposed to the two burial plots in our local cemetery, I remained magnetically drawn to the place where Patty and Patrick had made their transition from this life to the next, taking every opportunity to return to the field in Roselawn, Indiana. While I usually made the trip with friends, on one occasion, I decided to go alone. After spending some time lingering in the peaceful and serene ambiance of the roadside memorial, I made my way out into the field. In the past, I had made such treks before the crop was planted or after it had been harvested. But this particular visit occurred toward the end of summer, and the healthy, strong stalks of corn towered well above my head. Refusing to be deterred, I disappeared into the thick rows of corn, only able to see a couple feet in any direction. I cut back and forth as I instinctively maneuvered my way through the maze toward the point of impact.

Several minutes into my trudge, an eerie feeling crept over me, which I initially ignored, continuing to forge ahead through the dense crop. But after another couple of minutes, my sense of discomfort had transformed into inescapable fear, as though I was consumed with all the panic that had been endured by everyone on board the plane. It was as if somehow the horror experienced by those sixty-eight people continued to seep out of the land into which the plane had plunged.

In a state of hysteria, I turned and began to flee as fast as my legs would carry me. Depending on what direction I needed to take, I either dashed through the paths established by the rows of corn, or created new rows by plunging directly through the crops. Having no point of reference, since all I could see was blue sky above and corn everywhere else, I just continued to run. I wondered if I had gotten turned around in my frenzy to escape because it seemed like I was trapped amid the endless stalks obstructing my passageway to freedom. The density of the corn hampered my efforts, making it seem as though I had been sprinting a lot longer than my casual stroll into the field had indicated was necessary.

I at last reached the safe haven of the gravel road. Upon exiting the field, all the haunting sensations instantly seemed to vanish. It was not until some time later that I began to understand those frightening feelings as ripples that continued to emerge not only from the destruction of the crash, but also from the trauma I had lived through afterward. Even though I had traveled to a place far from where I stood after first learning of the crash, I would still face occasional reminders of the experiences that in many ways served as definitive landmarks, tracing how I had moved into a life so different from that I had known.

I realized that the many people that had come into my life because of the tragedy had been essential to my rebuilding an identity that was for the most part centered in peace and happiness. Thus, as the fifth anniversary of the crash drew near, I felt it necessary to do something special for Helen, Julie, and Chuck to honor their steadfast commitment in taking care of the memorial site and making arrangements for our gathering after each anniversary service. They had always given an unrelenting effort to ease the families' pain, and I wanted to express my deep appreciation for their quiet devotion.

The fifth anniversary of the crash fell on a Sunday, and that morning a surprise lay waiting in the newspaper that Julie went to retrieve from the end of her driveway. Featured on the front page was a large picture of Patty's and Patrick's crosses, with a pumpkin sitting in front of Patrick's, next to which was an article honoring the contributions made by Helen and her family, who, despite not having known any of the victims on board the plane, had incorporated those most affected by the tragedy into their lives. Below the pictures of Patty's and Patrick's crosses, the paper also contained a piece I had written entitled "Angels in Her Midst," which first gave an overview of the trauma I suffered at the onset of the crash, and then went on to explain my journey to move forward over the past five years. At the end, I thanked Helen and her family for all they had done for us, and I closed my tribute with the words, "Your generosity and warmheartedness have touched so many souls, and lifted so many spirits. Thank you for being our angels."

Helen and her family later expressed to me that they were so touched by this story that it took them five or six attempts before they were able to read through it in its entirety. Due to the humble way in which they assisted us, many of their friends and neighbors hadn't known of their involvement with the families of Flight 4184 until opening the newspaper that day; upon the release of my article, the community responded by visiting the crash site, along with an outpouring of support for the efforts of Helen, Julie, and Chuck.

The fifth anniversary was the first major milestone commemorating the crash since the one-year anniversary, and thus I found myself deeply impacted by the arrival of this day. However, my emotional strain was eased by the presence of many friends, as well as by the communal and loving atmosphere that presided throughout the day, all of which served to remind me of the many wonderful things I had gained out of my devastating loss. I agreed to give press interviews following the ceremony, during which I maintained that our gathering was not focused on negatively recollecting upon the past, but rather on the process of moving on in our lives with those who could truly empathize and celebrate with us. I spoke of the positives that had manifested since this same day five years prior, reassuringly explaining that I had allowed the sun to again shine in my life, and that the rays were emerging from new relationships and the fond memories of the loved ones who had passed.

❧ 38 ❧

In much the same way that the aftermath of the crash over time had afforded me opportunities for personal growth, the issues spawning from Flight 4184 eventually induced a flow of progress within the airline industry as well. Specifically, throughout the years following the settlement, I noticed the callous manner in which business had been conducted at American Airlines giving way to a more caring and compassionate approach.

Soon after the fifth anniversary of the crash, the insurance company representing American Airlines sent a letter to the families. In it, they announced their intent to request that the court vacate the preservation order my attorney had entered the week of the preliminary hearing four and a half years earlier, which would allow them to dispose of all items that had been protected under it. The letter went on to state that, as a courtesy, American Airlines would voluntarily retain the small inventory of the remaining fifty-eight unclaimed personal effects, a photographic record of which had been sent to the families two years prior; these items would be preserved for an indefinite period of time, and would again be made available for the families to view and claim upon reasonable notice. I found it admirable that the airline was offering to hold onto these personal items, especially since they were in the process of eliminating their legal requirement to do so, giving them no other incentive outside of a genuine desire to do the right thing. After years of being disrespected, I felt as though the airline was finally trying to acknowledge the families' needs.

The following year, the airline sent another letter disclosing that

252

five additional boxes of unclaimed personal effects had been discovered, and that a booklet of color photographs of the items would soon be sent so we could view them for identification purposes. The airline went on to apologetically mention that due to poor record keeping, the pictures would contain items not only from the crash of Flight 4184, but from a subsequent crash as well. I was impressed by the airline's divulgence of this information, especially considering the fact that the protective order had been terminated the previous year, effectively freeing them from any obligation to safeguard these belongings. Although this news did conjure up some negative associations spawning from the airline's history of unreliability, the company's decision to notify families of the findings indicated that they were progressively working to amend their previous failings.

I was floored by the impact that the families of Flight 4184 eventually had upon the conduct of American Airlines. I noticed a marked difference between the airline's misguided policies in the immediate aftermath of the crash and what at this point seemed to be their considerate response to the concerns and needs that we had voiced.

This more humanitarian business approach was the work of visionaries within the airline's upper management, as individuals involved in handling our crash began to come forward with reformed perspectives from what they had learned. In a 2001 interview with Dr. Carolyn Coarsey, Robert Baker, Vice Chairman of American Airlines, made statements about his commitment to educating people on the importance of appropriately responding to air disasters, and these claims were substantiated and elaborated upon by company employees I had come to know. Mr. Baker had been an employee of American Airlines since 1968, and at the time of the crash of Flight 4184 he was serving as Vice President of Operations for the company. In his interview as well as in his day-to-day interactions, he emphasized prioritizing the needs of survivors and family members over any legal concerns. One of his coworkers told me that he maintained a healthy perspective, in that he refused to let lawyers dictate his actions and instead remained focused on doing the right thing for people. Mr. Baker also articulated the essential need for management to offer assistance and encouragement to the Care Team members instead of impeding their efforts. He felt that his job as a corporate executive included doing whatever he could to help those trained to respond to disasters, and was willing to devote himself to getting the job done. Additionally, Mr. Baker emphasized management's responsibility to evaluate the airline's handling of all crashes, so that the company could grow from their own errors and amend their policies for the future.

Mr. Baker had spoken with his coworkers about the toll that the crash of Flight 4184 had taken on him, admitting that his business perspective had become more considerate and compassionate due to what he had learned from this crash. In fact, he had been so dramatically moved by what had taken place on October 31, 1994 that he made annual trips to Roselawn, Indiana, to pray in solitude for the deceased victims of the tragedy.

Men like Robert Baker represented the new face of management's response to tragedies; it was both fulfilling and relieving to know that our efforts had inspired people like him to assure that never again would families suffer the way that we had. Things appeared to have taken a turn for the better, and as the years continued to elapse, no one foresaw any new developments arising that pertained to Flight 4184. However, at the tenth anniversary of the crash, while visiting the mass grave, Jenny and I decided to meet with one of the members of the cemetery's board of directors. We wanted to thank him for the great job that had been done in commemoration of this anniversary, both on the landscaping, as well as the bricks that had been laid out in the shape of angel wings framing the memorial stone. The many families in attendance disclosed how touched they were by this gesture memorializing the tragedy, as they continued to mourn and honor the lives of their loved ones even after so much time had passed. After we expressed our appreciation, he mentioned his surprise that over the past ten years, no one had taken the cemetery board up on their offer. Jenny and I were completely bewildered by his reference, and so we asked him to elaborate. Suddenly, we found ourselves listening to details about a decision the board had made after the mass burial to set aside approximately three hundred plots of land adjacent to the mass grave for family members of those who had perished on Flight 4184. Jenny and I looked at each other incredulously, as this was the first we had heard of such a proposal. As it turned out, the cemetery directors had asked the officials at American Airlines to pass the offer on to the families, which had clearly never happened.

I was so flustered upon hearing this information that I needed a moment to collect my thoughts. Afterward, Jenny and I discussed the issue, and we concluded that while the airline's omission was undeniably frustrating, it was a product of the same mentality that had defined our relations with the airline for several years following the crash, but did not necessarily reflect the reformed policies that the company had since adopted. Therefore, after deliberating as to the best course of action, we decided to contact American Airlines in order to investigate this matter before jumping to any conclusions. However, we soon discovered that the majority of those who had been involved in the aftermath of Flight 4184 were no longer employed by the airline, and no one there currently was aware of the cemetery board's offer. Refusing to give up, we then contacted a Care Team representative at American Airlines, who eventually put us in contact with the CEO of American Eagle. He immediately inquired as to how the company could best handle the situation. We suggested that a letter from the airline be sent to the families notifying them of this information, which he promptly agreed to do, and furthermore, before mailing the final copy, he sent us a draft of the letter for comments.

Even though it wound up taking approximately six months to get this one letter out, the airline still fulfilled their promise to send it, and therefore had demonstrated significant progress by addressing our concern with appropriate action. The airline finally seemed to be making decisions *with* the families instead of *for* the families.

Along with the reforms taking place within the corporate policies of American Airlines, I was also witnessing additional transformations occurring within the airline industry as a whole. The Family Assistance Act of 1996 had required airlines to conduct trauma-response training sessions for their employees, and Dr. Coarsey's videotaped interviews became a tool used worldwide to demonstrate the impact of such tragedies on families. I began to speak more frequently at these training sessions, sharing my experience with airline employees, and I also delivered presentations on the subject at international symposiums. These engagements allowed me to give airline personnel a first-hand perspective about the impact of their decisions and actions and, hopefully, equip them with a better understanding as to the needs of families and survivors of air disasters. Through these opportunities I was also able to see the fruition of all the families' efforts, and I was often overcome with awe at what we had helped to accomplish. I felt that it was important for me to follow-up on our hard work by continuing to make some contribution to the goals of the legislation; even though it was still difficult to discuss certain aspects of my story, I knew I had unique insights to offer that would expand the industry's awareness.

During one such seminar, I was walking through Delta's headquarters with their training manager just prior to my presentation when three other airline employees approached us. Even though the manager introduced us using only first names and without revealing my purpose for being there, the next thing I heard was, "I know you. You're Patty's sister." This man went on to say that he had previously gone through the response-training class, and remembered my interview on Dr. Coarsey's video, as well as the pictures that were shown of Patty and Patrick. It was encouraging for me to know that my involvement was making an impact upon people, while simultaneously allowing me to assure that Patty's and Patrick's memories live on.

In many ways, I found my mere presence at these training sessions to be somewhat miraculous; ten years earlier, I would have never imagined that families of various crashes would have been able to come together, pushing beyond all the obstacles to make our voices heard, and yet somehow we had accomplished just that. Such thoughts would lead me to consider the ways in which my journey toward healing had been laced with unforeseeable and unexpected gifts; particularly, several inexplicable events took place at the roadside memorial over the years that seemed to indicate the presence of mystical forces. Many witnesses to these phenomena rejected such a possibility; however, because I had come to see my capacity to persevere through extraordinary adversity in part as a blessing bestowed upon me from the loving eyes of Patty and Patrick, I was able to more easily believe in the idea that these marvels were in some way connected with our loved ones. Helen and her family were among those that initially doubted the miraculous nature of the events, but the ongoing string of unusual occurrences eventually over-turned their skepticism.

One spring, there was an unprecedented rainfall; when the rain had finally stopped, Helen and her family set out to check on the me-morial site. After they parked their car, they began to trudge through the soggy, rain-soaked grass to the memorial, when Helen suddenly spotted a piece of paper lying upon the drenched earth. To her surprise, when she knelt down and picked up the paper, not only was it completely dry, but when she turned it over, she was staring at Patty's smiling face. Even though she was a bit shaken, Helen assumed the picture had fallen off of Patty's cross during the storm; however, when she went to reattach the image, she shockingly discovered that no pictures were missing from the cross, and since she knew that I had not visited the site in months, she could not rationalize the situation by assuming that I had left the picture behind. Moreover, this picture was not laminated for protection against the elements like those on the cross, and yet somehow it had re-mained in perfect condition, completely unaffected by the rainstorm.

On the day of our tenth anniversary service, a bout of severe weather once again encompassed the area; a terrible wind storm barreled through northern Indiana, knocking over billboards and blowing siding off of buildings. The winds were so intense that when we arrived at the roadside memorial, the minister asked why we were even going to bother trying to light the sixty-eight candles that stood in front of the crosses. We decided to go ahead as planned, despite the unfavorable conditions, and in an eerily similar fashion to what had occurred after the first anniversary service, not only were all the families able to light their candles, but somehow every single candle stayed lit throughout the duration of the service and then well on into the night.

Upon the arrival of the Christmas season, Helen, Julie, and Chuck would typically cut down evergreen trees and bring them to the memorial site, along with sixty-eight red bows and pine cones to use for decoration. One year, while collecting the exact number of pine cones they needed, Julie found one that was larger than the rest; upon closer examination, she realized that two pine cones had become stuck together. She figured that she could just separate the two, giving her the exact number to hang on the tree, but after several unsuccessful attempts to split the cones, Julie became frustrated. As she tightened her grip to pull even harder, she was suddenly overcome with a clear understanding as to why she could not separate them: they were not stuck, but had actually grown together. At that moment, Patty and I rushed into her thoughts, as she strongly felt that her inability to separate the cones symbolized the unique connection that Patty and I had shared and celebrated throughout our lives. That year the double pine cone was hung on the Christmas tree; I was so touched by this story that following that holiday season, I hung the double cone in my bedroom, where it has since remained—forever connected.

Over time, I came to notice that my own life was also filled with such everyday miracles, as I often seemed to stumble upon gifts that filled me with inspiration and love. One day, feeling apprehensive over the writing of this book while walking my dog, I saw something lying in my path on the sidewalk. At first I thought nothing of it, but after a few steps I suddenly froze, realizing what I had just walked past. Backtracking, I leaned over and picked up a sharpened pencil completely covered in penguin decorations, and topped with a large, unused eraser in the shape of a penguin. My thoughts immediately turned to Patty and the penguin collection we had acquired over the years, and in that moment I felt reassured of our everlasting bond. A smile emerged on my face and my heart filled with warmth, as I just knew this had been a message of encouragement from my sister.

Even though much of what I encountered to some seemed coincidental, in my eyes, these instances indicated that Patty remained very much alive…alerting me to her presence by exercising her wonderful sense of humor, finding great bargains, adding to our penguin collection, and above all, affording me the strength and love I needed to carry on. It seemed as though each time I found myself longing for help or guidance, there would be some sign or signal reminding me that I was not alone, and reassuring me of my own capabilities. My trust in the plausibility of these magical phenomena allowed for the continuation of the special relationship between me and my sister, for whether these occurrences manifested from my faith that Patty's and Patrick's spirits remained with me, or from my eternal love for my sister and nephew, they helped me summon the courage and fortitude I needed to keep living beyond the death of the life I had so loved.

I was finally in a place close to where I had been before the crash, having regained the joy and tranquility that had once enriched my life on a daily basis. In the natural progression of time, Halloween continues to arrive at the end of each October, conjuring up my memories of childhood innocence, and the celebrations Patty and I shared that have become forever etched into my mind and heart. While the poignant mark of October 31, 1994 always generates feelings of sorrow, my ability to accept Patty's lasting presence in my life eases the pain associated with that date, and endows me with the capacity to continue giving life to the memory of my sister and nephew.

Epilogue

He was my North, my South, my East and West,
My working week and my Sunday rest,
My noon, my midnight, my talk, my song;
I thought that love would last forever: I was wrong.

The stars are not wanted now: Put out every one;
Pack up the moon and dismantle the sun,
Pour away the ocean and sweep up the wood.
For nothing now can ever come to any good.

W. H. Auden, "Funeral Blues"

In the wake of losing my sister and nephew, I spent an indefinite period of time attempting to make sense out of the senseless, and trying to understand purposes that cannot be understood. There is no way to adequately articulate the unshakeable bond that defined the life that Patty and I shared, for I don't think I could ever find the words to do it justice. Therefore, I refer to W. H. Auden's poem, "Funeral Blues," as Patty truly was "my North, my South, my East and West"—in short, she was my everything—and I found it nearly impossible to imagine my sister as anything but alive. My many memories of the world we had created for ourselves represented what I understood life to be; thus, trying to process the fact that Patty was no longer here shattered my concept of reality. The day of her death, it seemed as though the world should have simply ground to a halt…the sun should not have risen the next day, and the cycles governing all of nature should have been fixed into a permanent state of frozen desolation. A storm had set in that brought an endless, murky, and impenetrable membrane of foreboding clouds that seemed to block any light from reaching the Earth.

For a long time after that marked day of October 31, 1994, it appeared as though I was forever doomed to live in the winter of my trauma; amid my daze of agonizing devastation, I found that I was plagued by unanswerable questions and paralyzed by the magnitude of my grief. In an instant, everything that I had been taught to believe appeared to have been compromised in such a way that a looming shadow of doubt was cast, causing me to incessantly contend with the flood of ambiguities that suddenly characterized my world. Before the crash, everything had seemed to make sense. I had no incentive to dwell upon ideas about fate, coincidence, and God, for I had never been given a reason to mistrust my faith, or to grapple with unknowable explanations concerning the determining forces of life and death. But the second I received the phone call from my dad informing me of Patty's and Patrick's deaths, everything I had so firmly held to be true seemed to disintegrate into a spiraling web of theoretical uncertainties. I found myself in what I now understand to be an existential crisis, as I fruitlessly delved into considerations of our purposes here on Earth, as well as the related and yet equally indecipherable concepts of fate, free will, and choice, desperately seeking to comprehend why this had happened to my family.

My ostensibly insurmountable task of coming to terms with losing two of the people I loved most in the world was further complicated by the airline's mishandling of the post-crash situation. I was already angry and devastated over their deaths, and my inconceivable grief was exacerbated and prolonged from what I endured in the days, months, and years following the crash of Flight 4184. It was exceedingly difficult for me to contain my frustration over the mind-boggling actions of the airline, which I would find nearly impossible to believe had I not experienced them directly. It was as though the indiscretions of this corporation made the already enveloping blanket of clouds hang down even lower, forming an even more dismal and ominous atmosphere.

The extent to which all of the families had been wronged by the airline inevitably incited my desire to proactively seek out some justice for our loved ones, as well as fighting to make changes to the system responsible for extending our anguish and sorrow. The more proactive I became, the more empowered I felt, allowing me to assume a less reactionary and victimized role. While at the time I did not understand that by taking action, I was embarking upon my long road to healing, I now realize that by making the choice to join together with the other families and present a unified stance against the airline, I prevented my anger from endlessly festering in the silence of my mind. The formation of Families of 4184 created a unique support system, as well as a forum in which we could collectively stand up and publicly voice the ways we had been mistreated. Even though I knew that these changes would never be able to bring back Patty and Patrick, or reverse all the pain that had been inflicted upon my family, I still found myself with a growing desire to ensure that, in the future, others would not have to undergo our same struggle.

The time that I spent working with the Families of 4184, as well as collaborating with those from other crashes to form the National Air Disaster Alliance, eventually resulted in the passing of the Family Assistance Act of 1996; while this law contained many stipulations, I felt the clause mandating that airlines submit training plans in order to assure that family and survivor rights are upheld following a tragedy was in part a direct reflection of my individual contribution. The enactment of this legislation marked a significant milestone in my personal journey toward recovery, in that I was able to witness how the will of a small group of individuals had the power to influence not only corporations, but also the government's regulations for the airline industry. Even though these changes would not provide an absolute solution to the problems we had encountered, I acknowledged that perfection is unattainable, and in that light I felt proud of what we had been able to accomplish, as our work had laid the foundation for later improvements. I still continue to speak in the industry, offering a reminder of past problems not only to help educate airline employees through a personal account, but also to provide a glimpse of the progress that has since been made. For the first time since Patty's and Patrick's deaths, the layer of clouds seemed to have thinned just enough to suggest the possibility that the sun's light might one day re-emerge and again shine down upon the Earth.

Over time, I became conscious of my need to forgive all the people and forces connected with the crash toward which I harbored feelings of resentment, for I knew that allowing myself to retain such intensely hostile feelings would in the long run only serve to deteriorate my emotional, mental, and physical well-being. I began by working at relinquishing my animosity toward the airline and the entire aviation industry, which was a process made easier by the individuals who approached me and shared their stories so filled with genuinely sympathetic and compassionate condolences. It ultimately became clear to me that the airline's callous decisions, which at the time I had perceived as deriving from malice and indifference, were actually more a product of oversight and/or a profound lack of awareness. I have come to recognize that the Care Team women dispatched to my home immediately after the crash had probably not meant to cause the confusion and distrust that ensued because of their abrupt disappearance. Rather, they had most likely been following orders given by the airline's management to cease contact when we attained legal representation, and had simply been unprepared and poorly trained to handle the situation. And most importantly, after spending years reflecting upon the entire chain of events, I now understand that what happened to us following the crash was not the result of any deliberate intentions on the part of individuals, but rather was an inevitable consequence of a flawed corporate system unprepared to handle the ramifications of human tragedy. My presentations throughout the industry have afforded me the chance to meet a number of American Airlines' personnel; their stories honor the many employees inside the company who cared very much, not only about the lives that were lost, but also about the families that were left behind, and in listening to these heartfelt accounts, I gradually learned to recognize that the actions of a corporation do not necessarily reflect the objectives of the individuals working within it.

Another crucial aspect of forgiving those associated with my painful memories of the tragedy's aftermath involved learning to identify the ways in which the traumatic nature of my situation impacted my perception of events. In the throes of my grief, it was difficult for me to realize that my sensitivities were heightened to such a degree that otherwise trivial instances suddenly invoked strong and unexpected reactions within me. In hindsight, I do not believe that the gentleman who announced birthday wishes to his coworker during the preliminary hearing did so to purposely cause me more pain; rather, I assume that he was simply entirely oblivious of the degree to which the families were grieving, and that many of us were facing the prospect of attempting to celebrate the first birthdays without our loved ones.

In time, I discovered that there were things for which I also had to forgive myself, mainly my unfulfilled promise to Patty to gain custody of Jonathon. Even though I accepted that what had taken place was not under my control, I still struggled to find some way to reconcile my lingering remorse; eventually, I decided that I could at least partially honor Patty's request by offering Jonathon a lasting portrait of Patty as very much alive. Therefore, when I first set out to write this book, my intention was to document the joy and vitality that characterized Patty and Patrick, so that when Jonathon grew up, he would have these memories forever at his disposal. While my initial purpose widened during the time I worked on this book, I still hope that my account provides Jonathon with some insight and answers as to who his mother was, and the wonderful family with which he was blessed. Following the airline settlement, Jonathon's father decided to move him out of state, which removed any chance I had to be directly involved with his upbringing; since then, I have only been able to see Jonathon on several occasions, but he is in my thoughts and prayers every day. I truly hope that upon reading this narrative, Jonathon will come to me ready to re-explore what are now probably only vague memories of his mother and brother, and I patiently look forward to again perusing the many photo albums that once directed our bedtime storytelling, when I would share with him tales about his childhood, as well as memories of me and Patty growing up.

Looking back, it is clear how important forgiveness was to my healing process, because without it I would have been held captive in a sea of negativity and become a prisoner of a time past. Letting go of my anger was truly one of the greatest challenges that I have ever faced, because absolving people for what occurred would not necessarily right any wrongs or hold people accountable for their actions. And yet the multifaceted process of forgiveness ultimately served to be the means by which I freed myself from oversensitivity to the airline's actions, as well as the way I was able to release myself from resentment.

Perhaps one of the most perplexing and disorientating parts of my experience arose from how easily and rapidly my entire construct of reality, along with my beliefs, seemed to unravel. In the time I spent endlessly reflecting upon the circumstances of my sister's and nephew's deaths, I vacillated between different theories as to how it was that two people as beautiful, good, and alive as Patty and Patrick could have been taken away so suddenly. One detail that seemed especially prominent was the dream Eric had of a plane crash the night before the tragedy occurred, which had made Patty weary of flying home on that stormy Halloween afternoon. For a long time, I wondered whether Patty, by denying her own instinctive sense that something was wrong, in some way actually chose her fate. Such a thought provoked me to examine a myriad of ideas and questions, all of which focused on the extent to which we have control over the course of our lives; ultimately, I found myself considering whether free will actually exists, or whether our lives have all been predetermined to take a given direction, rendering our illusions of control obsolete. And, in a contradictory vein, I also entertained the possibility of life being completely coincidental and haphazard, without existent purposes as to why things happen. I felt like I was trapped in a web of paradoxes, as my various speculations seemed to stand in stark contrast to one another, leaving no apparent resolution.

Basically, I examined the events from every angle, frantically searching for some explanation or some form of understanding...anything to somehow justify the purpose of my loss…but I never found any such enlightenment. However, what I have discovered is the importance of acceptance, because regardless of whether or not we are able to understand the reasons behind why our lives change or head in unforeseeable directions, without accepting that things will inevitably happen that are out of our control, we will spend the rest of our lives drowning in questions. And so, in the absence of concrete answers as to why things happen, I have chosen instead to focus on the fact that even though we don't always have power over the events that occur in our lives, we can regulate how we react to them—either by succumbing to negativity, or by adopting a positive outlook toward the future. In retrospect, I consider the concept of acceptance to be one of the most pivotal aspects of the healing process, because if I had not been able to accept what had changed, then I would to this day be floating in an abyss of disorientating and debilitating emotions.

The tragedy of Flight 4184 irreversibly transformed and reshaped my life, forever influencing the spectrum of complexities that define the person that I am…but the loving imprint that Patty and Patrick left on my heart will always be a shaping force in my life as well. My experience has taught me that while I will undoubtedly be affected by external circumstances, only I can choose how I will live and who I will become, and it is up to me to accept the changes life throws at me. I have finally arrived at a place where I can acknowledge that I was lucky enough to have the best sister and friend in the world for thirty-seven years, and that my life has irrevocably changed because of her death…but I also came to appreciate that I am still blessed with the gift of life—something far too precious and fleeting to waste in anger and uncertainty.

My long road to recovery has been filled with many obstacles and steep passages, and has taken me to unexpected places. I cannot mark a definitive beginning or end to this journey, for I have come to realize that healing truly is a process—one that is not linear but rather takes place in cycles, moment to moment, often without any conscious effort. And after so many years, I can now clearly see that there is no end to healing, no ultimate destination to reach, but only the continuation of a lifelong journey. I believe that everybody takes their own path when trying to overcome traumatic events, but for me, one of the most essential aspects of moving forward resided in learning how to better care for myself and remain in tune with what I needed and felt. I found out how eager others were to help, but that it was also my responsibility to ask for assistance; and most importantly, I discovered how to follow my own time frame in traversing through my grief, instead of adhering to what is dictated by textbook definitions, or even the advice of well-meaning friends.

In the immediate aftermath of the crash, I found myself desperately seeking for any way to find some form of closure...almost as though I thought of closure as something tangible that I could concretely obtain in an instant. Thus, I wound up inadvertently prolonging and intensifying my own grief by believing that in attending just one service or receiving back just one item, I would suddenly and miraculously arrive at this ambiguous and abstract concept. Friends would often inquire as to whether certain milestones had brought about closure; while I realize that their sincere desire was for me to regain some peace, that question typically served to generate anxieties in my own mind as to why I could not seem to arrive at that place. I now understand that closure is unattainable, for while I have come to terms with the fact that my sister and nephew are no longer physically present, the tragedy will never cease to impact my life. And in hindsight, I recognize the problematic nature of placing emphasis on a word signifying an end or conclusion to the many emotions I was living through at the time, for even now, I can still be overcome with a multitude of feelings when thinking of my sister and nephew, some sad and some happy, but I know that I will never stop missing them, nor do I believe that I should.

I don't remember exactly when the clouds started to break, but at some point, I began to notice rays of sunlight emerging from behind the dense, hazy barrier lining the sky, beaming down into my life for the first time since that pivotal date of October 31, 1994; slowly, the storm seemed to be passing, as inescapably happens with all natural phenomena, and I found myself living in a spring of new beginnings. Over time,

I began to understand that just as the storms of early spring invariably give rise to the season's burst of blooming new life, so too do our trials and tribulations give us the opportunity to reflect, learn, and ultimately flourish. While there were still moments that I felt great pain, there were also many moments when I was again able to experience great joy and love; somehow, I managed to mesh the life I was rebuilding together with the one I had known before the tragedy, and I achieved some sort of balance between looking ahead to the future while simultaneously incorporating the memory of the past. Over the years, I have come to understand that Patty and Patrick are still very much a part of me, and that the love that existed between us did not die, but simply changed. I have held onto the belief that Patty and Patrick exist somewhere in eternal states of perfection, and that they are able to look down upon us, finding ways to signal their endless encouragement and love. And I have no doubt that Patty will always be a significant presence in my life, for I carry her in my heart wherever I go…I can still relish in all the wonderful memories we created together, I can continue to love her every minute of every day, and I can believe that somewhere, she and Patrick are watching over me, returning my everlasting love for them that has so profoundly shaped who I am, where I have been, and where I am going. So as I trek forward in my new life built upon hope, memories, faith, love, joy, and strength, my connection with my sister will continue on as well, for enough love exists between us to last for an eternity of lifetimes.

Perhaps the most telling insight I gained from this whole experience has been that the only true constant that life offers is change…for as all of nature is marked by cycles of transformation, so too is our time here on Earth. Due to the events that took place in the town of Roselawn, I came to perceive the rose as a symbol of the regenerating power of all natural rotations, for just as plants that die in the winter help to fertilize the soil so that flowers can surface in the spring, all endings eventually signal the emergence of new beginnings and new hope. In the immediate aftermath of the tragedy, I was standing underneath an expansive stretch of grayish-black sky that had no discernable beginning or end, enduring what seemed to be an ongoing torrent of gusting winds and pounding rain; however, the storm eventually passed, as all things inevitably do, and the sky above me is now blue, with the distant clouds slowly fading into the horizon. The sun has finally set upon Roselawn, and from the receding cloud-line has burst dusk's brilliant and beautiful shades of pink, orange, and purple, signifying the close of a cycle; but in the morning, when the sun's light again breaks through the darkness and lines the eastern sky with the different and yet equally magnificent colors of dawn, a new cycle is begun in which life and promise manifest out of the ashes of Flight 4184.

Acknowledgements

I am forever grateful for the endless loyalty and support of my family and friends.

Love and thanks to Mom and Dad for being my foundation and my mentors. You are the best parents ever and I am blessed to always have your support.

All my love to Jimmy, Andy, and Nikki. I am so proud of how bravely you took on the many challenges you were faced with in your young lives. I admire the balanced perspective you've developed on life and the lighthearted, fun-loving ways that so readily define who you are. Thank you Andy and Nikki for your ongoing support of this project and Jimmy, thank you for the time and honesty you have so freely given to assist me.

Heidi, I was so fortunate to have your endless loyalty and I'm so appreciative of you never walking on the piles of papers that occupied so much floor space during the writing of this book.

Because of the scope of this work, I have been blessed with the suggestions and support of many special people and I am thankful for their expertise and their encouragement. I am grateful to the friendships that have developed as a result of this journey and cherish those I now consider among my extended family. I am especially appreciative to everyone who cared for my sister and nephew in death as if my family were theirs.

Special thanks to my editor, Danielle Auslander and to the interest you have taken in this project. You have made the many long hours and sometimes grueling process of editing seem almost effortless. "This is a mess," or "Let me try this" are phrases that preceded your magic touch of giving greater clarity to my story. Thank you for your attention to detail in all aspects of your work. It has truly been my pleasure to work with you.

Jim Hall, your earlier efforts on behalf of all the families helped to catapult change in the industry. Thank you for your continued support and contribution to my book.

Mary Schiavo, your introduction beautifully represents the foundation of my book and your support for me and the families over the years has been invaluable.

Richard Mack I am grateful for your generous support on this project. Thank you for so freely sharing your creative as well as business talent in helping bring my book to completion. The ease with which you established my website, designed flyers, or pointed me toward my next step is appreciated more than I could ever say. And I proudly display your photography on the dust jacket, as it is unmatched!

Rich Nickel, your talent in design has creatively brought all the pieces of this project together. Thank you for your expertise.

Mark Livesay and Julie Mosley, thank you for your friendly yet professional manner in helping to create a great finished product.

Mike Ryder, your valuable advice and everything beyond your skillful proofreading has been greatly appreciated. It has truly been a pleasure to work with you.

Jeanne Miller, from the moment you first learned of my story you have been so supportive and encouraging. Thank you for all your help and guidance in keeping me on the right track.

Amy Taylor, I am so grateful for your unconditional friendship. Your honesty and encouraging words throughout the years have meant more than you can imagine. Also, thank you for your eagerness to assist Families of 4184 in any way possible through your creative flair.

David Aubrey and Jeff Maziarek, thank you for your enthusiasm and belief in this project and for helping me in any way you could.

Tom Pope, your encouragement, support, and sense of humor from the earliest stages of writing to the very end, is deeply appreciated. Thank you for your dedication in helping to preserve the roadside memorial and for the beautiful crosses you engraved for Patty and Patrick.

Citations

Chp. 10, p. 63: *Funk and Wagnall's Standard Desk Dictionary. Volume 2.* Funk & Wagnall's, Inc., New York, 1979, p. 446.

Chp. 13, p.75: American Airlines' letter informing families of undisclosed mass burial, Jan. 27, 1995.

Chp. 14, pp. 82-84: Crash sequence information obtained/quoted from several different sources: *Unheeded Warning: The Inside Story of American Eagle Flight 4184*, by Stephen A. Fredrick. New York: McGraw-Hill, 1996, pp. 218 ff.

All direct quotations/specific data come from either National Transportation Safety Board (NTSB) press kit; *NTSB Aircraft Accident Report, Volume I* (1996); *NTSB Aircraft Accident Report, Volume II* (1996).

Chp. 14, pp. 98-99: Press release, March 1, 1995.

Chp. 14, p. 99: PWI Environmental press releases, March 2, 1995.

Chp. 14, p. 101: Emergency motion for protective order to preserve effects/wreckage, press release, March 2, 1995.

Chp. 14, p. 102: Fredrick, *Unheeded Warning*, p. 229.

Chp. 14, p. 102: Press release, March 1, 1995.

Chp. 14, pp. 106-107: Article on state commissioner's re-inspection of the crash site, *The Indianapolis Star*, March 3, 1995, p. A2.

Chp. 17, p. 126: *Families of 4184 Roselawn*, newsletter, April, 1995.

Chp. 18, p. 133: American Airlines' letter informing families of undisclosed mass burial, Jan. 27, 1995.

Chp. 18, p. 134: personal correspondence, May 19, 1995.

Chp. 18, pp. 134-136: Letter from insurance company representing American Airlines, December 7, 1994.

Chp. 18, pp. 137-138: *Families of 4184 Roselawn*, newsletter, May 1995.

Chp. 19, p. 143: "Summary of NTSB/DOT Meeting with Families of Airline Crash Victims," June 20, 1995.

Chp. 19, pp. 145-146: *Families of 4184 Roselawn*, newsletter, July 1995.

Chp. 21, pp. 150-155: Personal correspondence from American Airlines, July 1995.

Chp. 21, p. 152: Third amended complaint, filed with United States District Court, September 30,1996.

Chp. 22, p. 168: Articles on memorial services: *The Post-Tribune*, August 19, 1995, p. A5; *The Times, Indiana Edition*, August 19, 1995, p.1.

Chp. 24, p.176: Third amended complaint, filed with United States District Court, September 30, 1996.

Chp. 27, pp. 195-198: Author appearance on "The Geraldo Show," May 30, 1996. Two quotes included by Jim Burnett, an expert on the panel for the "The Geraldo Show."

Chp. 29, pp. 203-206: Source of all quotations: NTSB final hearing in Washington D.C., July 1996. *NTSB Aircraft Accident Report, Volume I* (1996); *NTSB Aircraft Accident Report, Volume II* (1996).

Chp. 31, pp. 210-214: "Pretrail Settlement Memorandum," filed with United States District Court.

Chp. 32, pp. 216-217: Aviation Disaster Family Assistance Act of 1996 (P.L. 101-264), October 9, 1996.

Chp. 33, pp. 220-227: National Guard Reports regarding clean-up efforts at crash site, December 28, 1994 and February 4, 1995.

Chp. 34, p. 229: Third amended complaint, filed with United States District Court, September 30,1996.

Chp. 35, p. 238: *The Daily Herald*, September 23, 1997, p.6.

Chp. 36, p. 242: *The Daily Herald*, September 23, 1997, p.6.

Chp. 37, p. 250: *The Times, Indiana Edition*, October 31, 1999.

Chp. 38, p. 252: Letter from insurance company representing American Airlines, September 21, 1999.

Chp. 38 pp. 252-253: American Airlines' letter, March 14, 2001.

Chp. 38, pp. 253-254: *Handbook for Human Services Response: A Practical Approach for Helping People*, by Dr. Carolyn Coarsey. Blairsville, GA: Higher Resources, Inc., 2004, pp. 224-230.